Sunset

Fresh Produce

P9-BYO-159

Vegetables once considered exotic now appear regularly in supermarkets.

By the Editors of Sunset Books
and Sunset Magazine

Sunset Publishing Corporation • Menlo Park, California

BOOK EDITOR
PHYLLIS ELVING

RESEARCH & TEXT
JOAN GRIFFITHS
MARY JANE SWANSON

COORDINATING EDITOR
LINDA J. SELDEN

DESIGN
WILLIAMS & ZILLER DESIGN

PHOTOGRAPHERS: **Glenn Christiansen:** Pages 15, 25, 35 lower right, 36–37, 80, 98, 123. **Norman A. Plate:** Pages 4, 5 (all), 9, 11, 19 right, 31, 38–39, 42–43, 50–51, 52 top. **Teri Sandison:** Pages 1, 12, 35 upper left, 40, 52 lower right, 94. **David Stubbs:** Pages 2, 19 left, 27, 29, 32, 34, 41, 45, 55, 113. **Darrow M. Watt:** Pages 6, 16, 20, 21, 22, 28, 33, 46, 48, 49 (both), 53, 54, 56, 57 (both), 58, 59, 60, 62 (both), 64, 65, 67, 69, 71, 72, 73, 74, 75, 76, 77, 78, 81, 84, 86, 87, 88, 90, 92, 96, 97, 101, 102, 105, 107, 108, 110, 111, 115 (both), 117, 119, 120 (both), 122, 124 (both), 125, 126.

COVER: The array of fruits and vegetables available today enchants the eye as well as the palate. Design by Williams & Ziller Design. Photograph by Darrow M. Watt. Photo styling by Elizabeth Ross. Food styling by Mary Jane Swanson.

Editor, Sunset Books: Elizabeth L. Hogan

Third printing March 1991

FRESHNESS MAKES THE DIFFERENCE

From apples to tamarillos and from artichokes to turnips, this book offers an encyclopedic look at fresh fruits and vegetables. Whether you're searching for new ideas for preparing some of the familiar favorites or you're baffled by the many exotic varieties now appearing on supermarket shelves, you're sure to find the answers right here.

We explain how to select each fruit and vegetable at peak quality, how to recognize all types of produce, and how to choose from the many varieties currently on the market. And since buying fresh produce is only the first step, we give storage, preparation, and cooking suggestions that will best preserve the freshness and flavor of your purchases.

To inspire you to new taste adventures, try the recipes at the end of each listing—they were specially selected to show off each fruit or vegetable's distinctive flavor, texture, and appearance.

For her careful editing of the manuscript, we extend special thanks to Rebecca La Brum. Our thanks, also, to Marianne Lipanovich for her assistance with research and text, to Elizabeth Ross for her contribution in photo styling, and to Dug Waggoner for graphics work on pages 6 and 56. We're also grateful to Jean Gentry of the International Apple Institute, Charlie Bettencourt of Sunset Produce Co., Berkeley Bowl Produce, and Draeger's Supermarket.

Midsummer shopper can choose from among many kinds of berries at their peak of ripeness.

Contents

A FRESH APPROACH — 4

FRUITS — 6

Apples 7
Apricots 9
Avocados 10
Bananas 11
Berries 13
Carambolas 18
Cherimoyas 18
Cherries 19
Citrus 20

Dates 24
Feijoas 26
Figs 28
Grapes 30
Guavas 32
Kiwi Fruit 33
Litchis & Longans 34
Mangoes 34
Melons 35

Nectarines 38
Papayas 39
Passion Fruit 42
Peaches 43
Pears 44
Pepinos 47
Persimmons 47
Pineapples 48
Plums 50

Pomegranates 51
Prickly Pears 52
Quinces 53
Rhubarb 54
Sapotes 54
Tamarillos 55

VEGETABLES — 56

Artichokes 57
Asparagus 58
Beans 59
Beets 62
Bok Choy 63
Broccoli 64
Brussels Sprouts 65
Cabbage 68
Carrots 69
Cauliflower 70
Celery 73

Celery Root 74
Chayote 75
Corn 76
Cucumbers 77
Eggplant 79
Fennel 81
Garlic 82
Greens with a Bite 83
Jicama 85
Kohlrabi 86
Leeks 87

Mushrooms 89
Okra 92
Onions 93
Parsnips 94
Peas 95
Peppers 97
Potatoes 99
Radishes 102
Rutabagas 103
Salad Greens 104
Salsify 106

Sorrel 107
Spinach 109
Sprouts 110
Squash 111
Sunchokes 115
Sweet Potatoes & Yams 116
Swiss Chard 117
Tomatillos 118
Tomatoes 118
Turnips 121

A GLOSSARY OF TECHNIQUES — 122

INDEX — 127

SPECIAL FEATURES

"Can't Miss" Fruit Pies 17
Unlocking the Coconut 21
No-Fuss Fruit Jams 28
Icy Fruit Refreshment 41
Dressing Up Vegetables 66
Versatile Vegetable Purées 71
High-Potency Produce—Ginger & Horseradish 75
Produce Exotica 86
Adding Flavor with Herbs 108
Freezing Fruit 125
Extending the Tomato Season 126

A Fresh Approach

A revolution of sorts has been taking place in the produce department of your supermarket. Fruits considered strictly exotic a decade ago are displayed side by side with apples and oranges. Vegetables once found only in ethnic markets have become as readily available as carrots and celery. Even the old standbys have been appearing in more and more new varieties.

This increasing range of choices is exciting, but at the same time it poses a challenge. What do you do with a prickly pear or a carambola? How do you go about selecting the best daikon, and how can you tell when tomatillos are fresh? For that matter, what guidelines are there for choosing and using even commonplace fruits and vegetables, which are now often available in widely expanded seasons and regions?

To answer these questions, this book offers a basic market-to-menu guide to fresh produce. Easily recognizable types as well as exotic new ones are presented in A to Z listings complete with shopping tips, preparation instructions, and cooking and serving ideas—along with specific recipes. We take the mystery out of even the most unfamiliar fruit or vegetable, and we bring you up to date on the latest varieties of your old favorites.

THE NEW BASICS

Since the late 1970s, supermarkets have more than doubled the number of produce items they carry. Restaurants, too, report a big jump in the consumption of fresh fruit and main-dish salads. And farmers' markets, specialty produce stores, and ethnic food shops seem to be springing up everywhere.

Brimming boxes of nectarines, on sale at a low price—it's time to stock up.

Why this surge of interest in fresh produce? Part of the impetus comes from the increased public focus on healthful eating, on diet as a key to fitness. Fresh produce is a rich natural source of fiber, vitamins, and minerals—and most vegetables and fruits have a relatively low calorie count. But that doesn't tell the whole story. The modern consumer also has a heightened interest in *quality* food—in food as an experience encompassing taste and texture and color.

Over the past decade or so, the advent of lighter, innovative cooking styles has placed new emphasis on the fresh taste and appearance of basic ingredients. Increased exposure to different foods through travel and the influence of new ethnic groups in this country have also increased our appetite for new flavors. We are more willing to experiment—and in fact more demanding that choices be made available.

The success of the kiwi fruit is a case in point. First imported from New Zealand in the 1960s, it took off in popularity after being promoted by a few produce wholesalers. Its acceptance set a precedent that has encouraged the introduction of many more types of produce, from strange-looking tropical fruits to "designer" vegetables—blue potatoes, purple string beans, and orange beets, for example. And if you prefer to stick with familiar vegetables, but want them in a smaller size, you can now choose all sorts of "babies"; some are familiar varieties harvested immature, while others are hybrids that remain tiny when fully grown.

Modern distribution methods

also influence what we can buy. Only a few decades ago, much produce was sold within a few hundred miles of where it grew. As local farms gave way to suburban development, growing shifted to big agricultural districts. Many varieties were developed to be sturdy enough to withstand long-distance shipping. But you can still find some flavorful but fragile old-fashioned varieties at local and farmers' markets.

You won't always find varieties labeled at your produce market. If you want to know what type of onion or peach you're buying, ask the produce manager. The variety and shipper's name are printed on the container in which the produce was shipped to the market.

USING THIS BOOK

For each fruit or vegetable, this book tells you how to select the best of its type, when you're most likely to find it in your market, and how to store it when you get it home. Next we outline the basic steps necessary to prepare the produce for cooking or for eating raw, and we tell you which methods of cooking are most suitable. You'll also find seasoning and serving suggestions —along with *Sunset-*tested recipes.

For fruits, which are often sold before they're fully ripe, we give instructions for further ripening at home. Keep in mind that most kinds of fruit must reach a certain stage of maturity before picking or they will never ripen satisfactorily. There's no excuse for markets to sell fruit picked too early; return any that doesn't ripen properly.

Simple freezing instructions are also given for fruits, since many are in abundance for much shorter seasons than vegetables. For detailed instructions on preserving both fruits and vegetables, refer to the *Sunset* book *Canning, Freezing & Drying.*

Nutritional highlights are summarized for each fruit and vegetable. Keep in mind that nutritional content may be altered by cooking and storage time; vitamin C, for example, decreases substantially when food is cooked.

Food values given for each recipe were calculated primarily from statistics in Agriculture Handbook Number 456, *Nutritive Value of American*

Foods, a publication of the Agricultural Research Service, United States Department of Agriculture. If a recipe offers a choice of ingredients, values are figured on the basis of the ingredient listed first. For example, if a recipe lists "butter or margarine," the values are calculated for butter; margarine would yield a lower cholesterol content. Optional ingredients are not included when calculating values.

Amounts are figured on the basis of the largest suggested serving size unless otherwise indicated.

"A Glossary of Techniques," on pages 122 to 126, is designed to serve as a basic reference guide to the cooking methods you'll be using most often in preparing fresh fruits and vegetables. Use it in conjunction with the cooking instructions given in the individual produce listings.

After picking, nectarines are gently released from bag into large bins. Filled bins go into hydrocooler for quick cool-down.

In packing house, fruit is sorted out. Scarred and damaged fruit is discarded; the rest moves along to be cleaned, sized, and packed in containers.

Packaged nectarines, in cartons strapped to pallets, are moved with fork lifts to minimize damage during handling.

Refrigerated trucks travel day and night to transport fruit to market quickly. Most California-grown nectarines reach Western cities within a day or two of harvest.

Celebrate the seasons with fruits at their peak of flavor. Sweet or tart, crunchy-crisp or butter-soft, fruits are adaptable to every mealtime course.

Apples

It is only fitting to begin this book with America's favorite fruit—the apple, whose seeds were brought to our shores by the first European colonists. The apple has figured in American legends, and apple pie has even been held up (along with Mom and the flag) as a patriotic symbol.

Many scholars believe that apples originated in Southwest Asia—the same area where, according to the Bible, Eve picked the irresistible fruit in the Garden of Eden.

Over the years, horticultural journals have recorded more than 7,000 varieties of apples. But today, just 12 to 15 varieties represent 90 percent of U.S. commercial apple production. Washington is the largest producer, followed by New York, Michigan, California, Pennsylvania, and Virginia. Some apples are also imported from New Zealand and Europe.

Of the many apple varieties grown in years past, some have simply gone out of style. Others were planted primarily for their convenient harvest times, regardless of whether they were especially flavorful; the advent of modern cold storage put an end to their popularity. Surviving commercial types are those that can be stored and shipped well.

Nutrition. One large raw apple contains about 125 calories. Apples provide bulk and aid digestion.

■ **The top varieties.** Each apple variety has its own distinctive flavor and texture. Crisp, crunchy, juicy types

---

As autumn approaches, apples and pears fill market bins with seasonal shades of red, green, yellow, and russet. The photo shows several of the most popular varieties of each fruit. Apples include Red Delicious (top left), red and green Gravenstein in box; Granny Smith (top) and McIntosh at upper right; Rome Beauty (left) and Golden Delicious below box. Pears include red and yellow Comice at left below box, Bosc at bottom left, and Bartlett.

---

are excellent for eating out of hand; those that retain their shape and flavor during cooking are good for baking or making into pies or sauce.

The top-selling varieties in the United States are described below.

Red Delicious. The most popular eating variety in the United States, the Red Delicious has dark red skin and crisp, sweet, juicy flesh. It is not a good cooking apple, since it doesn't retain its shape when cooked. Available nationwide, almost all year.

Golden Delicious. This apple is catching up with the Red Delicious in popularity. It has yellow-green to yellow skin and sweet, aromatic flesh that doesn't darken after cutting. Excellent for eating out of hand as well as for baking, pies, and sauce. Available nationwide, almost all year.

McIntosh. This two-toned (red- and green-skinned) apple has juicy-crisp, tender flesh with a pleasantly tart flavor. Though best loved as an eating apple, it also makes excellent sauce and pies; it collapses when baked. Available nearly nationwide, mid-September through July.

Rome Beauty. Large, shiny, dark red Rome Beauties are considered by many to be the ultimate baking apple; the fruit holds its shape well during cooking. These aren't the best choice for eating fresh, since the yellow flesh is somewhat mealy-textured when raw. Available nationwide, October through July.

Jonathan. This old variety has bright, shiny red skin and firm, yellow, spicy-tasting flesh; it's good fresh and in pies and sauces, but collapses when baked. Availability of Jonathans is declining; they are sold predominantly in the mid-Atlantic, Midwest, and Southwest areas of the country, September through March.

York Imperial. Red, shiny York apples have firm, tart, wine-flavored flesh and a characteristic lopsided shape; they're especially good for baking. Available in the mid-Atlantic area and Southeast, late October through July.

Granny Smith. Large, bright green-skinned Granny Smiths, first grown in Australia, capture a larger share of the American market every year. Today, many are grown domestically on the West Coast. Sweet-tart and crisp, they're excellent for eating out of hand, as well as for pies, sauce, and baking. Available nationwide, almost all year.

Stayman. This close relative of the Winesap has deep red skin with purplish undertones; the snow white flesh is mildly tart and quite juicy and tender. Staymans are favorites for eating out of hand and can also be used for cooking. Available in Central and South Atlantic regions, October through early spring.

Newtown Pippin. Simply called Pippin in California, this is a bright green to yellow-green, tomato-shaped apple. Its firm, tart flesh isn't exceptionally juicy, so it's better for cooking than for eating fresh. Available on the West Coast, mid-September through April.

Winesap. An apple on the decline in production, the Winesap has dark red skin and firm, coarse-textured yellow flesh with a sweet, winelike flavor. These apples are excellent for eating fresh and can also be used for baking, pies, and sauce. Available nearly nationwide, November through July.

Cortland. This red apple has tart, snowy flesh that retains its white color even after cutting. Cortlands are best for eating fresh or making into sauce. Available in the Northeast and Midwest, September through April.

Northern Spy. The Northern Spy is one of the finest all-purpose apples. Unfortunately, its production is on the decline. Juicy, tart, and crisp textured, it's well suited for eating fresh and for all cooking uses. Much of the crop is processed into pie fillings and applesauce. Available on a limited basis in the Northeast and Upper Great Lakes region, mid-October through February.

Other notable varieties. Tart, juicy Idared is a favorite in the Northeast and

Midwest for eating out of hand. Gravenstein, a spicy, firm-textured West Coast apple, is excellent for all cooking uses. The Northeast's mildly tart Rhode Island Greening is probably the best pie apple. Miniature lady apples are just the right size for garnishes in holiday punches.

New varieties include Empire, a cross between Red Delicious and McIntosh; Mutsu, a golden-skinned Japanese apple now grown in the Northeast; and several New Zealand imports, including Gala and Braeburn.

■ **Season.** Almost all year for some, thanks to cold storage; September through November is the peak season for many types (see preceding listings).

■ **Selection.** Make sure to choose a variety suitable for the purpose you have in mind. Then look for bright red or green color that's the right shade for the variety. The surface should be smooth, firm, unbroken, and free of bruises and blemishes. Brownish, freckled areas on the skin, usually caused by weather, mar appearance somewhat but don't affect flavor.

A ripe red apple has a soft, light green undercast or background color. Immature apples have a bright dark green undercast; overripe fruit has a dull, yellowish green background and soft, often bruised skin.

■ **Ripening & storage.** Apples ripen 10 times faster at room temperature than in the refrigerator—so to keep them crisp, refrigerate them in a plastic bag (this helps them retain moisture). You can also store apples in a cellar at 32° to 40°F; line the container with plastic and cover the apples with a damp towel to prevent moisture loss.

The old saying "one bad apple can spoil the whole barrel" is indeed true. Sort apples before storing them, and use defective ones immediately.

■ **Preparation.** Simply rinse to eat out of hand. Or cut into quarters and remove core from each section. Use a vegetable peeler or sharp knife to peel apples for cooking. To core, push an apple corer through center of fruit from top to bottom; pull out core and stem. Coat peeled or sliced apples with lemon juice to prevent darkening.

■ **Amount.** One pound of apples (4 small, 3 medium-size, or 2 large fruits) yields 3 cups diced fruit or 2 ½ cups peeled, sliced fruit.

■ **Freezing.** Peel and core apples. Freeze in light syrup (see page 125).

■ **Serving ideas.** Apples can be diced to add to granola cereal, sautéed in butter to accompany pork sausages and waffles or pancakes, or baked in apple juice. For snacks, serve apple slices spread with peanut butter or Cheddar cheese spread. Add diced apples to curry-seasoned tuna or chicken salads; add slices to toasted cheese, liverwurst, or bacon sandwiches. For dessert, pair apples with soft-ripened cheeses.

■ **Cooking with apples.** Apples are the most versatile of all fruits. They're suitable for a variety of cooking techniques and can be used in many, many recipes.

Baking. Peel and core apples; quarter lengthwise. Glaze and bake (see page 122) until hot (about 20 minutes).

For whole baked apples, see recipe for Honey Crunch Baked Apples.

Grilling. Core apples. Cut small to medium-size fruit in half lengthwise; cut large apples lengthwise into ¾-inch wedges. Grill (see page 123) until hot and streaked with brown (about 6 minutes for wedges, 10 to 12 minutes for halves).

Poaching. Peel and core 4 or 5 medium-size firm apples; coat with 2 tablespoons lemon juice. Simmer in poaching liquid (see page 124) until tender when pierced (10 to 12 minutes).

Sautéing. Peel and core apples; cut into ½-inch-thick slices. Sauté (see page 124) until hot and tender when pierced (3 to 5 minutes).

MOLDED WALDORF SALAD

Per serving of salad: 129 calories, 2 g protein, 21 g carbohydrates, 5 g total fat, 0 mg cholesterol, 11 mg sodium

Per tablespoon of dressing: 26 calories, .38 g protein, .80 g carbohydrates, 2 g total fat, 5 mg cholesterol, 6 mg sodium

- 1 envelope unflavored gelatin
- 2 cups unsweetened clear apple juice
- 1 tablespoon lemon juice
- ½ cup thinly sliced celery
- ½ cup sliced pitted dates
- 2 cups diced unpeeled red apples
- ½ cup chopped walnuts
  Orange Dressing (recipe follows)

In a small pan, sprinkle gelatin over apple juice; let soften for 5 minutes. Then stir over low heat until gelatin is completely dissolved. Stir in lemon juice. Refrigerate until mixture has the consistency of unbeaten egg whites

(about 45 minutes). Stir in celery, dates, apples, and walnuts. Spoon mixture into a 6-cup mold. Cover and refrigerate until firm (at least 4 hours) or until next day. Meanwhile, prepare Orange Dressing.

To serve, unmold salad onto a serving plate. Pass dressing to spoon over salads. Makes 8 to 10 servings.

Orange Dressing. Blend ½ cup **sour cream** or mayonnaise and 1 ½ to 2 tablespoons **orange juice.**

HONEY CRUNCH BAKED APPLES

Per serving: 323 calories, 2 g protein, 61 g carbohydrates, 10 g total fat, 18 mg cholesterol, 83 mg sodium

- 6 large apples, peeled (if desired) and cored
- ⅓ cup *each* granola-type cereal and chopped pitted dates
- ¼ cup chopped almonds or walnuts
- ½ teaspoon ground cinnamon
- ¼ teaspoon ground nutmeg
- 2 teaspoons lemon juice
- 6 tablespoons honey
- 3 tablespoons melted butter or margarine
- ¾ cup apple juice or water

Place apples in a 9-inch square baking pan. In a bowl, combine cereal, dates, almonds, cinnamon, nutmeg, lemon juice, and 3 tablespoons of the honey. Spoon equal amounts of filling into each apple, packing in lightly.

Stir together melted butter, remaining 3 tablespoons honey, and apple juice. Pour over apples. Cover and bake in a 350° oven for 30 minutes. Uncover; continue to bake, basting often with pan juices, until tender when pierced (about 35 more minutes). Serve warm or cooled. Makes 6 servings.

APPLE CRISP

Per serving: 569 calories, 6 g protein, 94 g carbohydrates, 20 g total fat, 57 mg cholesterol, 252 mg sodium

- 8 cups peeled, cored, thinly sliced apples (3½ to 4 lbs.)
- ¼ cup lemon juice
- 1 cup sugar
- ½ teaspoon ground cinnamon
- 1 cup water
  Oatmeal Topping (recipe follows)

In a 9- by 13-inch baking dish, combine apples, lemon juice, sugar, and cinnamon. Pour water over mixture. Prepare Oatmeal Topping and squeeze over fruit mixture in large lumps. Bake in a 375° oven until topping is golden brown (about 50 minutes). Makes 10 to 12 servings.

Oatmeal Topping. In a bowl, stir together 1 ½ cups *each* **all-purpose flour** and firmly packed **brown sugar,** 2½ cups **rolled oats,** ¼ cup **instant non-fat dry milk,** 1½ teaspoons **ground cinnamon,** and ½ teaspoon **ground ginger.** Using a pastry blender or 2 knives, cut in 1 cup (½ lb.) firm **butter** or margarine until mixture resembles coarse crumbs.

■ *See also* **Fruit Pie** *(page 17),* **Gingered Carrots & Apples** *(page 70).*

Apricots

Delicately sweet apricots start the parade of summer fruits. Grown in China thousands of years ago, apricots were first planted in Southern California missions in the 1700s. Today, 97 percent of the U.S. market supply comes from California.

Unfortunately, ripe apricots are one of the softest and most difficult to handle of all fruits; as a result, many new varieties have been developed for their shipping qualities. In general, these new types are larger, firmer, smoother, brighter in color, and more acid in flavor than the old varieties such as Royal Blenheim, Derby Royal, and Tilton.

Royal Blenheim sets the standard for classic sweet-tart apricot flavor. But since it ripens unevenly, it's only rarely sold in markets. Derby Royal is larger than Blenheim and usually ripens more evenly, but it never gets as intensely sweet. To keep these two "royal" varieties straight, remember that Derby Royal ripens early, while Royal Blenheim doesn't start until the second week of June. Tilton ripens later yet.

In *Sunset* tests of the nine apricot varieties shown below, some tasters preferred the livelier flavor of the new apricot varieties. But most rated Royal Blenheim and Derby Royal tops both for eating fresh and for cooking. Among the new varieties, Castlebrite, Improved Flaming Gold, and Katy came out ahead.

Nutrition. Apricots are an excellent source of vitamin A and a fair source of vitamin C. Three apricots contain about 50 calories.

■ **Season.** Mid-May through mid-August (peak in June) for the domestic crop; December through January for New Zealand and Chilean fruit.

■ **Selection.** Look for plump fruit with as much golden orange color as possible. Blemishes, unless they break the skin, will not affect flavor. Avoid fruit that is pale yellow, greenish yellow, very firm, shriveled, or bruised. Soft-ripe fruit has the best flavor, but must be used immediately.

■ **Ripening & storage.** Ripen apricots at room temperature until they give to gentle pressure. To hasten ripening, group fruit in a loosely closed paper bag; check daily. Refrigerate ripe fruit, unwashed, in a paper or plastic bag for up to 2 days.

■ **Preparation.** Simply rinse to eat out of hand; discard pit. To cut fruit, slice around seam, twist in half, and lift out pit. To peel, dip in boiling water to cover for 20 seconds; cool quickly in cold water, then slip off skins.

■ **Amount.** One to 1¼ pounds apricots (about 12) yields about 2 cups halved or sliced fruit.

■ **Freezing.** Halve and pit apricots. Freeze in light syrup (see page 125).

■ **Serving ideas.** Fill apricot halves with Brie or other soft-ripened cheese and serve as an appetizer or dessert. Serve slices on hot or cold cereal or on pancakes or waffles. Add apricots to fruit, fish, or poultry salads. For dessert, sprinkle halves with orange liqueur or top with ice cream and slivered almonds.

■ **Cooking with apricots.** Cooking apricots with a little sugar intensifies their flavor. Use soft-ripe apricots for jam or sorbet, firm-ripe fruit in most other recipes.

Baking. Peel fruit, but leave whole. Glaze and bake (see page 122) until hot and tender when pierced (about 15 minutes).

Grilling. Halve and pit apricots. Thread on metal skewers, making sure they lie flat. Grill (see page 123) until hot and tender when pierced (4 to 6 minutes).

Poaching. Peel, halve, and pit 10 to 12 firm-ripe apricots. Simmer in poaching liquid (see page 124) until tender when pierced (6 to 8 minutes).

Sautéing. Halve and pit apricots. Sauté (see page 124) until hot and tender when pierced (about 5 minutes).

Continued on next page

Royal-Blenheim   Perfection

Katy   Pomo   Patterson   Tilton

Derby-Royal

Castlebrite   Improved Flaming Gold

Apricot varieties are look-alikes—but the new varieties are bigger, brighter in color, and easier to ship. They're also more acid in flavor than old favorites such as Derby Royal, Royal Blenheim, and Tilton.

APRICOT-ONION SALAD

Per serving: 260 calories, 3 g protein, 31 g carbohydrates, 16 g total fat, 0 mg cholesterol, 141 mg sodium

> 4 cups water
> ¼ cup red wine vinegar
> 1 small mild red onion, thinly sliced
> 2 pounds apricots
> ½ cup pitted ripe olives
> ¼ cup olive oil or salad oil
> ¼ cup finely chopped fresh mint
> 3 tablespoons lemon juice
> Salt and pepper
> Mint sprigs

In a 2- to 3-quart pan, combine water and 2 tablespoons of the vinegar. Bring to a boil over high heat; add onion and cook, uncovered, until pink and limp (about 10 minutes). Drain; pour into a deep salad bowl.

Halve and pit apricots; add to onion along with olives, oil, chopped mint, lemon juice, and remaining 2 tablespoons vinegar. Mix gently. Season to taste with salt and pepper. Cover and let stand at room temperature for at least 1 hour or up to 4 hours, mixing gently once or twice. Garnish with mint sprigs. Makes 4 to 6 servings.

APRICOT UPSIDE-DOWN GINGERCAKE

Per serving: 506 calories, 6 g protein, 89 g carbohydrates, 15 g total fat, 86 mg cholesterol, 469 mg sodium

> 7 tablespoons butter or margarine, softened
> ½ cup firmly packed brown sugar
> 12 to 16 apricots, halved and pitted
> 1½ cups all-purpose flour
> 1 teaspoon *each* baking soda, ground cinnamon, and ground ginger
> ¼ teaspoon salt
> ½ cup granulated sugar
> 1 egg
> ½ cup *each* light molasses and milk

Place 3 tablespoons of the butter in a 9-inch round baking pan; place in oven while it preheats to 325°. When butter is melted, remove pan from oven. Tilt pan to coat bottom evenly with butter; distribute brown sugar evenly over butter. Arrange apricots, cut side down, in a single layer over brown sugar.

In a bowl, stir together flour, baking soda, cinnamon, ginger, and salt; set aside. In a large bowl, cream remaining 4 tablespoons butter and granulated sugar. Add egg, molasses, and milk; beat until blended. Add flour mixture and beat until blended. Pour batter over apricots.

Bake in a 325° oven until a pick inserted in center comes out clean (50 to 60 minutes). Immediately invert cake onto serving plate. Serve warm. Makes 6 servings.

■*See also* **Fruit Pie** *(page 17),* **Fruit Jam** *(page 28),* **Fruit Sorbet** *(page 41).*

Avocados

The first record of the avocado is in Mayan and Aztec picture writings from 290 B.C. But it wasn't until centuries later—in the mid-1800s—that the Spaniards introduced the nonsweet, buttery-textured fruit to this country.

Though once considered exotic, avocados are now widely available all year from California and Florida. The main varieties of California avocados are pictured on page 11; these account for 85 percent of all avocados marketed in the United States. Oval-shaped Hass, available from April through November, is the principal market variety. Its thick, bumpy skin changes from emerald green to black as the fruit ripens; its flesh is rich and nutty.

Milder-flavored Fuerte is pear shaped, with smooth green skin. It's the most popular winter avocado. Bacon and Zutano are medium-size autumn/winter fruits with smooth, green, medium-thin skin and watery, mild-flavored flesh. Other California avocados include Pinkerton, available December through April, and summer-ripening Reed.

Florida avocados tend to be larger than the California types and, because they're lower in fat, less rich tasting. They usually have smooth, bright green skin. The main Florida varieties include Booth 7 and 8, Lula, and Waldin.

Nutrition. Half an average-size California avocado contains about 180 calories. It's a fair source of vitamins A, C, E and many minerals.

■ **Season.** All year; best prices April through August.

■ **Selection.** Avocados are best for eating when they yield to gentle pressure. In many markets they're sold while still hard; if you buy hard fruit, be sure to allow time for ripening at home. Avoid avocados that look badly bruised or have dark, soft, sunken spots.

■ **Ripening & storage.** To ripen hard avocados as quickly as possible, store them in a loosely closed paper bag at room temperature; check frequently. Fruit will not ripen once cut. Refrigerate cut or whole ripe avocados in a paper or plastic bag for up to 2 days.

■ **Preparation.** To halve an avocado, cut it lengthwise from top to bottom, twisting around pit; pull halves apart. Spear pit with a knife to remove. To slice avocados, peel and cut lengthwise. Coat cut surfaces with lemon or lime juice to prevent browning.

■ **Amount.** One large avocado (about 12 oz.) yields about 1 cup mashed fruit.

■ **Freezing.** Not recommended.

■ **Serving ideas.** Serve avocado slices on scrambled eggs or omelets. Fill an avocado half with shrimp or crab salad, or serve avocado slices with fruit, smoked meats, or tuna salad. Add cubed avocado to hot or cold soups, such as gazpacho. Make a sandwich of mashed avocado on toast, topped with crisp bacon.

■ **Cooking with avocados.** The avocado's smooth texture and mild flavor make it suitable for use in many recipes, but it tastes best uncooked.

GUACAMOLE

Per serving of dip: 193 calories, 3 g protein, 8 g carbohydrates, 19 g total fat, 0 mg cholesterol, 5 mg sodium

> 3 large soft-ripe avocados
> 3 tablespoons lemon juice or lime juice
> ¼ cup finely minced green onions (including tops)
> 1 tablespoon minced fresh cilantro (coriander)
> 1 to 2 tablespoons canned diced green chiles
> ⅛ to ¼ teaspoon liquid hot pepper seasoning
> Salt
> Dippers (suggestions follow)

Pit and peel avocados. Place in a bowl; mash coarsely with a fork, blending in lemon juice. Mix in onions, cilantro, chiles, and hot pepper seasoning. Season to taste with salt. Serve; or cover and refrigerate until next day (stir before serving). To eat, scoop guacamole onto dippers. Makes about 3 cups (6 to 8 servings).

Fuerte

Hass

Zutano

Bacon

California-grown smooth green Fuerte and nubby-skinned Hass are the most popular types of avocados.

Dippers. Choose **tortilla or corn chips;** cold **cooked shrimp;** or **fresh vegetables** such as cherry tomatoes.

AVOCADO HUEVOS RANCHEROS

Per serving: 467 calories, 16 g protein, 21 g carbohydrates, 38 g total fat, 273 mg cholesterol, 1017 mg sodium

- **2 tablespoons olive oil or salad oil**
- **1 medium-size onion, chopped**
- **1 can (15 oz.) tomato sauce**
- **1 clove garlic, minced or pressed**
- **1 can (4 oz.) diced green chiles**
- **1 teaspoon *each* ground cumin and oregano leaves
   Salt and pepper**
- **2 avocados**
- **2 tablespoons lemon juice or lime juice**
- **4 to 8 poached eggs**
- **½ cup shredded jack cheese
   Shredded lettuce**

Heat oil in a frying pan over medium heat; add onion and cook, stirring occasionally, until soft (about 10 minutes). Stir in tomato sauce, garlic, chiles, cumin, and oregano. Simmer, uncovered, until slightly thickened (about 10 minutes). Season to taste with salt and pepper. Remove from heat.

Halve, pit, and peel avocados. Coat on all sides with lemon juice and arrange, cut side up, in a 9-inch baking pan. Place 1 or 2 eggs in each half. Spoon 1 to 2 tablespoons of the tomato sauce over each avocado; sprinkle evenly with cheese. Broil about 6 inches below heat just until cheese is melted. Serve each avocado half on a bed of lettuce. Pass remaining sauce to spoon over all. Makes 4 servings.

■ *See also* **Citrus-Avocado Salad** *(page 24),* **Cauliflower-Spinach Toss** *(page 72).*

Bananas

Native to southern Asia, bananas were one of the first cultivated fruits. Today, they are the third most popular fruit in American markets, ranking just behind apples and oranges. Yet except for a small Hawaiian crop, the entire U.S. supply of this tropical fruit is imported, primarily from Central America.

Why are bananas so readily available? Like pears, they actually ripen better off the tree. Consequently, they can be picked and graded in the tropics, shipped while still green and easy to handle, then ripened domestically in specially equipped rooms.

Continued on next page

There are two principal commercial varieties of bananas, though you probably won't find them labled as such. Mild-flavored Gros Michel, a long banana with a tapered tip, is very resistant to bruising but sensitive to tropical disease. Disease-resistant Cavendish, also mild flavored, is a curved banana that's more sensitive to bruising.

A look through the banana section of many U.S. markets reveals quite a few newcomers. Easy-to-spot Red Spanish or Red Cuban bananas (pictured on page 27) have purplish-red skin and sweet, creamy flesh. Saba (shown at right) and look-alike Brazilian are very straight, clear yellow bananas with squared-off sides and a prominent blossom end. They're tart even when ripe, astringent when unripe. Short, stubby, pale gold Manzano, Apple, or Finger bananas come in bristly bunches. They're refreshingly tart and crunchy when ripe, but puckery if green.

Plantains resemble bananas, but they're longer, thicker, and starchier in flavor. In their native countries, plantains are used more like a vegetable than a fruit; they're usually baked or fried and served like potatoes. They are not suitable for eating raw unless very ripe, when they turn completely black.

Nutrition. Bananas are an almost perfect food. A fully ripe large banana contains only about 100 calories; it's very low in sodium, high in potassium, and quite high in 11 other minerals and six vitamins.

Plantains contain about 120 calories per 3-ounce cooked portion (not including oil if fried). They're a good source of potassium and phosphorus.

■ **Season.** All year; sporadic for specialty bananas.

■ **Selection.** For eating raw, common yellow bananas may be firm and greenish yellow to clear yellow with a few black spots, depending on personal preference. Soft, black-spotted bananas are best for mashing to use in baked goods; firm-ripe fruit is best for most other recipes.

Red Spanish bananas are soft when ripe; their skins turn from purplish red to darker purple. Saba and Manzano types are covered with black spots when ripe; Manzano will also feel soft.

Plantains are usually cooked when green or yellow with some black spots. Plantains to be eaten raw should be entirely black.

■ **Ripening & storage.** Ripen bananas at room temperature, uncovered, out of direct sun; turn daily. Use ripe fruit quickly. You can refrigerate ripe bananas to preserve their flesh, though their skins will turn black.

Plantains should be ripened in the same way as bananas. Store ripe fruit at room temperature.

■ **Preparation.** Simply pull back the peel to eat out of hand; or remove peel and fibrous strings and then slice. Coat cut bananas with lemon, lime, or orange juice to prevent darkening. To mash soft-ripe bananas for cooking, peel and slice, then mash with a fork or potato masher.

To prepare plantains for cooking, cut off ends; then peel, removing fibrous strings. Slice.

■ **Amount.** About 1 pound bananas (2 large or 3 medium-size) or 1 pound plantains yields 1 cup mashed or 1½ cups sliced fruit.

■ **Freezing.** Not recommended.

■ **Serving ideas.** Start the day with banana slices on cereal, pancakes, or waffles. Serve banana chunks in fruit, poultry, or smoked meat salads. For dessert, top banana slices with orange-, hazelnut-, or coffee-flavored liqueur; or top with chocolate sauce, chopped peanuts, and whipped cream. Purée bananas with chilled fruit juice to make banana slush.

■ **Cooking with bananas.** Our instructions are designed for common bananas; exotic types are best eaten raw. Use firm-ripe bananas when slices are called for; when you need mashed bananas for recipes, use soft-ripe fruit.

Like potatoes, starchy plantains can be baked or fried (see recipe) to serve alongside meats or poultry.

Baking. Cut bananas in half lengthwise; do not peel. Glaze and bake (see page 122) until hot throughout (about 15 minutes).

To bake plantains, pierce with a fork in several places; do not peel. Place on a baking sheet and bake in a 400° oven until tender when pierced (about 1 hour). Pull back peel and season to taste with butter, salt, and pepper; eat from skin.

Grilling. Cut bananas in half lengthwise; do not peel. Grill (see page 123), cut side down, until hot throughout (about 5 minutes).

Sautéing. Peel bananas, cut into ½-inch slices, and coat with lemon juice. Sauté (see page 124) just until hot (about 3 minutes).

Banana family newcomers include short and stubby Manzano (or Apple or Finger), medium-size Saba (or Brazilian), and large, starchy plaintain.

FLAMING DESSERT BANANAS

Per serving: 166 calories, .82 g protein, 21 g carbohydrates, 9 g total fat, 27 mg cholesterol, 106 mg sodium

> 2 or 3 large firm-ripe bananas
> 3 tablespoons butter or margarine
> ½ teaspoon grated orange peel
> 2 tablespoons sugar
> ¼ cup Cointreau or curaçao, warmed

Peel bananas; cut in half lengthwise and then crosswise. Melt butter in a chafing dish over direct flame. Add orange peel and bananas, cut side up. Cook quickly until lightly browned; turn over. Sprinkle with sugar. Simmer until fruit is hot (2 to 3 more minutes).

Add Cointreau and ignite (not beneath a vent or fan). Spoon sauce over bananas to serve. Makes 4 servings.

FRIED PLANTAIN CHIPS

Per serving: 157 calories, 1 g protein, 41 g carbohydrates, .55 g total fat, 0 mg cholesterol, 7 mg sodium

> 3 plantains (about 2 lbs. *total*); choose yellow plantains spotted with black
> Salad oil
> 4 cups cold water
> Salt

Cut off and discard ends of plantains; peel, removing fibrous strings. Cut crosswise into ¾-inch slices.

In a deep 3- to 4-quart pan, heat 1½ inches of oil to 375°F on a deep-frying thermometer. Add plantain slices to oil, without crowding; cook until golden (about 3 minutes). Remove from oil with a slotted spoon; drain on paper towels.

With a flat-surfaced mallet, gently pound each plantain slice to a thickness of ⅛ inch. Place in water, without crowding; let stand until edges absorb water and look puffy (2 to 3 minutes). Lift out and lightly pat dry with paper towels.

Return to oil and cook until brown and crisp (about 3 minutes). Remove from oil with a slotted spoon; drain. Sprinkle with salt and serve hot. Or let cool, then cover and refrigerate for up to 2 days. To reheat, spread in a single layer on baking sheets and bake in a 450° oven until hot and crisp (5 to 7 minutes). Makes about 6 servings.

■ *See also Autumn Kiwi Fruit Salad (page 33), Fruit Sorbet (page 41).*

Berries

Plump, fresh berries are one of nature's most fragile—yet most glorious—fruits. Their seasons follow a sweet-to-sour succession—first strawberries, then raspberries, blackberries, blueberries, gooseberries, red currants, and cranberries.

Depending on their sweetness, berries are used quite differently. Naturally sweet strawberries, blackberries, raspberries, and blueberries are all delightful raw, often without added sweetening. Middle-of-the-road gooseberries can be enjoyed raw or cooked, with or without sweetener. Tart red currants and cranberries are almost always served cooked and sweetened with sugar.

Nutrition. Berries are low in calories and generally high in vitamin C (see individual listings).

■ **Season.** Seasons vary depending on the type (see individual listings), but you'll find the best selection of different types from May through July.

■ **Selection.** For the best quality and flavor, select firm, plump berries that are full colored for their variety. (For details on specific types, check the individual listings.)

■ **Ripening & storage.** Berries don't ripen after picking, but they do deteriorate quickly—so plan to use them within 1 or 2 days of purchase. To store, arrange berries, unwashed, in a shallow pan lined with paper towels. Top with more paper towels, then cover with plastic wrap and refrigerate for up to 2 days.

■ **Preparation.** Just before using, place berries in a colander and rinse with a gentle stream of cool water. Drain on paper towels. Remove strawberry caps with a huller or sharp knife; slice if desired. Pull stems from currants. Pinch stem and blossom ends from gooseberries.

■ **Amount.** One pound of any type of berries equals about 4 cups.

■ **Freezing.** To freeze firm-textured blueberries, gooseberries, red currants, or cranberries: arrange, unwashed, in a single layer on a shallow pan; freeze solid. Transfer to plastic bags and store in freezer for up to 6 months. Rinse before using. (Cranberries sold in plastic bags can be frozen as purchased.)

To freeze strawberries, raspberries, or blackberries: rinse well, then drain. Freeze in light syrup (see page 125).

■ **Serving ideas.** Serve strawberries, blackberries, raspberries, or blueberries on cereal, sweet omelets, pancakes, or waffles; or use them in fruit salads with cottage cheese or yogurt. For dessert, serve sweet berries with soft-ripened cheeses, drizzle with orange-flavored liqueur, or present in a stemmed glass with sparkling wine.

■ **Cooking with berries.** Not all types of berries are interchangeable in cooking, so be sure to use the types called for in recipes.

STRAWBERRIES

More than 70 percent of America's fresh strawberries are grown in California. Picking starts in January in the southern part of the state, then moves northward to the central coast by April. Typically, a surge in volume begins in mid-April; prices are lowest in May. From November through January, berries from Florida, Mexico, and New Zealand extend the strawberry season.

The cultivation of strawberries goes back to the mid-1600s, when early Massachusetts settlers enjoyed fruits grown by local Indians. But today's market strawberries evolved from five varieties developed at the University of California in 1945. Since then, hundreds of new strawberry varieties have been developed, with whole new generations introduced every 4 or 5 years. Of the types widely grown today, Chandler, Pajaro, and Douglas have outstanding flavor. Chandler is excellent for freezing.

Though there's no direct relationship between size and flavor, California strawberries are bred to be large—so any small or misshapen fruits probably grew poorly. The long-stemmed berries found in fancy markets aren't a special variety—they're just selected very carefully (usually, one picker is responsible for choosing them).

Fraises des bois are very tiny strawberries of European origin, now grown on a small scale in California. Both red and white varieties are very fragrant, with a sweet, mild flavor and slightly crunchy seeds. Look for them in upscale markets from May through October.

Nutrition. Strawberries are low in calories—about 55 per cup—and high in vitamin C.

RASPBERRIES

Though cultivated raspberries weren't introduced to the United States until the late 1700s, the wild berries are native to this country: red raspberries grow in the northern states, black raspberries farther south. Today, though, we see not only the familiar red and black raspberries, but also purple and golden types. California, Oregon, and Washington are the main producers.

Red raspberries remain the favorite; the photo on page 15 shows four Western varieties. Willamette (available mid-May through June) and Meeker (late June through July) are early-season berries; their soft, juicy texture makes them hard to ship, so they're frequently frozen or used in preserves. Late-bearing, firm-textured Heritage and Sweetbriar (mid-July through December, peaking in September) are the best varieties for shipping and for eating raw.

Black raspberries are small and seedy, with a distinctive mild-tart flavor. The purple raspberry is a hybrid of the red and black varieties; the golden raspberry is a novel variation of the red type, with a sweeter, milder flavor than its parent.

Continued on next page

Raspberries are the only cane berries that come free of their caps when picked, making them the most fragile of all. When selecting raspberries, choose plump, well-shaped fruit that's free of mold. Stained baskets indicate soft, overripe berries.

Nutrition. Red raspberries are rich in vitamins A and C. Red raspberries contain around 70 calories per cup, black raspberries about 100.

BLACKBERRIES

Wild blackberries didn't begin to flourish in this country until the forests were cleared, giving the plants enough sun and space to grow well. Blackberry cultivation began in about 1825.

There are actually two classes of blackberries—a trailing, ground-running kind, sometimes called dewberry, and the brambleberries that grow on erect plants.

Nutrition. Blackberries are high in vitamin C. One cup of berries has about 85 calories.

■ **Blackberry varieties.** Aside from loganberries, which are red, most blackberries range in color from dark maroon to glossy black. But though they look much alike, they may differ markedly in flavor and texture.

Boysen. Grown mainly in California but also to some extent in Oregon and Texas, boysenberries are plump, 1¼-inch-long dewberries with a deep maroon color and a tart, aromatic flavor. They make great pies. When sweetened, they're delicious with yogurt or ice cream. Their season runs from June through July.

Cherokee. Available in small quantities from California and Oregon, these are large, sturdy, glossy blackberries with a smooth, mellow flavor. They're sweet enough to eat alone; for pies, combine them with tarter berries. Look for California berries from late May through October; the Oregon season runs from mid-July through August.

Evergreen. This old Northwest variety is a medium-size berry with a glossy black color. Mild in flavor with little tartness, Evergreens are best paired with tarter berries for pies. For eating fresh, enliven their flavor with lemon juice and sugar to taste. These are late-season berries, available from mid-August through mid-September.

Logan. The oldest trailing blackberry variety on the Pacific Coast, the loganberry was developed in California (it now comes primarily from Oregon). Loganberries are large, long, dark red, and quite tart; combine them with sweeter berries in pies, or use them in jams. Their season extends from mid-May through mid-July.

Marion. Medium-size and slightly elongated, Oregon-grown marionberries are rather soft—therefore rather difficult to ship. They have an outstanding rich, tangy-sweet flavor. These berries are in season from mid-July to mid-August.

Ollalie. Developed at Oregon State University and now grown extensively in California, ollalieberries are a cross between a black logan and a youngberry (yet another blackberry hybrid). They're long berries, more slender than boysens, with shiny black skin when fully ripe; if the fruit is still dark maroon, it will be very tart. Ollalies are great for pies. Their season runs from late May through early July.

BLUEBERRIES

Wild blueberries have been a cherished part of the American heritage since the nation's earliest years. In colonial times, they were the basis of such classic dishes as "grunt," "slump," "buckle," and "flummery."

Cultivation of large blueberries began in the early 1900s; today, they are found all over the world, in French *clafouti*, German *kuchen*, Swedish pancakes, Jewish blintzes, and Scottish jams.

The United States and Canada are still the largest producers and consumers of this North American native. The berries in American markets in mid-April come from the southern and eastern United States; from late June through September, the fruit comes from Washington, Oregon, Michigan, Maine, and British Columbia.

Blueberry varieties differ slightly in size and flavor, but it's hard to tell them apart. Most are seedless, with a crunchy texture and a sweet, mild flavor that's enhanced by a little lemon juice. Fresh berries should be plump and firm, with a light grayish bloom.

Nutrition. Blueberries are rich in vitamin C. One cup has about 90 calories.

GOOSEBERRIES

Gooseberries aren't a common sight in American markets, yet some 50 species are grown worldwide. In recent years, there has been an increase in the commercial supplies coming from New Zealand and a few growers in California and Oregon.

Crunchy-textured gooseberries are light green in color, quite tart in flavor. A new, larger variety, Poorman, is sweeter and can be eaten "as is"—but most gooseberries are used to make pies and preserves.

Domestic fruit is in season from May through August, peaking in June; New Zealand supplies are sold from October through December.

Bright yellow cape gooseberries, sometimes called Physalis, are larger and sweeter than green gooseberries—you can eat them out of hand. Each has a brown, papery husk. The season for these New Zealand imports runs from February through June.

Nutrition. Gooseberries have about 120 calories per cup and contain a good supply of vitamin C.

RED CURRANTS

Tart, intensely flavored red currants, excellent for preserves and meat sauces, grow in small clusters or bunches. Select slightly underripe berries for jelly, since greener fruit contains more natural pectin. (The dried currants used in baking are really a type of grape; see page 30.)

Almost all the currants in U.S. markets come from Oregon; the season is short, running from early July to early August. When you buy, look for currants firmly attached to the cluster stems.

Nutrition. Low in sodium and high in vitamin C, currants contain 62 calories per cup, unsweetened.

CRANBERRIES

Since the first Thanksgiving, Americans have been harvesting these tart, bright red native berries from the swampy bogs where they grow. Originally hand picked, then gathered with wooden rakes, cranberries are picked mechanically today—the only berry to be harvested by machine.

North America remains the sole producer of cranberries. Massachusetts

Strawberries

Fraises des Bois (red)

Fraises des Bois (white)

Pajaro

Heidi

Chandler

Blackberries

Boysen

Olallie

Logan

Marion

Cherokee

Raspberries

Willamette

Heritage

Meeker

Sweetbriar

Brandywine (purple)

Munger (black)

Gooseberries

Oregon Champion

Red currants

Cherry

Blueberries

Patriot

Earliblue

Bluetta

and Wisconsin produce the bulk of the crop, followed by New Jersey, Washington, Oregon, and western Canada.

Of more than 100 different cranberry varieties, just four types make up most of the commercial supply. Two of these are Massachusetts berries: Early Black, a small, blackish red berry harvested in September, and oblong Howe, medium red and fairly large. Searles is a Wisconsin berry; deep red McFarlin, grown in the Northwest, is named for the man who started cranberry cultivation in that part of the country.

Like red currants, cranberries need to be sweetened with sugar. They are especially tasty in preserves and relishes—as an accompaniment to meats and, of course, turkey and other poultry.

Cranberry season runs from September through November. Choose firm, plump berries; avoid those that look withered.

Nutrition. Unsweetened raw cranberries contain just 44 calories per cup. They're very high in vitamins A and C.

WINE & BERRY COMPOTE

Per serving: 274 calories, 4 g protein, 51 g carbohydrates, 7 g total fat, 27 mg cholesterol, 45 mg sodium

- 1 to 1½ pounds (4 to 6 cups) mixed berries (strawberries, raspberries, any of the blackberries, blueberries, gooseberries, or red currants)
- 1 cup *each* dry red wine and water
- ¾ cup sugar
- 6 tablespoons lemon juice
- 1 vanilla bean (6 to 7 inches long), split lengthwise; or 1 teaspoon vanilla
- 1½ to 2 pints vanilla ice cream

Hull berries or remove blossom and/or stem ends, as necessary. Rinse and drain berries; set aside.

In a 4- to 5-quart pan, combine wine, water, sugar, lemon juice, and vanilla bean. Bring to a boil over high heat, stirring until sugar is dissolved; then boil, uncovered, until reduced to 1¼ cups.

Remove vanilla bean and scrape seeds into syrup. (If using vanilla, add at this point.) If made ahead, cover and refrigerate for up to 3 weeks; bring to a simmer before continuing. Gently stir berries into hot syrup; set aside to cool slightly.

For each serving, place 1 large scoop ice cream in a dessert bowl. Spoon berries in syrup around ice cream. Makes 6 to 8 servings.

Tart red cranberries are most plentiful in autumn, just in time to go into fresh-tasting relishes for holiday meals.

BLUEBERRY CRUNCH COFFEE RING

Per serving: 390 calories, 5 g protein, 57 g carbohydrates, 17 g total fat, 65 mg cholesterol, 433 mg sodium

Walnut Streusel (recipe follows)
- 1½ cups all-purpose flour
- ¾ cup granulated sugar
- 1 tablespoon baking powder
- ½ teaspoon salt
- ¼ teaspoon ground nutmeg
- ⅓ cup firm butter or margarine
- 1 cup blueberries
- 1 egg
- ½ cup milk
- 1 teaspoon vanilla
  Powdered sugar

Prepare Walnut Streusel. Pat about half the streusel into a greased, flour-dusted 9-inch tube pan or layer cake pan with a removable bottom; set aside.

In a large bowl, stir together flour, granulated sugar, baking powder, salt, and nutmeg. Using a pastry blender or 2 knives, cut in butter until mixture resembles coarse crumbs. Gently stir in blueberries.

Beat egg lightly with milk and vanilla; stir into berry mixture just until combined. Spread half the batter in streusel-lined pan; sprinkle with remaining streusel, then spread with remaining batter.

Bake in a 350° oven until a pick inserted in center comes out clean (45 to 60 minutes). Let cool in pan for 20 minutes, then remove pan sides. Dust with powdered sugar. Serve warm or cool. Makes 8 to 10 servings.

Walnut Streusel. Mix ½ cup *each* finely chopped **walnuts** and firmly packed **brown sugar**, 2 tablespoons **all-purpose flour**, 2 teaspoons **ground cinnamon**, and 2 tablespoons melted **butter** or margarine.

BERRIES WITH CHANTILLY CUSTARD

Per serving: 228 calories, 5 g protein, 17 g carbohydrates, 16 g total fat, 231 mg cholesterol, 36 mg sodium

- ½ cup milk
- 1 piece vanilla bean (3 to 4 inches long), split lengthwise; or ½ teaspoon vanilla
- 1½ tablespoons sugar
  Yolks of 3 large eggs
- 1 tablespoon almond- or orange-flavored liqueur
- ½ cup whipping cream
- 3 to 4 cups berries (hulled small strawberries or fraises des bois, raspberries, any of the blackberries, or blueberries), rinsed and drained

In a 1- to 2-quart pan, combine milk and vanilla bean. Bring to scalding over medium heat. In a bowl, whisk together sugar and egg yolks; whisk about ⅓ of the hot milk mixture into yolk mixture, then pour all back into pan. Reduce heat to low and cook, stirring, until mixture coats the back of a metal spoon (about 15 minutes). Immediately remove from heat and stir until cool. If using vanilla, stir in; then stir in liqueur. Cover and refrigerate until cold (at least 2 hours) or until next day. Remove vanilla bean.

Beat cream until stiff; fold into chilled custard. Spoon into 4 or 5 (about 1½-cup) wine glasses or dessert bowls. Spoon berries over custard cream. Makes 4 or 5 servings.

GOOSEBERRY OR CURRANT RELISH

Per serving: 49 calories, .23 g protein, 12 g carbohydrates, .06 g total fat, 0 mg cholesterol, .42 mg sodium

- ¾ cup gooseberries or red currants
- ½ cup water
- ⅓ cup *each* sugar and orange juice
- 1½ tablespoons lemon juice
- ½ teaspoon finely grated orange peel

Remove stem and blossom ends from gooseberries (or stem currants). Rinse and drain berries.

In a 1- to 1½-quart pan, combine water, sugar, orange juice, and lemon juice; bring to a boil over high heat, stirring until sugar is dissolved. Add ½ cup of the berries; reduce heat to

"CAN'T MISS" FRUIT PIES

Traditional fruit pie, warm from the oven, may just be the all-time favorite dessert. Achieving the proper flaky crust and juicy fruit filling is a can't miss proposition with our easy pastry recipe and filling variations. And if you like, you can use a spicy streusel topping in place of the top crust. The proportions given here are for a 9-inch pie.

FRESH FRUIT PIE

    Fruit Filling (recipes follow)
    Flaky Pastry (recipe follows)
  2 tablespoons butter or margarine
    (for double-crust pie)
    Streusel Topping (recipe follows),
    optional

Prepare fruit filling of your choice; determine amount of sugar (within indicated range) by sweetness of fruit and personal taste. Sugar increases the liquid in pie, so if you use the maximum amount of sugar, or if fruit is juicy, use the maximum amount of cornstarch or tapioca. Set filling aside.

Prepare pastry; if making amount for a double-crust pie, divide into 2 equal portions. On a lightly floured board or pastry cloth, flatten one portion into a round. With a floured or stockinet-covered rolling pin, roll out from center in all directions with light, even strokes, making an 11-inch circle about ⅛ inch thick.

Gently fold pastry circle into quarters; transfer to a 9-inch pie pan, placing point of folded pastry at pan center. Carefully unfold, using fingertips to fit pastry gently onto pan sides.

For double-crust pie, pour filling into pastry shell; dot with butter. Roll out remaining pastry to an 11-inch circle; fold into quarters, transfer onto pie, and gently unfold to cover filling. Trim, leaving a 1-inch overhang; then seal by folding edge of top pastry under edge of bottom pastry. Flute edge. Cut several slashes in top to allow steam to escape.

For streusel-topped pie, trim bottom pastry, leaving a 1-inch overhang. Fold edge under and flute, hooking edge slightly over rim. Pour in fruit filling. Prepare Streusel Topping; squeeze into large chunks over fruit.

Set oven at 400°. To prevent overbrowning, wrap edge of pie with a foil strip 2 to 3 inches wide. Set pie on a rimmed baking sheet and bake on lowest oven rack for recommended time, until juices bubble vigorously and pastry is well browned. Check all streusel-topped pies after they have baked 15 to 20 minutes; if they are browning too fast, loosely cover streusel with foil. Remove foil strip from double-crust pie 15 to 20 minutes before pie is done. Remove foil from streusel topping about 5 minutes before pie is done.

Let cool on a rack. Serve warm; cover cooled pie and refrigerate to serve cold; or reheat, uncovered, in a 350° oven until heated through (10 to 15 minutes).

Apple Filling. Combine 8 cups peeled, cored, thinly sliced **apples,** ¾ to 1 cup **sugar,** 2½ to 3 tablespoons **cornstarch** or quick-cooking tapioca, 1 teaspoon **ground cinnamon,** and ¼ teaspoon **ground ginger.**
Bake pie for 50 to 60 minutes.

Apricot Filling. Combine 8 cups quartered and pitted fully ripe **apricots** (slice if large), 1¼ to 1½ cups **sugar,** 3½ to 4 tablespoons **cornstarch** or quick-cooking tapioca, 1 tablespoon **lemon juice,** and 1¼ teaspoons **ground coriander.**
Bake pie for 55 to 75 minutes.

Berry Filling. Combine 6 cups whole **blackberries** or blueberries, 1½ to 1¾ cups **sugar,** and 3½ to 4 tablespoons **cornstarch** or quick-cooking tapioca. For blueberry pie only, stir in 1 tablespoon **lemon juice.**
Bake pie for 55 to 60 minutes.

Peach or Nectarine Filling. Combine 8 cups peeled, thinly sliced **peaches** or thinly sliced unpeeled nectarines, ¾ to 1 cup **sugar,** 3 to 3½ tablespoons **cornstarch** or quick-cooking tapioca, 2 tablespoons **lemon juice,** and ½ teaspoon **ground nutmeg.**
Bake pie for 45 to 75 minutes.

Pear Filling. Combine 8 cups peeled, cored, thinly sliced **pears,** ¾ to 1 cup **sugar,** 2½ to 3 tablespoons **cornstarch** or quick-cooking tapioca, 2 tablespoons **lemon juice,** and ½ teaspoon **ground ginger.**
Bake pie for 55 to 60 minutes.

Plum Filling. Combine 8 cups pitted and sliced **plums,** 1½ to 2 cups **sugar,** 6½ to 7 tablespoons **cornstarch** or quick-cooking tapioca, 1 teaspoon grated **lemon peel,** and ½ teaspoon **ground cinnamon.**
Bake pie for 1 hour.

Flaky Pastry. In a large bowl, combine 2¼ cups **all-purpose flour** and ½ teaspoon **salt.** Using a pastry blender or 2 knives, cut in ¾ cup **solid vegetable shortening,** lard, or firm margarine until particles are about the size of peas. Sprinkle 4 to 5 tablespoons **cold water,** a tablespoon at a time, over flour mixture, stirring lightly and quickly with a fork just until all flour is moistened. Dough should be neither dry and crumbly nor wet and sticky. Stir with a fork until dough almost cleans sides of bowl. Press lightly into a ball. Makes enough pastry for a double-crust 9-inch pie; prepare half the recipe for a streusel-topped 9-inch pie.

Streusel Topping. In a bowl, combine 1 cup **all-purpose flour,** ½ cup firmly packed **brown sugar,** and ½ teaspoon **ground cinnamon.** With your fingers, rub in 6 tablespoons **butter** or margarine until mixture resembles course crumbs. Stir in ½ cup chopped **nuts,** if desired. Makes enough topping for a 9-inch pie.

... Berries continued

medium and boil, uncovered, until reduced to 1 cup (about 30 minutes). Add remaining ¼ cup berries and continue to cook just until some of them begin to pop (about 3 minutes). Stir in orange peel. Serve relish warm or cool, as a sauce on ice cream or as an accompaniment for lamb, pork, or chicken. Makes 1¼ cups (about 7 servings).

CRANBERRY-ORANGE RELISH

Per ¼ cup: 86 calories, .25 g protein, 22 g carbohydrates, .27 g total fat, 0 mg cholesterol, 1 mg sodium

Using a food chopper fitted with a fine blade, grind 1 pound (4 cups) **cranberries** and 1 large unpeeled **orange,** cut into quarters. In a small pan, stir together cranberry mixture and 1 cup **sugar;** bring to a boil over medium heat, stirring constantly. Remove from heat, cover, and refrigerate until cold (at least 3 hours) or up to 4 days. Makes 3 cups.

■ *See also* **Fruit Pie** *(page 17),* **Fruit Jam** *(page 28),* **Raspberry Sauce** *(page 33),* **Fruit Sorbet** *(page 41),* **Rhubarb-Strawberry Pie** *(page 54).*

Cactus Pears see Prickly Pears, page 52

Carambolas

When sliced crosswise, the yellow-gold carambola reveals the striking shape that has earned it the nickname "starfruit." Both decorative shape and bright color make sliced carambolas very attractive as a garnish for beverages, salads, and meats. *(Photo on page 27.)*

Native to the Malay Archipelago, carambolas are now grown commercially in southern Florida. The fruit is oval in shape, with four to six prominent longitudinal ribs; it has edible waxy skin and yellow flesh that's crisp like an apple. The flavor ranges from sweet-tart to quite sour, depending on the variety.

Two basic carambola types are sold in American markets. Cultivated Arkin is grown from rootstocks; it has a pleasant sweet-tart flavor. A second class of

carambolas, grown from seed, tends to be tarter than Arkin.

■ **Nutrition.** Carambolas are a good source of vitamin C. One-half cup of sliced fruit has just 35 calories.

■ **Season.** September through February, in limited quantities.

■ **Selection.** Ripe fruit turns yellow-gold, with a slightly brown tinge on the prominent ribs. Fruit will ripen at room temperature, but avoid carambolas that are more green than yellow.

■ **Ripening & storage.** Ripen fruit at room temperature, uncovered, out of direct sun; turn frequently. Refrigerate ripe fruit, unwashed, in a loosely closed paper or plastic bag for up to 1 week.

■ **Preparation.** Wash carambolas well; pat dry. Cut crosswise into thin slices.

■ **Amount.** One pound carambolas (2 large or 3 medium-size fruits) yields about 2 cups sliced fruit.

■ **Freezing.** Not recommended.

■ **Serving ideas.** Use sliced raw carambolas as a garnish for beverages, ham, roast pork, or poultry. Add raw slices to fruit, mixed green, or poultry salads. For appetizers, top toasted French bread with cream cheese or salami and sliced carambolas.

■ **Cooking with carambolas.** Because carambolas are quick to prepare—they needn't be peeled or coated with lemon juice to prevent browning—they are especially easy to use in recipes. Though they're most often eaten raw, they are also delicious sautéed; if cooked quickly, they retain their appealing tender-crisp texture.

Sautéing. Cut unpeeled carambolas crosswise into ½-inch slices. Sauté (see page 124) until hot and tender-crisp when pierced (3 to 5 minutes).

CARAMBOLA SPINACH SALAD WITH PASSION FRUIT DRESSING

Per serving of salad: 40 calories, 4 g protein, 7 g carbohydrates, .46 g total fat, 0 mg cholesterol, 82 mg sodium
Per tablespoon of dressing: 66 calories, .06 g protein, 2 g carbohydrates, 7 g total fat, 0 mg cholesterol, .49 mg sodium

> Passion Fruit Dressing
> (recipe follows)
> 1½ pounds spinach
> 1 small red onion, thinly sliced and separated into rings
> 2 cups sliced carambolas

Prepare Passion Fruit Dressing. Discard spinach stems and any tough or wilted leaves. Then thoroughly rinse

spinach and pat dry with paper towels. On each of 6 salad plates, arrange ⅙ of the leaves in concentric circles. Decoratively arrange ⅙ of the onion rings and ⅓ cup of the carambolas atop spinach leaves on each plate. If made ahead, cover and refrigerate for up to 1 hour. To serve, offer dressing to spoon over individual portions. Makes 6 servings.

Passion Fruit Dressing. Whirl ¼ cup **passion fruit pulp** (2 to 3 fruits, see page 42) in a blender or food processor until seeds resemble coarsely ground pepper. Add 6 tablespoons **lemon juice,** 2 tablespoons **sugar,** and 1 teaspoon *each* grated **lemon peel** and **dry mustard.** Whirl until blended. With motor running, pour in ¾ cup **salad oil.** Season to taste with **salt.** If made ahead, cover and refrigerate for up to 3 days.

Cherimoyas

Native to the cool, dry slopes of the Andes, cherimoyas (sometimes called "custard apples") now grow readily along the California coast. These heart-shaped, 4- to 6-inch-long fruits have pale green, leathery skin and luscious, cream-colored flesh with a custardy texture and a flavor something like pineapple crossed with banana. The flesh is generously studded with black seeds.

Nutrition. Cherimoyas are low in sodium and high in niacin, phosphorus, and thiamin. A ⅓-pound serving provides 94 calories.

■ **Season.** November through April; peak in February and March.

■ **Selection.** Cherimoyas sold in grocery stores are usually still pale green and quite firm. When ripe, the fruit turns a dull brownish green; some varieties will have tan freckles. Ripe fruit yields to gentle pressure like a ripe peach.

■ **Ripening & storage.** Ripen fruit at room temperature, uncovered, out of direct sun; turn frequently. Firm, light green fruit may take up to 1 week to ripen. Refrigerate ripe fruit in a paper or plastic bag for up to 2 days.

Serve soft, ripe cherimoyas in wedges, accompanied with orange or lemon wedges to squeeze on top. Eat fruit from skin with a spoon; discard seeds.

■ **Preparation.** Cut cherimoyas into wedges and sprinkle with lemon or orange juice to prevent darkening. To eat, scoop flesh from skin with spoon, discarding seeds. Or peel fruit with a knife and cut into 1-inch cubes; discard seeds.

To purée, coarsely mash seeded cubes with a fork, or purée in a blender or food processor.

■ **Amount.** One large cherimoya (about 1½ lbs.) yields about 2 cups cubed fruit or 1½ cups purée.

■ **Freezing.** Not recommended.

■ **Serving ideas.** Combine cherimoya and fresh orange chunks for breakfast. Use chunks in fruit salads, or sprinkle with orange-flavored liqueur and serve over orange sherbet for dessert.

■ **Cooking with cherimoyas.** The cherimoya is a soft, delicate fruit that is best served raw.

CHERIMOYA CHIFFON PIE

Per serving: 352 calories, 5 g protein, 43 g carbohydrates, 19 g total fat, 40 mg cholesterol, 166 mg sodium

  1 **large ripe cherimoya (about 1½ lbs.)**
  ¼ **cup orange juice**
  ¼ **cup sugar**
  1 **envelope unflavored gelatin**
  ¼ **cup cold water**
  3 **egg whites**
  6 **tablespoons sugar**
  1 **cup whipping cream**
      Baked 9-inch pie shell
  1 **small orange, sliced**

Cut cherimoya in half. Scoop out pulp, discarding seeds; whirl pulp in a blender or food processor until puréed (you should have 1½ cups purée). In a small bowl, combine purée, orange juice, and the ¼ cup sugar.

In a small pan, sprinkle gelatin over cold water; let soften for 5 minutes. Heat over medium heat, stirring, until gelatin is dissolved. Stir gelatin mixture into cherimoya mixture and refrigerate just until mixture begins to thicken.

In large bowl of an electric mixer, beat egg whites on high speed until they hold soft peaks. Gradually add the 6 tablespoons sugar, beating until mixture holds stiff, moist peaks.

Beat cream until stiff. Fold fruit mixture and half the whipped cream into egg whites just until blended. Pour into pie shell and refrigerate until firm (at least 3 hours) or until next day. Cover and refrigerate remaining whipped cream.

To serve, garnish pie with remaining whipped cream and orange slices. Makes 6 to 8 servings.

■ *See also **Fruit Sorbet** (page 41).*

Cherries

By the time agricultural historians began keeping records, cherries were already well established in Asia, in Europe, and (in wild form) in America. Cultivated European varieties were brought to North America by early colonists, and today the United States grows more cherries than any other country.

The West, led by Washington, is the top producer of sweet cherries in the United States. East of the Rockies, cherries are grown from the southern side of the Great Lakes basin to New York's Hudson River Valley.

There are two commercially important sweet cherry types: dark red to purple-skinned cherries and yellow-skinned ones. In the dark-colored category, extra-sweet Bing is the dominant commercial sweet cherry, followed by Lambert. Black Tartarian, Chapman, Burlat, and other Bing look-alikes can be found in smaller supplies at roadside stands.

Yellow-fleshed, red-blushed Royal Anns are best known among the lighter-skinned sweet cherries. Though

Dark red Bing and Lambert are the most popular sweet cherries; Rainier is a new yellow-skinned type.

they're a bit too fragile to ship, they can be found at roadside stands and local markets. Rainier is a promising new commercial variety of yellow-skinned cherry.

Aside from sweet cherries, there's another kind of cherry—the sour cherry ("pie cherry," as it's often called). You may find some of these high-acid fruits at roadside stands, but most are processed for canning or freezing. Montmorency, the chief sour cherry variety, is grown in New England, the Great Lakes region, and the Great Plains.

Nutrition. Cherries are a fair source of vitamin A. One cup of raw sweet cherries contains 65 calories.

■ **Season.** Mid-May through July; peak in June. Domestic cherries sold after the first week of August have probably been in cold storage. A small supply of sweet cherries imported from New Zealand is available from mid-November through January.

■ **Selection.** Sweet cherries increase in size, sweetness, and depth of color as they ripen. Look for plump, bright-colored cherries; those with mahogany or reddish brown skin promise the most flavor. Avoid overly soft or shriveled cherries and those with dark stems. Sour cherries should also be plump and bright colored.

■ **Ripening & storage.** Cherries are quite perishable. To keep them fresh for several days, line a shallow pan with several layers of paper towels. Arrange cherries, unwashed, on towels in a single layer; then top with more paper towels and plastic wrap. Refrigerate for up to 3 days.

■ **Preparation.** Simply rinse cherries to eat fresh; discard stems and pits. To pit cherries for use in recipes, use a cherry pitter—an inexpensive tool sold at hardware and cookware shops.

Continued on next page

■ **Amount.** One pound of cherries yields about 2 ½ cups pitted fruit.

■ **Freezing.** Pit cherries and freeze in light syrup (see page 125).

■ **Serving ideas.** Sprinkle pitted cherries on cereal, pancakes or waffles, or sweet omelets. Add pitted cherries to fruit, gelatin, or poultry salads. For dessert, serve cherries over ice cream with cherry-flavored liqueur. Or pair with any soft-ripened cheese.

■ **Cooking with cherries.** Since almost all sour cherries are processed, our recipes feature sweet cherries. While cherries lose much of their fresh taste when cooked, they stay firm and have rich, sweet flavor when poached.

Poaching. Rinse 3 cups stemmed and pitted dark sweet cherries. Simmer in poaching liquid (see page 124) until hot and tender (about 3 minutes).

CHERRY SALAD WITH SESAME DRESSING

Per serving: 293 calories, 5 g protein, 52 g carbohydrates, 10 g total fat, 17 mg cholesterol, 123 mg sodium

> **Sesame-Orange Dressing (recipe follows)**
> 1 **medium-size head iceberg lettuce**
> 1 **small pineapple (2 to 2½ lbs.), peeled, cored, and cut into 1-inch pieces (see page 49)**
> 2½ **cups dark sweet cherries (about 1 lb.), stemmed and pitted**

Prepare Sesame-Orange Dressing; set aside.

Line a 1½- to 2-quart salad bowl with about 4 of the largest lettuce leaves. Break remaining lettuce into bite-size pieces and place in bowl. Add pineapple and cherries.

To serve, pour dressing over salad and mix to coat evenly. Makes about 6 servings.

Sesame-Orange Dressing. Toast 2 tablespoons **sesame seeds** in an 8- to 10-inch frying pan over medium heat until golden (about 5 minutes), shaking pan frequently. Set aside. In a bowl, stir together 1 cup **sour cream,** 3 tablespoons *each* **lime juice** and **frozen concentrated orange juice,** and ¼ teaspoon **salt.** Add sesame seeds; stir until well blended.

For a showy tart, arrange circles of dark red pitted cherries on a rich butter crust and glaze with melted red currant jelly.

CHERRY RAISINS

Per ¼ cup: 114 calories, 2 g protein, 28 g carbohydrates, .40 g total fat, 0 mg cholesterol, 3 mg sodium

> 4 to 5 **cups dark sweet cherries (about 2 lbs.), stemmed and pitted**
> 1 **tablespoon sugar**

Place cherries in a single layer, slightly apart, on a 12- by 17-inch rimmed baking sheet. Sprinkle evenly with sugar. Bake in a 200° oven just until juice oozes from fruit (about 30 minutes).

Cover baking sheet with cheesecloth to keep out leaves and insects. Then place in a sunny location and let dry for 2 to 4 days; turn cherries once daily, and bring them inside at night.

Cherries are ready to store when shriveled and leathery, but still tacky to the touch. Store in airtight containers in a cool place. Makes 1 to 1⅓ cups.

DARK CHERRY TART

Per serving: 368 calories, 4 g protein, 62 g carbohydrates, 13 g total fat, 67 mg cholesterol, 146 mg sodium

> **Butter Crust (recipe follows)**
> 6 **cups dark sweet cherries (about 2 ½ lbs.), stemmed and pitted**
> ½ **cup sugar**
> 2 **tablespoons cornstarch**
> 2 **tablespoons lemon juice**
> ⅛ **teaspoon ground cinnamon**
> ⅓ **cup red currant jelly**

Prepare Butter Crust and set aside. Choose enough of the prettiest cherries to make 4 cups. Set aside. Whirl remaining 2 cups cherries in a blender or food processor until puréed. In a 2- to 3-quart pan, combine sugar and cornstarch; stir in cherry purée, lemon juice, and cinnamon. Cook over medium heat, stirring constantly, until thick and bubbly. Remove from heat and let cool slightly, then pour into Butter Crust. Refrigerate until set (about 1 hour).

Arrange reserved cherries evenly over cherry filling. Place jelly in a small pan; stir over medium-low heat until melted. Brush jelly over cherries to glaze. Refrigerate tart until glaze is set (at least 1 hour) or until next day.

To serve, remove sides of pan; cut tart into wedges. Makes 8 to 10 servings.

Butter Crust. In a food processor (or in a bowl), combine 1⅓ cups **all-purpose flour,** 3 tablespoons **sugar,** and ½ cup (¼ lb.) firm **butter** or margarine, cut into pieces. Whirl (or rub with your fingers) until mixture resembles coarse crumbs. Add 1 **egg yolk** and whirl or mix with a fork until combined. Shape dough into a ball; press over bottom and up sides of an 11-inch tart pan with a removable bottom. Bake in a 300° oven until light brown (about 30 minutes). Let cool.

Citrus

You'll find many members of the citrus family represented in American markets, including oranges, lemons, limes, grapefruit, mandarins (tangerines, tangelos, and tangors), and kumquats. These fruits vary in taste from extra-sweet to mouth-puckering, and they offer a diversity of color and texture as well.

Native to Asia, citrus fruits thrive in mild subtropical climates. Florida and California produce the biggest share of the U.S. crop, followed by Arizona and Texas.

Nutrition. Citrus fruits are exceptionally high in vitamin C; a single

UNLOCKING THE COCONUT

Coconut is a tough nut to crack—but a trip to the toolbox will yield the proper equipment for the job.

At the market, choose a coconut that sloshes when you shake it; if you don't hear anything, it may be dried out. To open the coconut, pierce the three dark-colored eyes at the top of the nut with a screwdriver or an ice pick. Pour out the liquid inside; reserve to serve as a beverage, if desired. Place the drained coconut on a rimmed baking sheet in a 350° oven for about 15 minutes, or just until shell begins to crack. Let cool briefly, then place on a sturdy surface. Using a hammer or mallet, hit hard along the crack; the nut should break into pieces.

Pry white coconut flesh from shell with a screwdriver or knife with a rounded end. If desired, pare off brown skin with a small knife or vegetable peeler. Grate the coconut to use in fruit salads, baked goods, or confections, or as a condiment to serve with curries. Or cube it to make fresh coconut milk, often called for in Asian and tropical dishes.

To make coconut milk, cut fresh coconut into ½-inch chunks. For each cup of coconut chunks, mea-

Briefly baking a coconut makes it easier to crack; use a screwdriver and hammer to complete the job.

sure 1 cup hot water. Whirl together in a blender or food processor until mixture is thick and pulpy (about 20 to 30 seconds); then let steep for 30 minutes. Strain through a double thickness of cheesecloth, squeezing out liquid; discard coconut. Cover and refrigerate "milk" for up to 3 days; or freeze for longer storage. One cup *each* coconut and hot water makes about 1 cup coconut milk.

---

serving of the fresh fruit or juice provides a full day's supply of this vitamin. Citrus fruits are also relatively low in calories—about 70 per medium-size orange, 50 for half a grapefruit.

■ **Season.** All year; see variety listings for specifics.

■ **Selection.** For the juiciest, sweetest citrus, select firm, thin-skinned fruit that's full colored for its type and heavy for its size.

■ **Ripening & storage.** Citrus fruits are sold ripe and ready to eat. They can be stored at cool room temperature (60° to 70°F) for up to 1 week, in the refrigerator for up to 2 weeks.

■ **Preparation.** *To peel citrus for eating out of hand,* wedge thumb between peel and flesh; pull off peel a piece at a time. Break fruit into sections to eat. *To remove peel and all white membrane,* run a sharp knife between peel and flesh; peel fruit spiral fashion.

To section peeled fruit for salads, run a sharp knife along sides of dividing membranes to core; twist knife at core to release sections.

To eat oranges or grapefruit from shell, cut in half crosswise. Using a curved knife, cut around each section; eat with a spoon.

To juice citrus, roll fruit on a firm surface to soften; then ream on a lemon juicer. *To grate* citrus peel, rub colored part only against small holes of grater. *To cut citrus zest* (colored outer part of peel), drag a zester across peel; or use a vegetable peeler to remove colored part of peel, then chop finely.

■ **Amount.** Three medium-size or 2 large oranges make 1 pound. One lemon yields about 3 tablespoons juice; you'll get 2 tablespoons from a lime, about ½ cup from an orange.

■ **Freezing.** Not recommended for the fruit itself, but citrus juice can be frozen in plastic containers for up to a year.

■ **Serving ideas.** Add orange, grapefruit, or mandarin sections to fruit, poultry, fish, smoked meat, or green salads. Use lemon or lime juice to season beverages, salads, fish, poultry, and cooked vegetables. For dessert, serve poached oranges or oranges sprinkled with orange liqueur over pound cake or ice cream.

■ **Cooking with citrus.** Sliced or sectioned oranges, mandarins, grapefruit, and kumquats are all used in cooking. Lemons and limes, on the

other hand, are frequently used just for their juice.

Baking. Cut peel and all white membrane from oranges, grapefruit, or mandarins. Cut fruit in half crosswise. Glaze and bake (see page 122) until hot (15 to 25 minutes, depending on size of fruit).

Grilling. Cut large unpeeled oranges crosswise into ¾-inch slices; cut mandarins or small oranges in half crosswise. Grill (see page 123) until hot and streaked with brown (about 5 minutes for slices, 10 minutes for halves).

Poaching. Cut peel and all white membrane from 8 to 10 small oranges or mandarins (or 4 or 5 large fruit, cut in halves); or use 3 cups whole kumquats. Simmer in poaching liquid (see page 124) until hot (about 10 minutes).

Sautéing. Cut peel and all white membrane from oranges or mandarins. Cut fruit crosswise into ½-inch slices. Sauté (see page 124) until hot (about 3 minutes).

GRAPEFRUIT

This sweet-tart giant of the citrus family has been grown in Florida since the 1800s, but it wasn't until the turn of the

Marsh grapefruit

Ruby grapefruit

Eustis limequat

Nagami kumquat

Kara mandarin

Clementine mandarin

Owari Satsuma mandarin

Dancy mandarin

Valencia orange

Tarocco blood orange

Sampson tangelo

Minneola tangelo

Rangpur lime

Washington navel orange

Robertson navel orange

Improved Meyer lemon

Eureka lemon

Bearss lime

century that it was sent to other parts of the country. Now Texas, California, and Arizona are also important producers of grapefruit.

Florida still produces 75 percent of the U.S. crop. Grapefruit grown in the Indian River Valley—a strip of land along the eastern Gulf Coast—are considered prime-quality fruits; they're identified with a label.

Just one variety, the virtually seedless Marsh, accounts for all the golden-fleshed commercial grapefruit grown today. Ruby Red and Star Ruby, grown primarily in Texas, are the leading varieties of pink grapefruit; other pink-fleshed types include Marsh Pink, Foster Pink, and Burgundy Red. Pink grapefruit usually cost more than golden-fleshed ones, but it's strictly a matter of eye appeal—flavor and juiciness are the same.

The best grapefruit are smooth, thin skinned, and flat at both ends. Avoid fruit with a pointed end or thick, deeply pored skin.

The pear-shaped *pummelo* (or *pomelo*), a forerunner of the modern grapefruit, is up to double the size of its descendent. Pummelos have a thick rind and flesh that's sweeter, firmer, and less juicy than that of grapefruit. Look for them in Asian markets.

■ **Season.** All year; peak January through June.

KUMQUATS

Native to China, kumquats are still highly prized in that country—and in areas of the United States with large Asian populations.

You eat these tiny, bright orange fruits whole, skin and all; their skin is quite sweet and perfumy, their orange flesh tart and refreshing.

Two varieties of kumquats are sold in U.S. markets: Nagami, shown on page 22, and the smaller, milder Meiwa. Choose bright orange fruits; avoid those with green skins.

Limequats, a kumquat hybrid, are olive-size fruits that taste like limes and can be used like them in cooking.

■ **Season.** December through May.

LEMONS

The commercial lemon industry got its start during the California Gold Rush, when production was stepped up to help in the prevention of scurvy, a

vitamin C-deficiency disease. Most of the U.S. crop is still grown in California.

Lemons are probably the most useful of all citrus fruits. Though they're too tart for out-of-hand eating, their juice is used to flavor everything from fish to salads to fruit desserts. Weight watchers enjoy lemon juice as a low-calorie seasoner—a good substitute for salad dressings and sauces.

The two main commercial varieties are the Eureka and the smoother-skinned Lisbon. The milder Meyer is a home garden lemon often grown as an ornamental and frequently sold at farmers' markets.

Select lemons on the basis of skin texture and clearness of color, not size. In fact, large lemons typically have thicker, less desirable skin; small to medium-size fruits that are thin skinned and heavy for their size are usually a better buy (they're juicier).

■ **Season.** All year; prices are highest during summer.

LIMES

Though similar in flavor to lemons, limes are more fragrant and less acid. Sweet limes are popular in some subtropical and tropical areas of the world, but only the acid varieties grow in the United States—primarily the large Tahiti strain and the small, thin-rinded Mexican limes.

Tahiti limes include a number of types, among them Persian (called Tahiti in California), Bearss, Idemore, and Pond. Persian is the most popular commercial lime; it's a large, bright green fruit with fine-grained pulp and a very acid flavor. Smaller (but otherwise similar) Bearss grows in California.

Mexican limes are distinguished by their small size, oval shape, and thin, leathery yellow-green skin. The Key lime of Florida belongs to this category. Taken as a group, these limes tend to be tarter than the Tahiti type.

Choose bright green or yellow-green, fresh-looking limes with firm texture.

■ **Season.** All year; best prices during summer.

MANDARINS

The most diverse group of edible citrus fruits, mandarins include all the "zipper-skinned" (easy-to-peel) family members: tangerines, tangelos (a tangerine-grapefruit hybrid), and

tangors (a tangerine-sweet orange hybrid).

When cut crosswise, a mandarin looks just like an orange—the segments are arranged petal fashion, with a core in the center. But when these fruits are peeled, their most distinctive feature is revealed: the segments separate easily into sweet bites.

Florida is the largest producer of mandarins in the United States; California and Arizona also have become increasingly significant growing areas. Mexico and Japan export a substantial amount of mandarins.

The most common commercial tangerine varieties are Dancy and Robinson. These two types resemble each other in texture, flavor, and color, but they differ in size (Robinson is larger). Other available varieties include extra-sweet, juicy Clementine, imported from Spain and North Africa; California-grown Kinnow and Fairchild; large, seedy, flavorful Kara; very sweet and nearly seedless Owari (Satsuma); firm, juicy (but hard to peel) Honey tangerines; and the Rangpur lime, which isn't a lime at all, but rather a tangerine with a sour flavor.

Among tangelos, the most popular is the Minneola, which resembles its tangerine parent more than its grapefruit parent. It's easy to recognize by its large size and the knob on one end. Other commercial tangelo varieties are Nova, Florida-grown Early K and Orlando, and extra-tart, grapefruit-flavored Sampson.

Temple is the most important tangor variety. Resembling an overgrown tangerine, it's a seedy fruit with an excellent sweet, juicy flavor.

When purchasing any type of mandarin, look for firm, full-colored, thin-skinned fruit.

■ **Season.** November through April; peak December through February.

ORANGES

The United States is blessed with the best sweet oranges in the world. The first trees were planted in the mid-1700s at Spanish missions in both Florida and California; most of the U.S. supply still comes from these two states. But due to differences in soil and climate, Florida and California oranges—even those of the same variety—vary in color, texture, and juiciness.

Continued on next page

Florida oranges are thin-skinned, very juicy—and very easy to squeeze. For this reason, much of the crop is sold to the commercial juice industry. Varieties include Hamlin, a somewhat pulpy and seedy fruit in season from October through December; Pineapple (November through February), quite seedy and very juicy; and Florida Valencia (January through July), considered at maturity to be the finest juice orange. Late-blooming Pope Summer finishes the season in August.

California oranges are rated the finest eating or table oranges. The seedless, easy-to-peel Navel variety is in season November through May. The thinner-skinned California Valencia, considered both an eating orange and a juice orange, is on the market from February through October. Arizona also grows these oranges.

Blood oranges, so called because of their deep pink to red flesh, are very popular in Mediterranean Europe but available only on a limited basis in the United States. The flavor is like that of a sweet orange, with berry overtones. Commercial varieties include burgundy-colored Moro and pink Tarocco and Sanguinelli.

For the sweetest, juiciest fruit, choose an orange variety that's right at the midpoint of its peak season.

■ **Season.** All year; for specific varieties, see individual descriptions above.

CITRUS-AVOCADO SALAD

Per serving: 263 calories, 4 g protein, 18 g carbohydrates, 21 g total fat, 0 mg cholesterol, 5 mg sodium

> 1 **large grapefruit**
> 1 **large orange** or
>   2 **mandarins**
> 2 **tablespoons** *each* **lemon juice** and **salad oil**
>   **Butter lettuce leaves**
> 1 **large ripe avocado**
> ⅓ **cup chopped salted cashews** or **peanuts**

Using a sharp knife, cut peel and all white membrane from grapefruit and orange. Holding fruit over a bowl to catch juice, cut sections free and drop into bowl. Add lemon juice and oil, mix gently, cover, and refrigerate for at least 1 hour or up to 4 hours.

Just before serving, arrange lettuce on 4 individual plates. Pit, peel, and slice avocado and arrange equally on lettuce, then top evenly with citrus mixture and juices; sprinkle with cashews. Makes 4 servings.

QUICK LEMON OR LIME CURD

Per tablespoon: 65 calories, 1 g protein, 7 g carbohydrates, 4 g total fat, 56 mg cholesterol, 43 mg sodium

In a blender, combine 2 teaspoons grated **lemon or lime peel**, ⅓ cup **lemon or lime juice**, 2 **eggs**, 1 **egg yolk**, and ½ cup **sugar**. Whirl until well blended. With blender on lowest speed, gradually add ¼ cup (⅛ lb.) melted **butter** or margarine in a thin stream. Transfer mixture to a 1- to 2-quart pan. Cook over low heat, stirring constantly, until mixture is thick enough to mound slightly (6 to 8 minutes). Refrigerate until cold (or for up to 2 weeks) before serving. Spread on biscuits, toast, or cookies as you would jam. Makes 1 cup.

BITTERSWEET MARMALADE

Per tablespoon: 29 calories, .05 g protein, 8 g carbohydrates, .01 g total fat, 0 mg cholesterol, .14 mg sodium

> 6 **medium-size thin-skinned oranges**
> 2 **thin-skinned lemons**
> 2 **medium-size thin-skinned grapefruit**
> 2 **cups water**
> 9 **cups sugar**

Rinse oranges, lemons, and grapefruit, but do not peel. Cut crosswise into ⅛-inch slices; discard seeds and end pieces. Cut orange and lemon slices into quarters; cut grapefruit slices into eighths.

Place fruit and water in a 6- to 8-quart pan. Bring mixture to a boil; reduce heat, cover, and simmer until peel is translucent and tender when pierced (25 to 30 minutes). Add sugar and stir until well blended. Cook over medium-high heat, uncovered, stirring often, until mixture thickens and reaches jell point (228°F on a candy thermometer or until 1 tablespoon of juice jells when refrigerated for 3 minutes); this takes about 30 minutes.

Sterilize eight 1-pint canning jars, lids, and rings as directed on page 28. Fill and process jars as directed. Makes 8 pints.

Kumquat Marmalade. Follow directions for **Bittersweet Marmalade**, but substitute 9 cups thinly sliced **kumquats** for oranges, lemons, and grapefruit. Add water and cook until fruit is tender when pierced (about 20 minutes). Add sugar and complete marmalade as directed.

BAKED LEMON CUSTARD

Per serving: 483 calories, 7 g protein, 53 g carbohydrates, 29 g total fat, 324 mg cholesterol, 343 mg sodium

> 1 **medium-size lemon**
> 4 **eggs**
> 1 **cup sugar**
> ½ **cup** (¼ **lb.**) **butter** or **margarine, softened**
>   **Boiling water**

Rinse lemon, but do not peel. Thinly slice crosswise; discard ends and any seeds. Place lemon slices in a blender or food processor with eggs, sugar, and butter. Whirl until smoothly blended.

Pour mixture into 4 individual ¾- to 1-cup baking dishes. Set in a 9-inch square baking pan; pour in 1 inch boiling water. Bake, uncovered, in a 300° oven until centers appear set when pan is gently shaken (about 30 minutes). Remove from water and let cool for at least 10 minutes. Serve warm or chilled. Makes 4 servings.

■ *See also* **Spinach, Date & Orange Salad** *(page 26),* **Feijoas in Orange Syrup** *(page 26),* **Cilantro Papaya Salad** *(page 42),* **Romaine & Tangerine Salad** *(page 106).*

Cranberries   *see Berries, page 13*

Currants   *see Berries, page 13; Grapes, page 30*

Dates

Dates have a history of cultivation reaching back 4,500 years, to the Middle East and North Africa. They're still making history today, but closer to home—in Southern California's Coachella Valley, where 98 percent of the U.S. crop is grown. Only Iraq produces more.

Though many people think of dates as a dried fruit, they are actually fresh. And dates aren't just a single kind of fruit; about 100 varieties exist today, though only the eight shown on page 25 are of commercial importance. Some are soft, others naturally dry or semi-dry. All are high in fruit sugar.

The Deglet Noor, which many people associate with true date flavor, dominates the market with a 95

Deglet Noor

Barhi

Thoory

Dayri

Medjool

Zahidi

Halawy

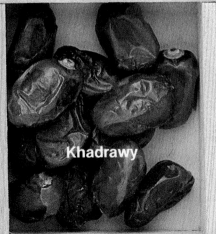

Khadrawy

percent share. It's followed at great distance by crunchy-fleshed Zahidi. Two varieties gaining in popularity are the large, attractive Medjool, often sold as fresh produce, and Barhi, the softest and most fragile date. The driest date, the Thoory or bread date, was carried by early nomads as a staple food. Backpackers and athletes still like to tote these dates along as snacks; look for them in health food stores.

Of the three remaining varieties, attractive black-skinned Dayri is least known. Halawy, the main variety imported from Iraq, has shriveled skin and must be plumped up by steaming. Khadrawy is an important early-ripening date.

Nutrition. An average date contains about 25 calories. In addition to a bit of protein and fiber, dates contain relatively large amounts of potassium, iron, and niacin.

■ **Season.** All year; best selection of numerous varieties is November through March.

■ **Selection.** Dates are like a convenience food—sold ripe and ready to eat. In the market, you'll find them alongside other fresh produce or with dried fruits. Health food stores also sell them, often offering a wider selection than supermarkets do. Except for Medjools, which are sold loose, dates are usually packaged.

■ **Ripening & storage.** All commercial varieties store well. They'll keep at cool room temperature for weeks, in the refrigerator for up to a year, or in the freezer for up to 5 years. Sugar crystals may form on the surface, but they don't affect flavor; just wipe them off with a damp cloth.

■ **Preparation.** To remove pit, make a small slit in date and push back flesh; pull out pit. To snip, cut pitted dates into small pieces with kitchen shears; rinse shears frequently with cold water to prevent sticking. Chop dates by hand with a knife, rinsing knife frequently with cold water.

■ **Amount.** There are about 50 medium-size dates in a pound.

■ **Freezing.** Package airtight in plastic bags or freezer containers; freeze for up to 5 years.

■ **Serving ideas.** For breakfast, sprinkle snipped dates on cooked cereal or granola, spoon onto pancakes as they bake, spoon over cooked waffles, or tuck a whole pitted date inside a muffin before baking. Add date halves to fruit,

. . . Dates continued

spinach, chicken, tuna, or smoked meat salads. For appetizers, fill pitted dates with cream cheese, Brie, pieces of cooked Polish sausage, or pieces of apple and bits of cooked bacon.

■ **Cooking with dates.** You can substitute snipped dates for raisins in recipes; they are especially good in breads, cookies, and puddings. Add whole pitted dates to the pan with pork or chicken during the last 15 minutes of roasting.

SPINACH, DATE & ORANGE SALAD

Per serving: 375 calories, 7 g protein, 53 g carbohydrates, 19 g total fat, 0 mg cholesterol, 233 mg sodium

> **Honey Dressing (recipe follows)**
> 1 pound **spinach,** rinsed well and patted dry
> 2 large **oranges,** peeled and cut into thin slices
> About 12 medium-size **dates,** pitted and cut in halves
> 4 to 6 tablespoons **slivered almonds**

Prepare Honey Dressing and set aside.

Arrange equal portions of spinach on 4 to 6 salad plates. Top evenly with oranges, dates, and almonds. (At this point, you may cover and refrigerate for up to 2 hours.)

Before serving, drizzle salads with Honey Dressing; let diners mix salads to coat all ingredients evenly. Makes 4 to 6 servings.

Honey Dressing. Stir together ¼ cup *each* **honey, salad oil,** and **red wine vinegar;** 1 teaspoon **Dijon mustard;** and ¼ teaspoon *each* **salt** and **pepper.**

DATE COOKIE PILLOWS

Per cookie: 133 calories, 2 g protein, 26 g carbohydrates, 3 g total fat, 15 mg cholesterol, 84 mg sodium

> **Date Filling (recipe follows)**
> 2½ cups **all-purpose flour**
> 1½ teaspoons *each* **cream of tartar and baking soda**
> 1½ cups firmly packed **brown sugar**
> ½ cup (¼ lb.) **butter** or **margarine,** softened
> 1 **egg**
> ¾ teaspoon **vanilla**
> 1½ teaspoons **vinegar**
> ½ cup **milk**

Prepare filling and set aside.

In a bowl, stir together flour, cream of tartar, and baking soda. In a large bowl, beat together sugar, butter, egg, and vanilla until creamy. Stir together vinegar and milk; add to creamed mixture alternately with flour mixture, stirring until well blended after each addition. Cover and refrigerate until firm (about 8 hours).

On a heavily floured board, roll out dough, a portion at a time, to a thickness of about ⅛ inch. Cut out cookies with a floured 2-inch cookie cutter. Place half the cutouts on greased baking sheets, spacing them 2 inches apart. Top each with about 2 teaspoons filling; cover with a second cutout and press edges to seal. Bake in a 350° oven until golden (about 12 minutes). Let cool on racks. If made ahead, store airtight for up to 1 week. Makes about 3 dozen cookies.

Date Filling. In a 2-quart pan, combine ¾ cup **orange juice,** ½ cup **sugar,** and 2 cups chopped or snipped **pitted dates.** Bring to a boil over high heat; then reduce heat to medium and cook, stirring constantly, until mixture is quite thick (about 5 minutes). Stir in ½ cup **chopped nuts,** if desired.

Feijoas

Better known to back-yard gardeners as the pineapple guava, the gray-green, egg-shaped feijoa is native to South America. Feijoas have recently enjoyed great commercial popularity in New Zealand; they've also been planted in some quantity in California.

Commercial feijoa varieties are uniformly 2½ to 3 inches long (garden varieties are usually smaller). Their pale yellow flesh is very sweet, aromatic, and juicy, not unlike that of the common guava. Some describe the flavor as a cross between pineapple and banana. Tiny seeds in the soft inner pulp are edible. The thick, waxy skin is too tart to eat fresh, but it can be used in pickles or preserves.

Nutrition. A good source of vitamin C, feijoas have about 35 calories per 3½-ounce serving.

■ **Season.** Sporadically from late February through early June for New Zealand fruit; early September through December for California feijoas.

■ **Selection.** Fruits sold in markets are usually very firm and bright olive green. When ripe, the fruit becomes as soft as a ripe plum and turns darker green; the aroma is pronounced.

■ **Ripening & storage.** Ripen fruit at room temperature, uncovered, out of direct sun; turn frequently. Refrigerate ripe fruit, uncovered, in a single layer on paper-towel-lined trays for up to 2 days.

■ **Preparation.** To eat fresh, cut feijoas in half and scoop flesh from shell with a spoon. To slice, peel fruit with a sharp knife, then cut crosswise into thin slices. Feijoas darken quickly when cut; to preserve their color, coat cut surfaces with lemon or lime juice.

■ **Amount.** Eight to 10 feijoas yield 1 cup pulp.

■ **Freezing.** Not recommended.

■ **Serving ideas.** For breakfast, offer feijoa halves ready to eat from the shell, or serve slices with pancakes, waffles, or sweet omelets. Slices are also good in fruit salads, especially those containing oranges. For dessert, drizzle slices with orange-flavored liqueur and serve with vanilla ice cream or with orange or lemon sherbet.

■ **Cooking with feijoas.** Since feijoas have the same aromatic, tropical flavor and soft texture as guavas do, you can substitute them for guavas in the chiffon pie recipe on page 32.

Sautéing. Peel feijoas, then cut fruit in halves lengthwise and coat with lemon juice. Sauté (see page 124) until tender when pierced (about 4 minutes).

FEIJOAS IN ORANGE SYRUP

Per serving: 145 calories, .93 g protein, 36 g carbohydrates, .17 g total fat, 0 mg cholesterol, 1 mg sodium

> 1 cup **orange juice**
> **Peel of 1 large orange (colored part of peel only)**
> ½ cup **sugar**
> ¼ cup **water**
> 4 or 5 **feijoas**
> 1 cup **orange segments**

In a 1- to 2-quart pan, combine orange juice, orange peel, sugar, and water. Bring to a boil over high heat; boil rapidly until reduced to 1 cup.

Peel feijoas, cut crosswise into ¼-inch slices, and drop into hot orange syrup. Add orange segments. Cover and refrigerate until cold (about 4 hours) or until next day. Makes about 4 servings.

■ *See also* **Fruit Sorbet** *(page 41).*

Pepino

Red banana

Papaya (Solo)

Kiwi fruit

Feijoa

Tamarillo

Carambola

Passion fruit

NO-FUSS FRUIT JAMS

Making jam is one of the simplest ways to preserve the good taste of fresh fruits for all-year enjoyment. There are several ways to go about it; two of the most reliable and time-saving methods are the short-cook procedure and the no-cook freezer technique presented here. Both methods require purchased pectin.

The short-cook method uses dry pectin (available in 1¾- or 2-oz. boxes) and a 2-minute cooking time. It's especially well suited to low-acid fruits such as figs, mangoes, papayas, peaches, and pears.

Fresh-tasting freezer jam, made with liquid pectin, requires no cooking. But because pectin's jelling power is reduced when it's not heated, this kind of jam needs extra sugar to achieve the right consistency. For best flavor, make freezer jam with tart fruits such as apricots, berries, kiwi fruit, nectarines, or plums.

Whichever method you choose, keep two rules in mind: you can't double jam recipes, and you can't reduce the amount of sugar. If you do either, you may end up with liquid jam.

SHORT-COOK JAM

> Fruit of your choice (see amount in chart)
> Lemon juice (see amount in chart)
> 1 box (1¾ to 2 oz.) dry pectin
> Sugar (see amount in chart)

Check yield for each fruit to determine how many canning jars you will need. Wash jars in hot, soapy water and rinse well. Immerse jars, rings, and new lids in boiling water to cover and hold at a gentle boil for 10 to 30 minutes. When ready to fill, drain jars on a clean towel.

Meanwhile, rinse fruit; then peel, seed, hull, or core as necessary (see basic preparation instructions in entries for individual fruits). Cut fruit into cubes. Mash fruit with a potato masher (or whirl briefly in a food processor, but do not purée).

In an 8- to 10-quart pan, combine mashed fruit, lemon juice, and pectin. Place over high heat; stirring constantly, bring to a rolling boil that cannot be stirred down. Still stirring, add sugar. Return to a boil that cannot be stirred down, then boil for exactly 2 minutes. Remove from heat and skim off foam.

Ladle hot jam into prepared jars, filling to ¼ inch

SHORT-COOK METHOD WITH DRY PECTIN
(1¾- or 2-oz. box)

	AMT. OF FRUIT	MASHED FRUIT	LEMON JUICE	SUGAR	YIELD
Fig	3¼ lbs.	5 c. + ½ c. water	½ c.	7 c.	8½ c.
Mango	6 lbs.	4 c.	¼ c.	6 c.	6½ c.
Papaya	5 lbs.	4 c.	¼ c.	6 c.	6½ c.
Peach	3 lbs.	4 c.	¼ c.	6 c.	6¾ c.
Pear	3 lbs.	4 c.	¼ c.	5½ c.	6½ c.

NO-COOK FREEZER METHOD WITH LIQUID PECTIN
(3-oz. pouch)

	AMT. OF FRUIT	MASHED FRUIT	LEMON JUICE	SUGAR	YIELD
Apricot	1 lb.	1½ c.	¼ c.	3 c.	4 c.
Berry	1 qt.	2 c.	2 T.	4 c.	4¾ c.
Kiwi	1¼ lbs.	2¼ c.	¼ c.	4 c.	5 c.
Nectarine	1 lb.	1½ c.	¼ c.	3 c.	4 c.
Plum	1¼ lbs.	2¼ c.	2 T.	4 c.	5 c.

from rims. Wipe rims clean. Lift lids from hot water and immediately place on jars; screw on rings tightly. Place jars on a rack in a canning or other deep kettle. Add boiling water to cover jars. Hold at simmering (180°F) for 10 minutes. Remove from water and let cool on a towel, away from drafts.

To test seal, press center of lid. If it stays down, seal is good; if it pops when pressed, there's no seal. Refrigerate unsealed jam and use as soon as possible. Store sealed cooked jam in a cool (50°F), dark place for up to about 2 years.

NO-COOK FREEZER JAM

> Fruit of your choice (see amount in chart)
> Sugar (see amount in chart)
> 1 pouch (3 oz.) liquid pectin
> Lemon juice (see amount in chart)

Rinse fruit; then peel, seed, hull, or core as necessary (see basic preparation instructions in entries for individual fruits). Cut fruit into cubes. Mash fruit with a potato masher (or whirl briefly in a food processor, but do not purée).

In a large bowl, thoroughly mix fruit and sugar; let stand for 10 minutes, stirring occasionally. Meanwhile, mix pectin and lemon juice; add to fruit mixture and stir (don't beat in air) for 3 minutes. Fill clean small canning jars or plastic containers, leaving a ½-inch headspace; place lids on. Let jam stand at room temperature until next day; then refrigerate for up to 3 weeks or freeze for up to 1 year.

Figs and prosciutto with yogurt dressing make an elegant first course or luncheon entrée (recipe below right).

Figs

One of the oldest cultivated fruits, figs are referred to in the Biblical story of the Garden of Eden. In the United States, the fig's history begins with California's first Spanish mission, established in San Diego around 1760. Here the Black Mission variety was named.

Today, California still produces the country's largest volume of both black and green figs. The crop hits markets in two seasonal splashes: first in June, again from August through early September. June figs are usually larger, but the autumn harvest is more abundant. Both crops come from the same trees.

The many varieties of figs usually vary only in color and shape. All have soft, sweet, slightly aromatic flesh that contains numerous edible blossoms and seeds.

The leading commerical types of fresh figs are Black Mission, with black skin and luscious pink flesh; brownish purple Brown Turkey, with richly flavored red flesh; Brunswick, a large, dark brown, mild-flavored fruit; violet-skinned Celeste, with tasty rose-colored flesh; and large, yellowish green Kadota, a violet-fleshed fig with an excellent flavor.

Smyrna, the common imported dried fig, and similar Calimyrna, grown in California, are rarely available fresh (they require a pollenizer and a specific wasp to carry the pollen).

Nutrition. Figs are a natural source of sugar without being too high in calories—about 50 per large fig.

■ **Season.** June; August through early September.

■ **Selection.** For the greatest sugar content and best eating quality, figs must be tree-ripened. However, since ripe figs are so perishable, the fruit is shipped firm-ripe. Ripe figs give readily to pressure. Avoid hard, dry figs and those with flattened sides, splits, or signs of mold.

■ **Ripening & storage.** Ripen at room temperature, uncovered, out of direct sun; turn frequently. Use ripe fruit as soon as possible. If you must store ripe fruit, arrange it in a single layer on paper-towel-lined trays; cover with plastic wrap and refrigerate for up to a few days.

■ **Preparation.** Trim off hard part of stem end. Some people pull off the thin skin, others don't; it's a matter of taste. For slices, cut lengthwise.

■ **Amount.** There are about 8 large or 12 to 16 small figs in a pound.

■ **Freezing.** Peel figs and remove stems. Freeze in light syrup (see page 125).

■ **Serving ideas.** For appetizers, wrap fig halves in sliced prosciutto or salami. Top open-faced cheese sandwiches with fig slices; broil until cheese is bubbly. For dessert, spread gingersnaps with cream cheese and top with fig slices; stuff figs with a small chunk of cherry-flavored Gourmandise cheese; or serve fig slices with custard sauce flavored with orange liqueur.

■ **Cooking with figs.** Exotic-looking, mellow-flavored figs add drama to many courses of a meal. When roasting ham or pork, set whole figs in drippings during the last 15 minutes of cooking.

Baking. Rinse figs. Glaze and bake (see page 122) until hot throughout (about 15 minutes).

Grilling. Rinse figs and cut in halves. Thread on skewers, making sure fruit lies flat. Grill (see page 123) until hot (4 to 6 minutes).

Poaching. Rinse 10 to 12 firm-ripe green or black figs. Simmer in poaching liquid (see page 124) until hot and tender (3 to 5 minutes).

FIG, PROSCIUTTO & YOGURT SALAD

Per serving: 216 calories, 8 g protein, 31 g carbohydrates, 8 g total fat, 26 mg cholesterol, 177 mg sodium

- ½ cup *each* lemon-flavored yogurt and sour cream
- 1 tablespoon shredded fresh mint
- 12 small or 6 large figs, stems trimmed
- 6 thin slices prosciutto (about 2 oz. *total*)
  Mint sprigs

In a small bowl, blend yogurt, sour cream, and shredded mint. Cut small figs vertically in halves; cut large figs into quarters. Cut prosciutto slices in half crosswise; roll up each piece.

Spoon yogurt mixture equally into centers of 4 salad plates. Divide figs and prosciutto evenly among plates, arranging figs cut side up atop dressing. Garnish with mint sprigs and serve at once. Makes 4 servings.

BUTTERY FIG BAR COOKIES

Per cookie: 148 calories, 2 g protein, 25 g carbohydrates, 5 g total fat, 14 mg cholesterol, 113 mg sodium

- 2 pounds fully ripe figs
- 2 tablespoons lemon juice
- ½ cup granulated sugar
- ¾ cup (¼ lb. plus ¼ cup) butter or margarine, softened
- 1 cup firmly packed brown sugar
- 1¾ cups all-purpose flour
- ½ teaspoon *each* baking soda and salt
- 1½ cups rolled oats

Remove stems and blossom ends from figs; coarsely chop figs, place in a 2- to

...Figs continued

3-quart pan, and add lemon juice and granulated sugar. Stir well. Cook over medium heat, stirring often, until reduced to 2 cups; as mixture thickens, reduce heat to prevent scorching. Remove from heat and let cool.

In a large bowl, cream butter and brown sugar. In another bowl, stir together flour, baking soda, and salt. Add to creamed mixture; blend well. Stir in oats.

Press half the mixture evenly over bottom of a 9- by 13-inch baking dish. Spread fig mixture on top. Top evenly with remaining oat mixture and pat down lightly.

Bake in a 400° oven until lightly browned (20 to 25 minutes). Let cool in pan on a rack. While still warm, cut into about 1½- by 2½-inch bars. Makes about 2½ dozen cookies.

Gooseberries see Berries, page 13

Grapefruit see Citrus, page 20

Grapes

Mission fathers pushing north from Mexico in the 18th century were the first to introduce grapes to California. Soon the same types of grapes that had been cultivated in other parts of the world since Biblical times were flourishing in the United States. Today, fresh table grapes are sold in American markets year round—seedless or seeded, in a range of colors, tastes, and textures.

Ninety-seven percent of U.S. commercial table grapes are grown in California's hot interior valley; Arizona produces most of the rest. In the winter, fresh grapes (the same varieties that grow here) are increasingly available from the Southern Hemisphere (particularly Chile) and, to a lesser extent, from Mexico.

Of the 18 varieties of table grapes shown on page 31, green and red seedless types are generally in the highest demand, though seeded grapes often have fuller and more interesting flavors. Most of the varieties pictured are widely sold, but you may have some difficulty locating Christmas Rose, Red Globe, Exotic, Tokay, Beauty Seedless, Niabell, and tiny, super-sweet Black Corinth—grown for dried currants and sometimes sold fresh as Zante currants.

Concord, a native American grape grown in the Northwest and East, is too fragile to ship well; it's primarily processed into juice, wine, and jelly.

Nutrition. Grapes are low in sodium. They contain about 70 calories per cup.

■ **Season.** All year; June through December for California grapes, January through June for imported grapes.

■ **Selection.** Since grapes don't get any sweeter or riper after picking, color is the best indication of ripeness and sweet flavor. Green grapes have the most flavor when they're yellow-green; red varieties are best when all grapes in the bunch are predominantly red; blue-black types should have a full, rich, dark color.

Look for plump grapes firmly attached to pliable green stems. Avoid soft or wrinkled fruits and those with bleached areas at the stem end.

■ **Ripening & storage.** Grapes are sold ripe and ready to eat. Refrigerate, unwashed, in a paper or plastic bag for 2 to 5 days, depending on variety.

■ **Preparation.** Just before serving, rinse grapes with a gentle spray of cool water. To serve fresh, cut into small bunches; discard any seeds as you eat the grapes. For cooking, seedless grapes are usually left whole. Cut seeded varieties in halves and remove seeds with the tip of a sharp knife.

■ **Amount.** One pound of seedless grapes equals about 3 cups.

■ **Freezing.** Not recommended.

■ **Serving ideas.** Serve grapes alongside wedges of soft-ripened cheeses as an appetizer or dessert. Use in fruit, mixed green, poultry, tuna, or ham salads. To garnish desserts, dip grapes in lightly beaten egg white, then in sugar; refrigerate until coating is firm.

■ **Cooking with grapes.** Though grapes are at their best served fresh, they're also easy to use in cooking. Unless you want to spend some time removing seeds, choose seedless varieties.

Poaching. Rinse 1 to 1¼ pounds seedless grapes and cut into small clusters. Simmer in poaching liquid (see page 124) until hot (2 to 3 minutes).

CHICKEN WITH PORT-FLAVORED GRAPE SAUCE

Per serving: 814 calories, 83 g protein, 16 g carbohydrates, 44 g total fat, 421 mg cholesterol, 440 mg sodium

  1 **roasting chicken (4 to 5 lbs.)**
      About 1 tablespoon butter or margarine, melted
      Salt and pepper
1½ **cups regular-strength chicken broth**
 ½ **cup tawny port**
  2 **tablespoons *each* cornstarch and water, stirred together**
  1 **tablespoon firmly packed brown sugar**
 ¼ **teaspoon thyme leaves**
  2 **cups seedless red or green grapes**

Remove chicken neck and giblets, then rinse chicken inside and out; pat dry. Place breast down on a rack in a roasting pan; brush with butter and sprinkle lightly with salt and pepper. Roast in a 325° oven for 45 minutes. Turn chicken breast up. Continue to roast until meat near thighbone is no longer pink; cut to test (about 45 more minutes).

Transfer chicken to a platter and keep warm. Pour broth into roasting pan and stir to scrape up browned particles; then pour into a 1- to 2-quart pan. Add port, cornstarch-water mixture, sugar, thyme, and grapes. Cook over high heat, stirring, until mixture boils, thickens, and turns clear.

Pour half the sauce over and around chicken on platter. Pass remaining sauce to spoon over individual servings. Makes about 6 servings.

GRAPES IN WINE JELLY

Per serving: 91 calories, 3 g protein, 21 g carbohydrates, .42 g total fat, 0 mg cholesterol, 4 mg sodium

  2 **envelopes unflavored gelatin**
 ⅓ **cup sugar**
  2 **cups water**
  2 **cups semisweet white wine, such as Chenin Blanc, Gewürztraminer, or French Colombard**
  1 **cup seedless red grapes**
      Small bunches of grapes

In a 2-quart pan, combine gelatin and sugar; stir in 1 cup of the water and let stand for 5 minutes to soften gelatin. Then stir over medium heat until gelatin and sugar are completely dissolved. Remove from heat; stir in wine and remaining 1 cup water. Refrigerate until mixture has thickened to the consistency of unbeaten egg whites.

Fold grapes into gelatin mixture and pour into a 6-cup mold. Cover and

Perlette
Seedless. Thick skin; crisp; mild sweetness. Late May to mid-July

Beauty Seedless
Firm skin; tender flesh. Mild, spicy-sweet. Late May to early July

Cardinal
Large, firm; mild, fruity, touch of tartness. Late May through August

Thompson Seedless
Crisp, juicy, refreshing; mild, sweet-tart taste. June through October

Flame Seedless
Crunchy bite; mild sweetness, slightly tart. Early June to September

Ribier
Plump and meaty. Mildly sweet; slightly bitter skin. Late July to January

Exotic
Meaty flesh, tender skin; juicy. Subtle sweetness. Early June to early August

Black Corinth
Zante currant. Crunchy, very sweet. Early to mid-August

Queen
Crisp, firm bite; juicy. Very mild sweetness. Mid-August to mid-September

Italia
Large, juicy, crisp. Rich muscat flavor. Mid-August to mid-October

Tokay
Crunchy bite. Fresh, mild, sweet flavor. Mid-August to November

Niabell
American-European hybrid. Slips skin. Tastes like Concord. August, September

Red Globe
Very large, firm; big seeds. Mild. Stores well. September to January

Ruby Seedless
Crisp and juicy; rich, sweet-tart taste. Mid-August through December

Emperor
Tender; small seeds. Mild cherry taste. Stores well. Mid-September to March

Christmas Rose
Very crunchy, juicy. Sweet, fruity flavor. Late September to January

Almeria
Firm, juicy; small seeds. Tangy sweetness. October through January

Calmeria
Crisp, juicy; thick skin. Rich, tangy-sweet. Mid-October to January

... Grapes continued

refrigerate until firm (at least 3 hours) or until next day. To unmold, dip mold to rim in lukewarm water for 10 seconds or until edges begin to soften; invert onto a platter. Garnish with bunches of grapes. Makes 6 to 8 servings.

SHERRIED CREAM WITH GRAPES

Per serving: 276 calories, 7 g protein, 39 g carbohydrates, 11 g total fat, 155 mg cholesterol, 219 mg sodium

- ⅓ cup sugar
- 2 tablespoons cornstarch
- ⅛ teaspoon salt
- 2 cups milk
- ¼ cup cream sherry
- 2 egg yolks, lightly beaten
- 2 tablespoons butter or margarine
- 1 teaspoon vanilla
  About 1½ cups seedless red or green grapes

In a 2-quart pan, stir together sugar, cornstarch, and salt. Gradually add milk and sherry, stirring until well blended. Bring mixture to a boil over medium heat, stirring constantly; boil for 1 minute. Remove from heat.

Stir some of the hot sauce into beaten egg yolks, then blend yolk mixture with remaining sauce in pan and cook, stirring, for 30 seconds. Remove from heat, add butter and vanilla, and stir until butter is melted.

Layer spoonfuls of pudding and grapes in 4 to 6 stemmed glasses. Refrigerate until serving time. Makes 4 to 6 servings.

Guavas

Now grown commercially in Hawaii and Florida, the common tropical guava (*guayaba* in Spanish) is native to the Caribbean. The large commercial variety, Beaumont, looks like a pale yellow lemon with smooth skin. Its juicy, shocking pink to salmon-colored flesh has a very sweet, flowery flavor; its seeds are edible.

Unfortunately, since the guava is an attractive host to the tropical fruit fly, some states will not accept the fresh fruit. For this reason, most of the U.S. guava crop is canned or processed into juices, purées, and preserves.

Guava's pink flesh encloses edible seeds.

Other types of guavas, including the lemon and strawberry varieties, are smaller than the common guava but taste much the same. Though these varieties aren't grown commercially, you may find them at farmers' markets or produce stands in Southern California and Florida. (Pineapple guavas—feijoas—are actually a completely different species of fruit; see page 26.)

Nutrition. Guavas are an excellent source of vitamin C. A 3½-ounce portion has 62 calories.

■ **Season.** August through October.

■ **Selection.** Ripe guavas have a fragrant aroma; their shells give to gentle pressure. Guavas sold in markets are usually quite firm and should be ripened further at home before using. Look for fruit that is free of bruises, blemishes, and soft spots.

■ **Ripening & storage.** Ripen guavas at room temperature, uncovered, out of direct sun; turn occasionally. Refrigerate ripe fruit in a plastic or paper bag for up to 1 week.

■ **Preparation.** Cut in half crosswise and scoop out flesh with a spoon. Or peel with a sharp knife and thinly slice.

■ **Amount.** One large guava yields ⅓ to ½ cup sliced fruit.

■ **Freezing.** Not recommended.

■ **Serving ideas.** Serve guava slices on pancakes, waffles, or sweet omelets; or add to fruit, poultry, or smoked meat salads. Accompany meat or poultry entrées with sautéed, baked, or grilled guavas. To serve

guavas for dessert, sprinkle slices with orange-flavored liqueur; or serve over ice cream or pound cake.

■ **Cooking with guavas.** Choose firm-ripe guavas for use in cooking. Guavas may also be substituted for feijoas in the recipe on page 26.

Baking. Peel guavas and cut in halves lengthwise. Glaze and bake (see page 122) until hot (about 15 minutes).

Grilling. Peel guavas and cut in halves lengthwise. Grill (see page 123) until tender and streaked with brown (4 to 6 minutes).

Sautéing. Peel guavas and cut lengthwise into quarters. Sauté (see page 124) until fruit is hot and tender when pierced (3 to 5 minutes).

GUAVA CHIFFON PIE

Per serving: 358 calories, 8 g protein, 45 g carbohydrates, 15 g total fat, 169 mg cholesterol, 270 mg sodium

- 2 cups peeled, thinly sliced guavas
- 2 tablespoons lemon juice
- 1 envelope unflavored gelatin
- ¼ cup cold water
- ¾ cup sugar
- 4 eggs, separated
- 2 tablespoons lime juice
- ⅛ teaspoon salt
- ¼ teaspoon cream of tartar
  Baked 9-inch pie shell

Whirl guavas and lemon juice in a food processor or blender until smoothly puréed; you should have 1 cup.

Sprinkle gelatin over cold water and let soften for 5 minutes.

Meanwhile, in the top of a double boiler, combine guava purée, ½ cup of the sugar, and egg yolks. Beat with a rotary beater until frothy. Place over simmering water; cook, stirring, until mixture is thickened (about 7 minutes). Remove from heat. Add gelatin mixture and stir until dissolved; stir in lime juice. Cover and refrigerate until thick and syrupy.

In a large bowl, combine egg whites, salt, and cream of tartar. Beat until mixture holds soft peaks. Gradually beat in remaining ¼ cup sugar until mixture holds stiff peaks. Fold thickened guava mixture into meringue until blended. Spoon mixture evenly into pie shell. Refrigerate, uncovered, until filling is set (about 3 hours). Makes 6 to 8 servings.

■ *See also* **Fruit Sorbet,** *page 41.*

Kiwi Fruit

Vine-grown kiwi fruit was originally called "Chinese gooseberry." But when New Zealanders began to market the fruit in Los Angeles in the mid-1960s, they renamed it "kiwi fruit" to associate with another, better-known New Zealand native—the kiwi bird. *(Photo on page 27.)*

New Zealand still exports large quantities of kiwi fruit to the United States, but California has proven to be an equally fertile growing area. For this reason, and also because the fruit can be kept in cold storage almost indefinitely, kiwi fruit is sold in U.S. markets all year at reasonable prices.

Beneath the fuzzy brown exterior of this 2-inch, oval fruit lies sparkling green flesh marked with a swirl of tiny black edible seeds. Some liken the kiwi fruit's refreshing flavor to that of strawberries, or strawberries crossed with pineapple.

Nutrition. Kiwi fruit is high in vitamin C. A 3½-ounce portion has about 35 calories.

Bright green kiwi fruit slices make Autumn Salad a standout (see recipe this page).

■ **Season.** March through October for imported fruit, November through April for the domestic crop.

■ **Selection.** When ready to eat, kiwi fruit is as soft as a ripe peach. Most markets display very firm fruit that needs to be ripened further. Choose evenly firm fruit free of mold and soft spots.

■ **Ripening & storage.** Ripen at room temperature, uncovered, out of direct sun; turn occasionally. Refrigerate ripe fruit in a plastic or paper bag for up to 1 week.

■ **Preparation.** Cut in half crosswise and scoop out flesh with a spoon. Or peel and thinly slice crosswise to show off the decorative pattern of the seeds.

■ **Amount.** One large kiwi fruit yields ⅓ to ½ cup slices.

■ **Freezing.** Not recommmended.

■ **Serving ideas.** For appetizers, pair sliced kiwi fruit with sliced smoked or cured meats, smoked salmon, or cheese. In salads, mix it with other fruits; or use to garnish poultry, fish, or ham salads. Offer wedges of kiwi fruit with barbecued or roasted poultry, pork, or lamb. To serve for dessert, drizzle slices with orange-flavored liqueur or serve over custard, pound cake, or yogurt.

■ **Cooking with kiwi fruit.** Kiwi fruit is best used uncooked, since it turns an unattractive shade of olive green when heated.

AUTUMN KIWI FRUIT SALAD

Per serving of salad: 242 calories, 3 g protein, 61 g carbohydrates, 1 g total fat, 0 mg cholesterol, 4 mg sodium

Per tablespoon of dressing: 50 calories, .29 g protein, 2 g carbohydrates, 5 g total fat, 5 mg cholesterol, 5 mg sodium

  6 **large kiwi fruits, peeled and sliced**
  1 **medium-size pineapple (3 to 3½ lbs.), peeled, cored, and cut into 1-inch cubes**
  3 **bananas, sliced diagonally**
  2 **firm-ripe Fuyu-type persimmons, cut into thin slices**
  1 **cup seedless red grapes**
    Honey-Yogurt Dressing (recipe follows)
    Chopped walnuts or pecans

In a large bowl, gently mix kiwi fruit, pineapple, bananas, persimmons, and grapes. Cover and refrigerate for 30 to 60 minutes to blend flavors. Meanwhile, prepare Honey-Yogurt Dressing. Pass walnuts and dressing

to spoon over individual servings. Makes 6 servings.

Honey-Yogurt Dressing. Combine 1½ tablespoons grated **orange peel**, 1 teaspoon grated **fresh ginger**, ¾ cup *each* **mayonnaise** and **plain yogurt**, 2 tablespoons **honey**, and 1 tablespoon **lemon juice.** Beat with a wire whisk until well blended. If made ahead, cover and refrigerate.

PAVLOVA (NEW ZEALAND MERINGUE DESSERT)

Per serving of Pavlova: 239 calories, 3 g protein, 27 g carbohydrates, 14 g total fat, 48 mg cholesterol, 59 mg sodium

Per tablespoon of sauce: 13 calories, .07 g protein, 3 g carbohydrates, .03 g total fat, 0 mg cholesterol, .08 mg sodium

  4 **egg whites, at room temperature**
  ⅛ **teaspoon salt**
  1 **cup sugar**
  1 **tablespoon cornstarch**
  1 **teaspoon** *each* **white wine vinegar and vanilla**
  6 to 8 **kiwi fruits**
  1½ **cups whipping cream**
    Raspberry Sauce (recipe follows)

Preheat oven to 400°. In a large bowl, beat egg whites and salt until mixture holds soft peaks. Stir together sugar and cornstarch. Beat egg whites, gradually adding sugar mixture, until mixture holds stiff peaks. Beat in vinegar and vanilla.

Lightly moisten a greased baking sheet. Pile egg white mixture onto damp baking sheet; shape into a 7-inch circle. Place in preheated oven; immediately reduce oven temperature to 250° and bake until meringue is lightly browned and dry to the touch (about 1½ hours). Let cool, then lift off baking sheet with a large spatula and transfer to a serving plate.

To serve, peel and slice kiwi fruit. Beat cream until stiff; swirl over meringue, then garnish with sliced fruit. Pass Raspberry Sauce to spoon over individual servings. Makes 10 to 12 servings.

Raspberry Sauce. In a pan, blend 1 tablespoon **cornstarch** and ½ cup **sugar.** Stir in ½ cup **water**, 2 teaspoons **lemon juice**, and ¼ teaspoon **vanilla.** Add 2 cups slightly crushed **raspberries.** Cook over medium heat, stirring, until sauce boils and thickens. Let cool, cover, and chill for as long as overnight.

■ *See also* **Fruit Jam** *(page 28),* **Fruit Sorbet** *(page 41).*

Kumquats see Citrus, page 20

Lemons see Citrus, page 20

Limes see Citrus, page 20

Litchis & Longans

Litchis—or lichees—have been popular in Asia for more than 2,000 years. Small (1 to 1½ inches in diameter) and warty skinned, the fruits are sold in clusters on woody stems. Beneath the thin, barklike, bright red to red-brown shell is a translucent white fruit centered with a smooth brown seed. In both texture and flavor, litchis are reminiscent of peeled Muscat grapes.

China still grows a substantial supply of the fruit, but most Chinese litchis sold in the United States are canned, frozen, or dried. Other sources of the fresh fruit include Hawaii, Florida, Southern California, Brazil, and Jamaica. Look for fresh or preserved litchis in Asian markets.

Very similar to litchis, longans (also called "dragon's eyes") are native to India and come to U.S. markets from Hawaii and the Dominican Republic. They have a smooth brown shell and a

Litchis, left, are bright red to red-brown. Brown-skinned longans, right, taste similar.

more transparent, less aromatic flesh than litchis. Like litchis, longans are sold in Asian markets.

Nutrition. An excellent source of vitamin C, litchis and longans contain about 120 calories per cup.

■ **Season.** June through July for litchis, July through August for longans.

■ **Selection.** After litchis are picked, their shells turn from strawberry red to a duller red-brown color. Choose bright red to red-brown fruit with fresh-looking shells. Litchis with brown, withered shells may have brown, fermented flesh.

Look for longans with fresh, pliable shells, free of cracks.

■ **Ripening & storage.** Litchis and longans are ripe and ready to eat when sold. To store, refrigerate in a plastic or paper bag for up to 1 week.

■ **Preparation.** Serve in clusters, like grapes. Break each fruit from the stem, then peel or break off shell and eat flesh; discard seeds.

For a more dramatic presentation, use scissors to pierce shell of each fruit at tip; then cut shell into "petals." Tuck each petal back under fruit so it resembles a flower. To eat, pluck fruit free from shell.

■ **Amount.** Twenty litchis or longans yield about 1 cup peeled, seeded fruit.

■ **Freezing.** Freeze litchis or longans, uncovered, in a single layer until firm. Place in plastic bags and freeze for up to 6 months.

■ **Cooking with litchis.** Litchis and longans make a good poached dessert fruit, but otherwise they are best served uncooked.

Poaching. Simmer about 2 cups peeled, seeded litchis or longans in poaching liquid (see page 124) just until hot throughout (about 2 minutes).

■ **Serving ideas.** Serve peeled, seeded litchis or longans, well chilled, in fruit salads. To serve for dessert, sprinkle prepared fruit with orange juice or orange-flavored liqueur; or serve poached litchis or longans over ice cream or custard.

For a refreshing treat, freeze prepared litchis or longans until firm; let stand at room temperature for 20 minutes before serving.

Mandarins see Citrus, page 20

Mangoes

The mango is as common in the tropics as the apple is in temperate zones. But until the past decade, this Southeast Asian native was a rare sight in American grocery stores.

Today, U.S. markets are supplied with mangoes of many varieties from the Caribbean, South America, Mexico, Haiti, and Florida. The first variety to appear each year is the early-season Manila mango—yellow skinned, sweet, and exceptionally juicy. Next in line is the big red Tommy Atkins mango, its flesh almost fiber-free. Haden mangoes, oval fruits with pink-blushed yellow skin, come third. Last to arrive is the meatiest mango—green-skinned Keitt, sometimes blushed with yellow and red, sometimes solid green even when fully ripe.

Whatever variety of mango you choose, it's sure to have somewhat stringy, bright orange-yellow flesh clinging to a large, flat, hairy pit. The mango's flavor is peachlike, its aroma flowery.

Nutrition. Mangoes are high in vitamins A and C. One medium-size mango has about 150 calories.

■ **Season.** Sporadically January through August; peak in June.

■ **Selection.** When ripe, a mango gives to gentle pressure like a ripe avocado. Mangoes are usually sold quite firm and need to be ripened further before eating. Choose plump mangoes; avoid those with shriveled or bruised skin.

■ **Ripening & storage.** Ripen all varieties of mangoes at room temperature, uncovered, out of direct sun; turn occasionally. Red-green mangoes will turn redder when ripe; yellow-green varieties will turn more yellow. (The exception is the Keitt mango, which may remain green even when ripe.) Refrigerate ripe fruit in a plastic or paper bag for up to 3 days.

■ **Preparation.** There are several ways to approach a juicy (and often messy) mango. *To eat banana-style,* score the skin into quarters from top almost to stem end. Holding stem end with a napkin, peel back skin as you would peel a banana; lean over a plate and eat fruit off the pit.

Sweet and juicy mangoes have peachlike flavor.

To eat a mango on the half-shell, cut the fleshy "cheeks" completely off each side of the pit with a sharp knife. Serve each half to eat from the skin with a spoon.

To slice fruit, score skin lengthwise in 4 to 6 places; pull skin off. Cut fleshy cheeks from each side of pit; cut into slices or chunks.

■ **Amount.** A 1-pound mango yields about ¾ cup sliced fruit.

■ **Freezing.** Not recommended.

■ **Serving ideas.** Serve mango slices on waffles or French toast, or mix them into a fruit or spinach salad. Offer uncooked or sautéed slices alongside grilled or roasted meats and poultry. For dessert, drizzle slices with orange-flavored liqueur or top with sour cream and brown sugar.

■ **Cooking with mangoes.** Choose firm-ripe fruit for sautéing.

Sautéing. Peel and slice mangoes, then sauté (see page 124) until slices are hot (about 3 minutes).

MANGO FLUMMERY

Per serving: 277 calories, 1 g protein, 70 g carbohydrates, .60 g total fat, 0 mg cholesterol, 10 mg sodium

> 2 large mangoes, peeled and
>   sliced
> 2 tablespoons lemon juice
> 1 cup orange juice
> ⅔ cup sugar
> ⅓ cup quick-cooking tapioca
> ½ teaspoon grated orange
>   peel
>   Banana slices and shred-
>   ded coconut (optional)

In a blender or food processor, whirl mangoes until puréed; you should have 3 cups.

Transfer purée to a 3-quart pan. Stir in lemon juice, orange juice, sugar, and tapioca. Let stand for 5 minutes; then bring to a full boil over medium-high heat, stirring constantly. Remove from heat; stir in orange peel. Let cool for 15 minutes; cover and refrigerate until softly set (about 2 hours).

To serve, spoon flummery into 4 to 6 stemmed glasses; top each with bananas and coconut, if desired. Makes 4 to 6 servings.

■ *See also Fruit Jam (page 28), Fruit Sorbet (page 41).*

Melons

Melons are sold in a tantalizing spectrum of colors, shapes, sizes, tastes, and textures. Of the 20 types shown on pages 36 and 37, most are major market varieties. The others are "specialty melons" (see page 36), sold at fancy food stores, farmers' markets, and produce stands.

Most melons fall into the broad category of "muskmelons." The exception is watermelon, actually a member of the gourd family.

More than two-thirds of all the commercially grown melons in the United States are raised in California's hot interior valley; the remainder come from 24 other states. Melons are also imported from Mexico, New Zealand, and Chile.

Nutrition. Most melons are good sources of vitamin C; those with deep orange or red flesh are rich in vitamin A. Half a 5-inch cantaloupe has about 80 calories; a 7- by 2-inch honeydew wedge has 50, while a 1-inch slice of a 10-inch-diameter watermelon has 110.

■ **Season.** Sporadically all year, depending on variety; peak August through September.

■ **Selection.** Signs of ripeness vary depending on the variety; see the individual listings. Most varieties are sold slightly underripe and need to stand at room temperature for a few days to develop maximum flavor.

In general, choose melons that are evenly ripe, with no soft, water-soaked areas or mold. If you shake a melon and it seems to rattle, it *may* be extra-sweet—but it's more likely to be over-ripe and sour tasting.

■ **Ripening & storage.** To hasten ripening, place whole melons inside loosely closed paper bags. Once cut, melons won't get any riper. Refrigerate cut melons or fully ripe whole ones in tightly sealed plastic bags (the ethylene gas melons give off can hasten spoilage of other produce in the refrigerator).

■ **Melon varieties.** Almost all the following varieties are shown in the photograph on pages 36 and 37.

Cantaloupe. Musky-sweet, slightly tart cantaloupes come in several look-alike varieties. Topscore is a quality fruit marketed both early and late in the season; Ambrosia has an extra-sweet flavor; Saticoy is named for a Southern California town where it grows exceptionally well.

The best cantaloupes are slightly oval and 5 inches or more in diameter, with yellow or golden (not green) background color. Signs of sweetness include pronounced netting and a few tiny cracks near the stem end.

Continued on next page

Hollowed-out honeydew shell makes attractive container for melon soup (recipe on page 37).

...Melons continued

Casaba. Hard-shelled Golden Beauty is the standard variety; it has smooth-textured flesh that is juicy and subtly sweet.

To be sure of getting ripe melon, buy Casaba in cut pieces. If you buy a whole melon, choose one that's golden yellow all over except for the stem area, which may have a greenish cast. Stored in a cool place, whole melons will keep for up to a month.

Crenshaw. This melon's pale salmon flesh is extra sweet and juicy, with a rather spicy aroma.

For best flavor, choose a Crenshaw that weighs at least 5 pounds. When ripe, the melon is medium yellow all over; the blossom end should give when lightly pressed. Avoid melons with bruised or water-soaked spots. Crenshaws are fragile, so handle them gently.

Green honeydew. A good honeydew is very juicy, with crisp, honeysweet flesh. For best flavor, choose honeydews weighing at least 5 pounds; look for a waxy white rind barely tinged with green. When fully ripe, the melon will have a cream-colored rind and a pronounced honey aroma; the blossom end should give to gentle pressure.

Orange honeydew. In color, taste, texture, and aroma, this small melon resembles cantaloupe more than honeydew. When the melon is ripe, the rind turns from white to light salmon pink.

Jaune Canari. Canaris are very sweet, fragrant, and juicy, with a pleasantly crisp texture. Choose a 4- to 5-pound melon; you'll know it's ripe when the rind has turned bright yellow all over.

Persian. Though they look like overgrown cantaloupes, Persian melons have firmer flesh with a more buttery texture.

Since these melons are hard to grow and are fragile when ripe, they're often picked immature. For best flavor, choose melons weighing 5 pounds or more, with a background color turning from gray-green to bronze.

Santa Claus. Green and gold-striped Santa Claus melons are crisp and juicy, but not quite as sweet as many other melons. You can judge this melon's ripeness by the color of the stripes on its hard shell; the brighter the yellow, the riper and more flavorful the melon will be. For best flavor, choose a melon that weighs at least 5 pounds.

Green Flesh Honey Dew

Orange Flesh Honey Dew

Jaune Canari

Casaba

Persian

Santa Claus

Crenshaw

Sharlyn

Sharlyn. Sharlyns are especially sweet and fragrant—almost perfumy. Their creamy-soft, juicy flesh is good eating all the way to the rind.

These melons are fully ripe when the background color (beneath the netting) turns from green to 100 percent orange. However, since Sharlyns become overripe quickly, you may want to buy them when the background is just 50 to 70 percent orange. If you're unsure about a melon's ripeness, shake it gently; loose seeds may mean an overripe melon.

Watermelon. Everyone wants a sweet, crisp-fleshed watermelon, whether it's the old-fashioned Cal-sweet type or the newer red Triple-sweet or yellow Orchid Sweet variety.

But how do you pick a good one?

The only sure way of getting the perfect watermelon is to buy it cut. If you buy a whole melon, look for these signs: symmetrical shape, a dull rather than shiny surface, and an underside that's yellowish or beginning to turn cream-colored.

Specialty melons. French Afternoon and the similar Charentais are both intensely sweet newcomers. French Breakfast is less sweet, with a crisp texture like that of green honeydew. Two varieties from Israel are Galia, which can be extremely sweet and powerfully aromatic, and delicately sweet Ha-Ogen. Newcomers from New Zealand include Prince and White.

Triplesweet watermelon

PMR 45 cantaloupe

French Afternoon

Topscore cantaloupe

French Breakfast

Orchid Sweet watermelon

Honeyloupe

Saticoy cantaloupe

Ha-Ogen

Galia

Ambrosia cantaloupe

Calsweet watermelon

groups of 4, as follows: lay wedges on a flat surface, with flesh of one piece against rind of the next. Push 3 sturdy bamboo or metal skewers through wedges to hold them together—one skewer through center, the others about 1 inch to either side of center. Grill skewered melon (see page 123) until hot and streaked with brown (about 5 minutes).

FRESH MELON PICKLES

Per serving: 34 calories, .67 g protein, 9 g carbohydrates, 0 g total fat, 0 mg cholesterol, 7 mg sodium

½ cup white wine vinegar

2 tablespoons sugar

1 teaspoon *each* minced fresh tarragon, fresh dill, and fresh mint; or ½ teaspoon *each* dry tarragon, dry dill weed, and dry mint

2 cups 1-inch melon cubes (Casaba, Santa Claus, green or orange honeydew, or Persian)

In a bowl, stir together vinegar, sugar, tarragon, dill, and mint until sugar is dissolved. Stir in melon. Cover and refrigerate for at least 2 hours or up to 1 day, stirring occasionally. Makes 2 cups (about 6 servings).

CHILLED MELON SOUP

Per serving: 138 calories, 2 g protein, 29 g carbohydrates, 2 g total fat, 0 mg cholesterol, 33 mg sodium

6½ to 8 pounds melon (green or orange honeydew, cantaloupe, Persian, Casaba, Santa Claus, Jaune Canari, or Sharlyn)

2 teaspoons salad oil

2 fresh serrano or jalapeño chiles, seeded and minced; or ¼ teaspoon liquid hot pepper seasoning

½ cup fruity white wine such as Gewürztraminer or Chenin Blanc

⅔ cup lime juice or lemon juice

2 tablespoons honey

¼ teaspoon white pepper

Cut melon in halves. Scoop out and discard seeds. With a spoon, scoop flesh from melon; you should have 8 to 10 cups. Set aside.

Heat oil in a 1- to 2-quart pan over medium-high heat. Add chiles and cook, stirring, until soft (about 3 minutes). Add wine and bring to a boil. (If using hot pepper seasoning, bring

■ **Preparation.** Cut melon in halves, scoop out seeds, and cut into serving-size wedges to eat with a spoon. Or cut rind from wedges and eat melon with a knife and fork. Watermelon is a special case because of its size and the seeds scattered through its flesh. Cut into wedges or slices to eat. If using watermelon in recipes, pick out the seeds.

Another way to present melon is to scoop it into balls using a melon baller—rotate the simple utensil as you would an ice cream scoop.

■ **Amount.** Two-thirds to 1 pound of melon yields about 1 cup cubed melon.

■ **Freezing.** Not recommended.

■ **Serving ideas.** For easy appetizers, wrap slices of any type of melon with prosciutto or dry salami. Season melon wedges with lemon or lime juice, fresh mint, or ground red pepper (cayenne). Use melon cubes or balls in fruit salads. To serve melon for dessert, top wedges with vanilla ice cream; sprinkle lightly with chopped crystallized ginger. Or drizzle melon pieces with hazelnut- or orange-flavored liqueur.

■ **Cooking with melons.** Firm-fleshed melons such as cantaloupe and Persian are suitable for grilling.

Grilling. Cut melon into 1½-inch-thick wedges. Skewer wedges in

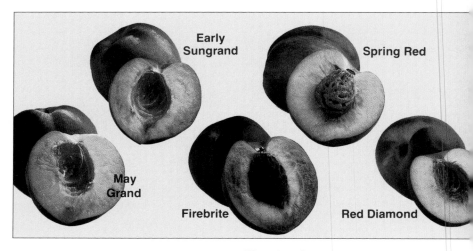

Early Sungrand · Spring Red · May Grand · Firebrite · Red Diamond

...Melons continued

to a boil with wine; omit oil.) Remove from heat.

In a large bowl, combine melon pieces, chile mixture, lime juice, honey, and white pepper. Whirl in a blender or food processor, a portion at a time, until smoothly puréed. Pour into a bowl and stir to blend. Cover and refrigerate until cold (at least 2 hours). Makes 6 to 8 first-course servings.

MELON & SMOKED MEAT SALAD

Per serving of salad: 543 calories, 92 g protein, 17 g carbohydrates, 10 g total fat, 224 mg cholesterol, 209 mg sodium

Per tablespoon of dressing: 82 calories, .09 g protein, .38 g carbohydrate, 9 g total fat, 0 mg cholesterol, 16 mg sodium

3 to 4 pounds melon (green or orange honeydew, Persian, Jaune Canari, Santa Claus, cantaloupe, or watermelon)

¼ pound edible-pod peas, ends and strings removed

1 smoked chicken (2½ to 3 lbs.), ½ pound thinly sliced pastrami, ⅓ pound sliced dry salami, or ¼ pound thinly sliced prosciutto
Herb Dressing (recipe follows)

3 or 4 butter lettuce leaves

Scoop out (or pick out) and discard melon seeds; cut off and discard rind. Cut melon lengthwise into 1-inch-thick wedges and set aside.

In a 2- to 3-quart pan, boil peas in 1 inch water until bright green (about 30 seconds); drain. Plunge peas into cold water; drain. Set aside.

Pull off and discard chicken skin. Pull meat from bones and tear into bite-size pieces; discard bones. (If using pastrami or other meat, do not cut into bite-size pieces.)

Prepare Herb Dressing. On a large platter, arrange melon, peas, and chicken pieces (or sliced meat). Garnish with lettuce leaves. Moisten with a small amount of dressing; pass remaining dressing at the table. Makes 4 servings.

Herb Dressing. Combine ½ cup **olive oil** or salad oil, 3 tablespoons **white wine vinegar,** 1 tablespoon *each* minced **onion** and **Dijon mustard,** and 1 teaspoon minced **fresh oregano** or ½ teaspoon dry oregano leaves. Makes about ¾ cup.

■ *See also Fruit Sorbet (page 41), Minted Pepino & Cantaloupe Salad (page 47).*

Nectarines

Neither a fuzzless peach nor a cross between a peach and a plum, the nectarine has been recognized as a distinct variety of fruit for some 2,000 years. But the nectarines seen in markets now bear little resemblance to those grown in the past. Today's eye-appealing nectarines are larger, redder, and firmer, and they're usually yellow-fleshed freestones.

Nectarines have become such favorites for fresh consumption that produce buyers expect they'll eventually surpass peaches in popularity. Virtually the entire U.S. crop is grown in California; some nectarines are also imported from Chile and New Zealand. The 12 commercially important varieties are shown in the photograph above. Favorites for eating fresh include Firebrite, Red Diamond, Flavortop, Summer Grand, Flamekist, and Red Gold. Best for cooking are Firebrite, Spring Red, and Red Diamond.

Nutrition. Nectarines are an excellent source of vitamin A. One medium-size fruit has 85 calories.

■ **Season.** Mid-June through mid-September (peak in July) for the domestic crop; mid-December through March for imported fruit.

■ **Selection.** Choose nectarines that have an orange-yellow (not green) background color between the red areas. Ripe nectarines give to gentle pressure, but they aren't as soft as a ripe peach.

■ **Ripening & storage.** Ripen firm-ripe nectarines at room temperature, uncovered, out of direct sun; turn occasionally. Refrigerate ripe fruit, unwashed, in a plastic or paper bag for up to 1 week.

■ **Preparation.** For eating out of hand, simply wash—it's not necessary to peel. Or cut around seam and twist fruit in half; lift or cut out pit, then slice fruit. Cut clingstone fruit away from pit in quarters or slices. To prevent browning, coat cut surfaces with lemon juice.

■ **Amount.** One pound nectarines (3 medium-size or 2 large) yields 1½ to 2 cups sliced fruit.

■ **Freezing.** Cut nectarines in halves, quarters, or slices; discard pits. Freeze in light syrup (see page 125).

■ **Serving ideas.** Serve sliced nectarines on breakfast cereal, pancakes, or waffles; or add to fruit, poultry, fish, or ham salads. Accompany meat or poultry entrées with sautéed, baked, or grilled nectarines. To serve nectarines for dessert, sprinkle slices with almond- or hazelnut-flavored liqueur; or serve over pound cake, ice cream, or fruit-flavored yogurt.

■ **Cooking with nectarines.**
Nectarines and peaches are interchangeable in cooking, though nectarines aren't as juicy as peaches. You may use nectarines in any of the peach recipes on page 44.

Baking. Halve and pit nectarines. Glaze and bake (see page 122) until hot (about 25 minutes).

Grilling. Halve and pit nectarines; coat cut sides with lemon juice to prevent browning. Grill (see page 123) until hot and streaked with brown (6 to 8 minutes).

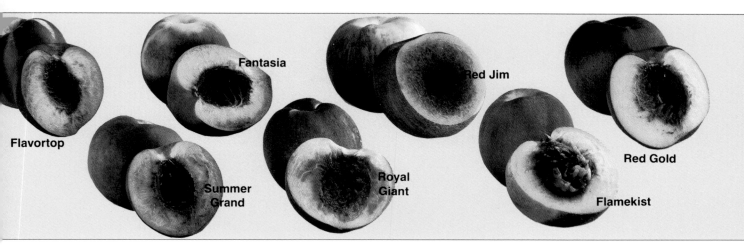

Flavortop

Fantasia

Red Jim

Summer Grand

Royal Giant

Red Gold

Flamekist

Poaching. Halve and pit 4 or 5 medium-size firm-ripe nectarines. Coat cut sides with 1 tablespoon lemon juice to prevent browning. Simmer in poaching liquid (see page 124) until fruit is tender when pierced (5 to 7 minutes).

Sautéing. Pit nectarines and cut in ½-inch-thick slices. Sauté (see page 124) until hot and tender when pierced (3 to 5 minutes).

BROILED CHICKEN WITH NECTARINES

Per serving: 692 calories, 95 g protein, 25 g carbohydrates, 22 g total fat, 346 mg cholesterol, 271 mg sodium

    1 frying chicken (about
       3½ lbs.), cut up
    ½ cup raspberry vinegar or
       red wine vinegar
    ½ cup finely chopped fresh
       basil
    2 tablespoons salad oil
    4 large firm-ripe nectarines
       Salt and pepper

Rinse chicken and pat dry. Place in a deep bowl. Combine vinegar, basil, and oil; pour over chicken and turn to coat. Cover and let stand at room temperature for 2 hours (or refrigerate until next day).

Lift chicken from marinade (reserve marinade) and arrange on a rack in a broiler pan. Broil 4 to 5 inches below heat for 20 minutes, turning as needed to brown evenly. Halve and pit nectarines; coat cut sides with marinade. Arrange nectarines, cut side up, on rack with chicken. Continue to broil until meat near thighbone is no longer pink; cut to test (about 10 more minutes). Season to taste with salt and pepper. Makes 4 to 6 servings.

NECTARINE SALAD RING

Per serving: 268 calories, 8 g protein, 43 g carbohydrates, 9 g total fat, 1 mg cholesterol, 89 mg sodium

    1 envelope unflavored
       gelatin
    1 cup buttermilk
    1 cup orange juice
    3 tablespoons honey
    3½ cups sliced nectarines
    ½ cup chopped walnuts
       (optional)

In a blender or food processor, sprinkle gelatin over buttermilk; let soften for 5 minutes. In a small pan, bring orange juice to a boil; add juice and honey to gelatin mixture. Whirl until blended. Pour mixture into a bowl; cover and refrigerate until thick and syrupy.

Stir nectarines and walnuts (if used) into gelatin mixture; pour into a 1½-quart mold. Cover and refrigerate until firm (about 4 hours).

To serve, dip mold to rim in warm water for 10 seconds; run tip of a knife around edge to loosen. Invert salad onto a serving plate. Makes 4 to 6 servings.

NECTARINE TART

Per serving: 346 calories, 3 g protein, 46 g carbohydrates, 18 g total fat, 148 mg cholesterol, 194 mg sodium

       Butter Crust (page 20)
    3 egg yolks
    ⅔ cup sugar
    4½ tablespoons lemon juice
    ⅓ cup butter or margarine,
       cut into pieces
    3 cups sliced nectarines
    ⅓ cup apricot or peach jam

Prepare and bake Butter Crust.

In a 1-quart pan, beat together egg yolks, sugar, 3 tablespoons of the lemon juice, and butter. Cook over

medium-low heat, stirring often, until thick (about 12 minutes). Let cool to room temperature, then spread in baked crust.

Toss together nectarines and remaining 1½ tablespoons lemon juice; arrange nectarines in overlapping concentric circles on custard. Serve; or cover and refrigerate for up to 4 hours.

To serve, remove pan sides. Stir jam over low heat until melted; brush over fruit. Makes about 10 servings.

■ *See also* **Fruit Pie** *(page 17),* **Fruit Jam** *(page 28),* **Fruit Sorbet** *(page 41).*

Oranges   *see Citrus, page 20*

Papayas

Native to tropical America and once considered exotic, papayas are no longer strangers to U.S. markets. Today, the Solo variety is extensively cultivated for export in Hawaii; smaller quantities are grown in Puerto Rico, Florida, and Southern California. The larger Mexican papaya is marketed in Southern California and in other areas with a large Mexican population.

Two strains of Solo papayas are grown in Hawaii. Solo Waimanalo, the more common, is shaped like a rounded pear with a short neck; it has bright yellow-orange flesh and tender green-yellow skin. Solo Sunrise looks almost the same, but it's slimmer, firmer, and less juicy, with salmon-pink flesh. In both varieties, the fruit's center cavity is filled with small black seeds.

The Hawaiian papaya industry has recently suffered some setbacks in getting its crop to market. The culprit is the tropical fruit fly, which bores into the fruit to lay its eggs. Various methods have been used to eradicate the flies, including spraying with EDB (ethyl dibromide), irradiation, and double dipping in hot water.

Mexican papayas taste muskier and less sweet than the Solo type; their skin is more green than yellow, their flesh salmon-red or bright orange. While an average Solo papaya weighs about 1 pound, Mexican papayas may reach 10 pounds. Because of their size, they're usually sold by the piece.

Nutrition. The milky juice of all papayas contains an enzyme called papain—a common ingredient in meat tenderizers, and highly prized by some as a remedy for indigestion. The fruit is also a rich source of vitamins A and C and potassium. Half a medium-size papaya contains about 60 calories.

■ **Season.** Usually all year; prices are lowest May through July and October through November. Availability varies with Hawaii's weather conditions.

■ **Selection.** Ripe papayas should be about as soft as a ripe peach, with more yellow than green in the skin. (Mexican papayas may remain mostly green even when fully ripe.) Most papayas are sold firm-ripe and need to be ripened further. Avoid bruised or shriveled papayas and those showing signs of mold or other deterioration.

■ **Ripening & storage.** Ripen firm papayas at room temperature in a loosely closed paper bag. Refrigerate ripe fruit in a plastic or paper bag for up to 3 days.

■ **Preparation.** Cut in half lengthwise and scoop out seeds, then eat from the skin with a spoon. Or peel with a vegetable peeler and cut into slices; discard seeds.

■ **Amount.** One medium-size Solo papaya (about 1 lb.) yields 1¼ to 1½ cups peeled, sliced, seeded fruit.

Mexican papaya, top, dwarfs Solo variety. Most common papaya in American markets is Solo Waimanalo, bottom right; Solo Sunrise, left, differs in flesh color.

■ **Freezing.** Not recommended.

■ **Serving ideas.** Sprinkle papaya with lime or lemon juice to enhance its flavor; add a sprinkling of ground red pepper (cayenne) for spicy contrast. Wrap slices of firm-ripe papaya in thinly sliced smoked or cured meat such as prosciutto. Add papaya chunks to fruit, spinach, poultry, or smoked meat salads. Serve sautéed, baked, or grilled papaya alongside meat or poultry entrées. To serve papaya for dessert, fill seeded halves with vanilla ice cream or lime, lemon, or orange sherbet.

■ **Cooking with papayas.** The following instructions are for Solo papayas. Mexican papayas can be used interchangeably, but you'll need to make adjustments for size.

Baking. Cut large papayas lengthwise into quarters; seed, but do not peel. Glaze and bake (see page 122) until hot (about 25 minutes).

Grilling. Peel papayas and cut lengthwise into quarters; remove seeds. Grill (see page 123) until hot and streaked with brown (5 to 8 minutes).

Sautéing. Peel papayas and cut lengthwise into 1-inch-thick slices. Discard seeds. Sauté (see page 124) until hot (3 to 5 minutes).

PAPAYA & SAUSAGE SAUTÉ

Per serving: 967 calories, 17 g protein, 62 g carbohydrates, 72 g total fat, 88 mg cholesterol, 1629 mg sodium

> 1¼ **pounds mild Italian sausages**
> ⅓ **cup water**
> 2 **tablespoons** *each* **lemon juice and honey**
> ½ **teaspoon** *each* **ground ginger, ground coriander, and curry powder**
> 2 **medium-size papayas (about 1 lb.** *each*)**, peeled, seeded, and cut lengthwise into ½-inch-thick slices**
> 3 **to 4 cups hot cooked rice**

Prick each sausage in several places, then place in a wide frying pan and add water. Bring to a boil over high heat; reduce heat, cover, and simmer until water has evaporated and sausages are brown and firm (about 10 minutes). Remove from heat. Discard all but 3 tablespoons drippings. Push sausages to side of pan; stir lemon juice, honey, ginger, coriander, and curry powder into reserved drippings. Roll sausages in spice mixture; transfer to a serving plate and keep warm.

Add papayas to pan. Cook over high heat, turning occasionally, until fruit is glazed and light brown (3 to 5 minutes). Pour papaya mixture around sausages. Serve with rice. Makes about 4 servings.

Continued on page 42

ICY FRUIT REFRESHMENT

Fruit sorbet is a naturally light and refreshing dessert that's simple to make: you just combine fresh fruit purée with a sugar syrup, then freeze. We offer you a choice of 20 different fruit flavors, from apricot to tamarillo; the recipe makes 3 or 4 servings (about 1½ cups).

FRESH FRUIT SORBET

    ½ cup *each* sugar and water
        Fruit of your choice (see amount
        in chart)
        Citrus juice (see amount in chart)

In a 1- to 2-quart pan, combine sugar and water. Bring to a boil over high heat; boil until mixture is reduced to ½ cup (about 5 minutes). Let cool. If made ahead, cover and refrigerate until ready to use (sugar syrup keeps indefinitely).

In a food processor or blender, whirl specified amount of fruit and citrus juice (if any) until puréed. You should have 1 cup purée. Mix syrup and fruit purée; pour into a 9-inch square metal pan. Cover and freeze until almost firm (about 1 hour).

Layered sorbets—papaya, tamarillo, kiwi—refresh the eye and the palate.

Break frozen fruit mixture into small pieces. Process briefly in a food processor just until smooth and slushy; do not overprocess. (Or turn mixture into a bowl and beat with an electric mixer.) Wrap airtight and freeze until firm (at least 2 hours) or for up to 1 month.

To serve, let sorbet stand at room temperature to soften slightly; then scoop out. Makes about 1½ cups (3 or 4 servings).

Note: You may also freeze fruit mixture in a self-refrigerated ice cream maker, following manufacturer's directions.

FRUIT	QUANTITY OF FRUIT	CITRUS JUICE
Apricot	1¼ cups peeled, cubed apricots (6 to 8 apricots)	1½ tablespoons lemon juice
Banana	1¼ cups cubed bananas (about 3 medium-size bananas)	1½ tablespoons lemon juice
Berry	1¼ cups berries (hulled, sliced strawberries or whole black-berries, raspberries, or blueberries)	1 tablespoon lemon juice for blueberry; none for other berries
Cherimoya	1¼ cups peeled, seeded, chopped cherimoya (about 1 large cherimoya)	2 tablespoons orange juice
Feijoa	1 cup feijoa pulp (scooped from centers of 8 to 10 large feijoas)	1½ tablespoons lemon juice
Fig	1¼ cups chopped figs (6 to 8 large figs)	2 tablespoons lemon juice
Guava	1 cup guava pulp (scooped from centers of 8 to 10 guavas)	1½ tablespoons lemon juice
Kiwi fruit	1¼ cups peeled, sliced kiwi fruits (4 or 5 kiwi fruits)	None
Mango	1 cup peeled, cubed mangoes (about 2 medium-size mangoes)	2½ tablespoons orange juice
Melon	1¼ cups peeled, seeded, cubed melon (about ⅓ of a cantaloupe)	2 tablespoons lemon juice
Nectarine	1¼ cups cubed nectarines (about 2 medium-size nectarines)	2 tablespoons lemon juice
Papaya	1¼ cups peeled, seeded, cubed papaya (a 1- to 1½-lb. fruit)	2½ tablespoons lime juice
Passion fruit	1 cup passion fruit pulp (scooped from 10 to 12 passion fruits); whirl until seeds resemble coarse pepper	None
Peach	1¼ cups peeled, cubed peaches (about 2 medium-size peaches)	2 tablespoons lemon juice
Pear	1¼ cups peeled, cored, cubed pears (about 2 medium-size pears)	2 tablespoons lemon juice
Pepino	1 cup peeled, seeded, cubed pepinos (4 to 6 pepinos)	1 tablespoon lemon juice
Persimmon	1 cup persimmon pulp (scooped from 1 large Hachiya or other soft persimmon)	1½ tablespoons lemon juice
Prickly pear	1¼ cups peeled, cubed prickly pears (5 or 6 large prickly pears)	2 tablespoons lemon juice
Sapote	1 cup peeled, seeded ripe sapote chunks (2 medium-size sapotes)	2 tablespoons lemon juice
Tamarillo	1 cup sliced tamarillos (4 or 5 tamarillos)	1 tablespoon lemon juice

CILANTRO PAPAYA SALAD

Per serving: 134 calories, 1 g protein, 14 g carbohydrates, 9 g total fat, 0 mg cholesterol, 51 mg sodium

   Cilantro Dressing
   (recipe follows)
1 medium-size papaya
   (about 1 lb.)
2 medium-size oranges
1 medium-size cucumber,
   peeled and sliced
   Lettuce leaves

Prepare Cilantro Dressing. Peel and seed papaya; then cut into bite-size chunks. Cut peel and all white membrane from oranges; cut between segments, then lift out segments. Combine papaya, oranges, and cucumber. Add dressing and stir gently to coat. Cover and refrigerate for 30 minutes to 1 hour. Serve on lettuce leaves. Makes 4 to 6 servings.

Cilantro Dressing. Stir together ¼ cup **salad oil,** 2 tablespoons **lime juice,** ¼ teaspoon **sugar,** ⅛ teaspoon **salt,** 3 to 4 tablespoons **canned diced green chiles,** 1 **green onion** (including top), chopped, and 2 tablespoons chopped **fresh cilantro (coriander).**

GINGERED PAPAYA WITH ICE CREAM

Per serving of sauce: 80 calories, .37 g protein, 12 g carbohydrates, 4 g total fat, 12 mg cholesterol, 52 mg sodium

1 medium-size firm-ripe
   papaya (about 1 lb.)
2 or 3 limes
2 tablespoons butter or
   margarine
2 tablespoons slivered
   crystallized ginger
1 tablespoon firmly packed
   brown sugar
   Vanilla ice cream

Halve, seed, and peel papaya; cut into ½-inch-thick slices. Pare green outer layer of peel from one lime; cut into thin strips. Squeeze juice from lime to make 2 tablespoons. Thinly slice remaining limes and set aside for garnish.

Melt butter in a wide frying pan over medium heat. Add papaya, ginger, and sugar. Gently turn papaya until heated through (about 3 minutes). Stir in lime peel and juice. Serve hot or cool over ice cream; garnish each serving with a few lime slices. Makes 4 to 6 servings.

■ *See also* **Fruit Jam** *(page 28),* **Fruit Sorbet** *(page 41).*

Today's peach varieties are nearly all yellow; an exception is white-fleshed Babcock. Most market peaches are freestone.

Passion Fruit

The passion fruit grows extensively in many tropical countries. It is said to have acquired its name when Christian missionaries first encountered the plant in South America: in its flower they saw the crown of thorns and other symbols of the Crucifixion. *(Photo on page 27.)*

Today, American markets carry fresh passion fruit from New Zealand and juices and jams from Hawaii. The egg-shaped, 2-inch-long fruit has a thick, hard shell—purple in the New Zealand variety, yellow in the Hawaiian type. The gelatinous, yellow-orange pulp is laced with many soft edible seeds; both pulp and seeds are very aromatic, with a sweet-tart, exotic flavor. Passion fruit is usually eaten fresh, though you can freeze it without loss of quality.

Nutrition. One passion fruit has about 16 calories.

■ **Season.** March through September.

■ **Selection.** If the dark purple shells are shriveled, wrinkled, or even a little moldy—that's great! It simply indicates that the fruit is ripe and ready to eat.

■ **Ripening & storage.** If fruit is smooth-skinned, ripen it until it's shriveled—at room temperature, uncovered, out of direct sun. Turn fruit occasionally as it ripens. Refrigerate ripe fruit in a plastic or paper bag for up to a few days; freeze for longer storage.

■ **Preparation.** Simply cut in half crosswise and scoop out pulp and seeds with a spoon.

■ **Amount.** Ten to 12 passion fruits yield about 1 cup pulp.

■ **Freezing.** Scoop pulp and seeds from halved fruit. Transfer to freezer containers; cover and freeze for up to 3 months.

■ **Serving ideas.** For an unusual appetizer, spoon teaspoonfuls of passion fruit pulp on toasted French

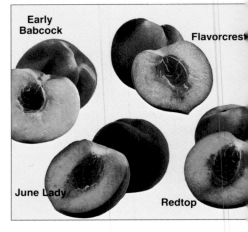

Early
Babcock

Flavorcrest

June Lady

Redtop

bread or crackers spread with cream cheese or Brie. Add dollops of passion fruit pulp to fruit, poultry, or gelatin salads. Serve over ice cream or sherbet for dessert.

■ **Cooking with passion fruit.** Passion fruit pulp may be cooked for use in pastry fillings, but it is generally used fresh.

PASSION FRUIT FILLING FOR PIES & CAKES

Per recipe: 1224 calories, 6 g protein, 231 g carbohydrates, 34 g total fat, 576 mg cholesterol, 305 mg sodium

1 cup sugar
¼ cup cornstarch
1 cup passion fruit pulp
1 cup water
2 egg yolks
2 tablespoons butter or
   margarine

Combine sugar and cornstarch in a 2-quart pan. Stir in passion fruit pulp and water. Bring to a boil over high heat, stirring constantly. Boil, stirring, for 30 seconds; remove from heat. Beat ¼ cup of the mixture into egg yolks, then beat egg yolk mixture into fruit mixture in pan. Add butter and continue to cook, stirring, until mixture is well blended and slightly thickened (about 1 minute). Remove from heat. Use hot or at room temperature to fill a baked pie or tart shell or to spread between cake layers. Makes about 3 cups filling.

■ *See also* **Carambola Spinach Salad with Passion Fruit Dressing** *(page 18),* **Fruit Sorbet** *(page 41).*

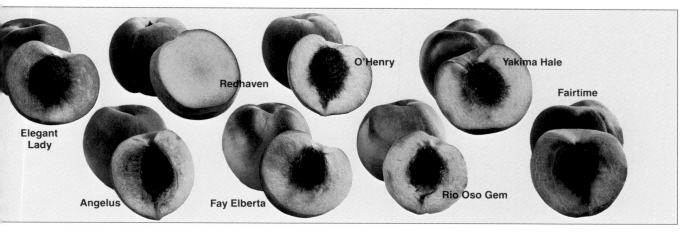

Elegant Lady

Redhaven

O'Henry

Yakima Hale

Fairtime

Angelus

Fay Elberta

Rio Oso Gem

Peaches

Peaches were probably first grown in China several thousand years ago. Early settlers brought them to the United States; today, they're among the most popular American fruits, ranking in sales just behind apples, oranges, and bananas.

The first modern peach variety was the Elberta—the ancestor of today's yellow-fleshed freestone peach. Today, however, there are hundreds of supermarket varieties. In general, the newer varieties are larger, firmer, and more acid in flavor than older types, and almost all are yellow-fleshed freestones. You may find the juicy, intensely flavored old-fashioned varieties such as Elbertas, Hales, and Rio Oso Gems in "you-pick" orchards and farmers' markets in your area.

Peaches are categorized as freestone or clingstone on the basis of how tenaciously the flesh adheres to the pit. Virtually no true clingstones are sold in markets today, but they are widely used for commercial canning.

Though grown commercially in almost all sections of the United States, peaches are also imported for winter consumption from New Zealand, Chile, and Mexico. Domestically, California produces the most (about 60 percent), followed by South Carolina and Georgia, where the Elberta was developed a century ago.

The photograph above shows 12 commercial varieties of California

peaches; varieties grown in other sections of the country vary slightly. In our taste tests, the two favorites for eating fresh were O'Henry and Rio Oso Gem. For cooking, O'Henry and Redhaven came out on top.

Nutrition. Peaches are a rich source of vitamin A. Each medium-size fruit contains about 50 calories.

■ **Season.** Mid-May through mid-October (peak in August) for domestic peaches; December through March for imported fruit.

■ **Selection.** A red color or blush is not a guarantee of good quality. Instead, look for fruit with a creamy or yellow—not green—background color. Ripe peaches give to gentle pressure; avoid green, extra-hard, and badly bruised fruit. Soft-ripe peaches can be used immediately; choose firm-ripe fruit for cooking or ripening at home. Peaches don't become any sweeter after they're picked, but ripening makes mature fruit softer and juicier.

■ **Ripening & storage.** Ripen firm-ripe fruit at room temperature in a loosely closed paper bag. Refrigerate ripe fruit, unwashed, in the same bag for up to 3 days.

■ **Preparation.** To eat out of hand, simply wash; or peel to remove fuzzy skin. (Modern commercial washing procedures remove much of the fuzz before peaches reach the market.) *To peel peaches*, dip in boiling water for 30 seconds, then lift out with a slotted spoon; cool quickly in cold water and slip off skin.

To cut, slice around seam, twist peach in half, and lift or cut out pit. Cut clingstone fruit away from pit in quarters or slices. To prevent browning, coat cut surfaces with lemon juice.

■ **Amount.** One pound peaches (3 medium-size or 2 large) yields 1½ to 2 cups sliced fruit.

■ **Freezing.** Peel and cut into halves, quarters, or slices; discard pits. Freeze in light syrup (see page 125).

■ **Serving ideas.** Serve peeled, sliced peaches on breakfast cereal, pancakes, or waffles; or add to fruit, ham, or poultry salads. Arrange sautéed, baked, or grilled peaches alongside grilled or roasted poultry. For an elegant dessert, drop peach halves in glasses of sparkling wine, or serve with raspberry sauce and ice cream to make peach Melba. Spoon slices over shortcake or offer with sour cream and brown sugar.

■ **Cooking with peaches.** Peaches don't gain flavor with cooking, but many varieties hold their shape well and have a pleasing, more mellow taste when cooked. You may also use peaches in recipes calling for nectarines (see page 39), but take into consideration that peaches are juicier.

Baking. Peel, halve, and pit peaches. Glaze and bake (see page 122) until hot (about 25 minutes).

Grilling. Peel, halve, and pit peaches; coat all sides with lemon juice. Grill (see page 123) until hot and streaked with brown (6 to 8 minutes).

Poaching. Peel, halve, and pit 4 or 5 large firm-ripe peaches. Coat all over with 1½ tablespoons lemon juice to prevent browning. Simmer in poaching liquid (see page 124) until tender when pierced (5 to 7 minutes).

Sautéing. Peel and pit peaches; cut into ½-inch-thick slices and coat with lemon juice. Sauté (see page 124) until hot (3 to 5 minutes).

Continued on next page

SHRIMP-STUFFED PEACHES

Per serving: 379 calories, 16 g protein, 28 g carbohydrates, 23 g total fat, 104 mg cholesterol, 449 mg sodium

> Curry Dressing
> (recipe follows)
> 1½ cups cold cooked rice
> ½ cup thinly sliced green onions (including tops)
> ½ pound small cooked shrimp, rinsed and drained
> Salt and pepper
> 4 large peaches
> Lettuce leaves

Prepare Curry Dressing. In a large bowl, combine rice, onions, and shrimp. Add dressing and stir gently to blend. Season to taste with salt and pepper. Cover and refrigerate for at least 2 hours or until next day.

Peel, halve, and pit peaches. Arrange lettuce leaves on 4 plates; place 2 peach halves on each plate. Mound shrimp mixture evenly on peaches. Makes 4 servings.

Curry Dressing. Stir together ½ cup **mayonnaise**, 1 tablespoon **lemon juice**, 2 teaspoons **curry powder**, and ¼ teaspoon **ground ginger**.

FROZEN PEACH YOGURT CHEESECAKE

Per serving: 432 calories, 6 g protein, 62 g carbohydrates, 20 g total fat, 57 mg cholesterol, 304 mg sodium

> Graham Cracker Crust
> (recipe follows)
> 1 large package (8 oz.) cream cheese, softened
> 1 cup peach- or vanilla-flavored yogurt
> ⅓ cup instant nonfat dry milk
> ½ cup honey or sugar
> 1½ cups peeled, coarsely chopped peaches
> Sliced peaches

Prepare Graham Cracker Crust.

In a blender or food processor, combine cream cheese, yogurt, dry milk, and honey; whirl until smooth. Add chopped peaches and whirl until blended. Pour mixture into crust and spread evenly. Freeze, uncovered, until firm (about 4 hours). Serve; or cover lightly and freeze for up to 3 days.

To serve, let stand at room temperature for 15 to 20 minutes to soften. Garnish with sliced peaches. Makes about 8 servings.

Graham Cracker Crust. Stir together 1½ cups **graham cracker crumbs**, 3 tablespoons **sugar**, 1 teaspoon **ground cinnamon**, and ⅓ cup **butter** or margarine (melted). Press over bottom and sides of an ungreased 9-inch pie pan.

HONEY PEACH COBBLER

Per serving: 211 calories, 3 g protein, 37 g carbohydrates, 7 g total fat, 22 mg cholesterol, 278 mg sodium

> 3 pounds peaches, peeled, pitted, and sliced
> 3 tablespoons lemon juice
> ½ cup honey
> 2 tablespoons *each* cornstarch and water, stirred together
> 3 tablespoons butter or margarine
> Whole Wheat Topping
> (recipe follows)

Place peaches in a shallow 3-quart baking dish. Stir in lemon juice, honey, and cornstarch-water mixture. Dot with butter.

Prepare Whole Wheat Topping; drop by spoonfuls onto peach mixture. Bake in a 400° oven until puffy and richly browned (about 30 minutes). Serve warm or cool. Makes 12 to 15 servings.

Whole Wheat Topping. Stir together 1¼ cups **whole wheat flour**, 2 teaspoons **baking powder**, ¾ teaspoon *each* **salt** and **ground cinnamon**, and ¼ teaspoon **ground nutmeg.** Using a pastry blender, cut in ¼ cup firm **butter** or margarine until uniformly blended. Stir together ½ cup **milk** and ¼ cup **honey;** stir into flour mixture just until blended.

■ *See also* **Fruit Pie** *(page 17),* **Fruit Jam** *(page 28),* **Fruit Sorbet** *(page 41),* **Plum & Peach Soup** *(page 51).*

Pears

The pear family is taking up more and more space in American produce markets. Joining the old-fashioned yellow pears these days are crimson-red varieties and small, round Asian pears. *(Photos on pages 6 and 46.)*

Pears fall into two different classes. The familiar European type has the typical pear shape; its flesh is soft and succulent, its skin yellow or red. Asian pears are round, with green-yellow or russet skin and crunchy flesh.

Nutrition. European pears are rich in levulose sugar—a valuable aid to diabetics able to digest this type of sugar more easily than glucose. A medium-size European pear contains about 100 calories.

EUROPEAN PEARS

Juicy European pears, one of the first fruits planted by American colonists, have been cultivated for thousands of years. Once nicknamed "butter fruit" due to their meltingly soft flesh, they're considered by many to be the most flavorful fruit grown in the temperate zone.

Of the many varieties of yellow- and red-skinned Europeans, four types are most often seen in U.S. markets: the summer Bartletts and the winter d'Anjou, Bosc, and Comice pears. Bartlett and Comice pears may be yellow or red; the red types differ from their yellow counterparts only in skin color, not in taste or texture.

The pear season begins with the bell-shaped Bartlett, famous for both its eating and cooking qualities. This pear has clear yellow or dark red skin and extremely juicy, smooth, and flavorful flesh.

The principal winter pear, d'Anjou, is on the market from October through May. It's oval and short necked, ranging from medium-size to large, with flesh that's slightly spicy and gritty near the center but generally buttery and sweet. The d'Anjou's yellow-green skin may remain very green even when the fruit is ripe.

Sometimes called the aristocrats of the pear family, Boscs have long, slender necks and dark yellow skin with brownish netting; their yellow-white flesh is buttery and juicy. This variety is excellent for both cooking and eating.

Large, rounded Comice pears, the showpiece pears shipped in Christmas packages, are rated by many as the best dessert pear. Their thick skin is either greenish yellow or dark red; their fine-textured flesh is meltingly tender. Because Comice pears don't keep well in cold storage, they are more limited in availability than the other types.

A number of lesser-known commercial European pears are also marketed at various times during the year: late summer Seckel, a small, sweet, russet-colored pear that's great for eating fresh; small to medium-size Winter Nellis, also russet skinned, with excellent cooking qualities; Forelle, a golden pear with a red blush; late winter Packham, a medium to large pear with a lumpy surface; and Eldorado, a winter pear resembling the Bartlett.

About 90 percent of the European pears sold in the United States are grown in California, Oregon, and Washington. Since pears are one fruit that ripens better off the tree, they can be shipped while still firm and green. Most varieties can also be held in cold storage for quite some time.

■ **Season.** All year; peak August through December.

■ **Selection.** Most pears are sold while still green. When selecting pears, don't be misled by a scar or minor surface blemish—it doesn't affect the fruit's flesh. In fact, most ripe pears have a highly russeted skin. Avoid fully ripe pears unless you plan to use them immediately.

■ **Ripening & storage.** Pears should be fully ripe for eating out of hand. For salads or cooking, though, they're best when firm-ripe. To ripen pears to the proper stage, place them in a loosely closed paper bag and let stand at room temperature until they give to firm pressure (for firm-ripe fruit) or gentle pressure (for ripe fruit). Turn pears occasionally as they ripen. Keep in mind that ripening takes 3 to 7 days; don't buy hard fruit and expect it to be soft and juicy 24 hours later.

With the exception of d'Anjou, yellow-green pears turn yellower as they ripen. Red pears attain their color before maturity; ripen these until they give to pressure and have a pronounced pear aroma. Refrigerate ripe pears, unwashed, in a plastic or paper bag for up to 3 days.

■ **Preparation.** Simply wash to eat out of hand. To core, insert an apple corer at stem end and push through base of fruit; pull out core. For slices, core pear, peel if desired, cut into quarters, and slice. (Or cut into quarters, remove core, and slice.) Coat cut surfaces with lemon juice to prevent darkening.

■ **Amount.** One pound pears (about 3 medium-size) yields about 2 cups sliced fruit.

■ **Freezing.** Not recommended.

■ **Serving ideas.** To serve pears as an appetizer, wrap slices with smoked meat, spear them with cheese cubes, or spread with Brie cheese. Use firm-ripe pears in fruit, poultry, smoked meat, or fish salads. Serve pears for dessert with sour cream flavored with orange peel and brown sugar.

■ **Cooking with European pears.** Firm-ripe Boscs, Bartletts, and d'Anjous are excellent choices for cooking.

Baking. Peel pears, cut lengthwise into quarters, and core. Glaze and bake (see page 122) until hot (about 20 minutes).

Grilling. Core pears. Cut small to medium-size fruit in half lengthwise; cut large fruit lengthwise into ¾-inch-thick wedges. Grill (see page 123) until hot and streaked with brown (about 6 minutes for wedges, 10 to 12 minutes for halves).

Poaching. Peel 8 to 10 small firm-ripe pears; or peel, halve, and core 4 or 5 large firm-ripe pears. Coat fruit with 2 tablespoons lemon juice. Simmer in poaching liquid (see page 124) until tender when pierced (10 to 12 minutes).

Sautéing. Peel and core pears, then cut into ½-inch-thick slices and coat with lemon juice. Sauté (see page 124) until hot and tender when pierced (3 to 5 minutes).

PEAR & CHEESE SALAD

Per serving: 260 calories, 8 g protein, 14 g carbohydrates, 20 g total fat, 15 mg cholesterol, 428 mg sodium

> **Dijon Vinaigrette (recipe follows)**
> 3 **medium-size red or yellow European pears**
> **About 1 tablespoon lemon juice**
> 4 **ounces chèvre (goat cheese), such as Bûcheron or Montrachet**
> **Freshly ground pepper**
> **Fresh cilantro (coriander) sprigs**

Prepare Dijon Vinaigrette; set aside. Cut pears in half lengthwise; core. Cut a wedge from base of each half, making a ¾-inch-wide cut (see photograph above right). Brush cut surfaces with lemon juice.

Cut cheese into 6 equal triangles and stuff into wedge-shaped spaces in pears. Place each pear half on a salad plate. Drizzle with vinaigrette, sprinkle with pepper, and garnish with cilantro. Makes 6 servings.

Red pear stuffed with goat cheese makes an unusual first course (recipe below left).

Dijon Vinaigrette. Thoroughly blend ½ cup **olive oil** or salad oil, 3 tablespoons **lemon juice**, and 1 tablespoon *each* **Dijon mustard** and finely chopped **shallot** or red onion. Season to taste with **salt**.

BAKED CINNAMON PEARS

Per serving: 301 calories, 2 g protein, 56 g carbohydrates, 10 g total fat, 30 mg cholesterol, 130 mg sodium

> 6 **medium-size red or yellow European pears**
> 1½ **tablespoons lemon juice**
> 5 **tablespoons butter or margarine, softened**
> ½ **cup firmly packed brown sugar**
> ⅔ **cup raisins**
> ½ **teaspoon ground cinnamon**
> ¼ **teaspoon ground nutmeg**
> ¼ **cup water**

Core pears, then pare off a ½-inch-wide strip of peel around stem end. Set pears upright in a 9-inch square baking dish. Sprinkle with lemon juice.

Thoroughly mix butter, sugar, raisins, cinnamon, and nutmeg. Divide mixture evenly among pear centers, packing in lightly. Distribute any remaining mixture in clumps in bottom of dish. Pour water into dish and cover tightly with foil.

Bake in a 400° oven until pears are tender when pierced (35 to 45 minutes). Serve warm; spoon any sauce remaining in baking dish over pears. Makes 6 servings.

■ See also **Fruit Pie** *(page 17),* **Fruit Jam** *(page 28),* **Fruit Sorbet** *(page 41),* **Beets & Pears with Dandelion Greens** *(page 84).*

ASIAN PEARS

Bursting with juice like a pear but crisp like an apple, the Asian pear is a relative newcomer to American markets. Though sometimes called "pear-apples," Asian pears aren't a hybrid of these two fruits; they're true pears.

The tree's original rootstock is said to have been brought to this country by Chinese immigrants seeking their fortunes in the California Gold Rush, but credit for perfecting the plant for commercial growing goes to researchers at the University of California. Most of the Asian pears sold in the United States today are grown in California, Oregon, and Washington.

Asian pears are generally much blander in flavor than ripe European pears, but their crisp texture makes them more suitable for salads and lunchbox snacks.

As shown in the photograph on this page, there are about 10 different varieties of Asian pears to choose from. The most popular are three yellow-green types. Twentieth Century has thin, tender skin and smooth, fruity-tasting, tart flesh; early-season Shinseiki looks much the same, but has a tarter flavor. New Kikusui stays green skinned even when ripe; its sweet-tart flesh is smooth textured. Two more yellow-green types, the pear-shaped Chinese varieties Ya Li and Tsu Li, are milder and less flavorful than their Japanese relatives.

Of the russet-colored Asian pears, the most widely sold is Chojuro, with a distinctive aromatic flavor that people seem either to love or hate. Milder Hosui is juicy and fine textured. Shinko was the favorite among *Sunset* tasters for its rich flavor and a fine, even texture; unfortunately, it's hard to find. Our tasters found Ishiiwase and Niitake somewhat undistinguished.

Most grocery stores stock only one or two varieties of Asian pears at a time. For a wider selection, check Oriental markets.

■ **Season.** July through October; peak in September.

■ **Selection.** Unlike European pears, Asians are usually sold ripe and ready to eat. Skin color is a fairly reliable guide to ripeness. Green-skinned Asian pears (with the exception of Kikusui) are at their best for eating when they turn the yellow-green color of the Ya Li pictured below; russet varieties should be the golden brown shade of the Hosui.

■ **Ripening & storage.** This fruit keeps exceptionally well. Store at room temperature, uncovered, out of direct sun, for more than a week; refrigerate, unwashed, in a plastic or paper bag for up to 3 months.

■ **Preparation.** Simply wash to eat out of hand (discard seeds). Or cut crosswise into thin slices; peeling is optional. Coat cut surfaces with lemon juice to prevent browning.

■ **Amount.** One pound Asian pears (4 or 5) yields about 2 cups sliced fruit.

■ **Freezing.** Not recommended.

■ **Serving ideas.** Try a squeeze of lime or a dash of salt on fresh slices. Offer Asian pears together with soft-ripened cheeses or soft dessert cheeses. For more ideas, check the serving suggestions for European pears.

■ **Cooking with Asian pears.** Unlike European pears, Asians are better suited to eating fresh or using in salads than to cooking. But they can be poached or used in pies.

Poaching. Peel 8 small Asian pears, leaving stems attached. Coat with 2 tablespoons lemon juice. Simmer in poaching liquid (see page 124) until tender when pierced (6 to 8 minutes).

PROSCIUTTO PEAR PLATE

Per serving of salad: 196 calories, 8 g protein, 16 g carbohydrates, 12 g total fat, 21 mg cholesterol, 372 mg sodium

Per tablespoon of dressing: 72 calories, .09 g protein, .96 n carbohydrates, 8 g total fat, 0 mg cholesterol, .39 mg sodium

>   Shallot Dressing (recipe follows)
> 2 large (3- to 3½-inch-diameter) Asian pears, peeled if desired
> 12 thin slices prosciutto or dry salami
>   Coarsely ground pepper

Prepare Shallot Dressing and set aside. Cut pears crosswise into thin slices. Arrange 3 or 4 pear slices on one side

Asian pears are rounder than familiar European types, crisp even when fully ripe.

of each of 4 salad plates; arrange 3 prosciutto slices on the other side. Spoon dressing over pears; sprinkle with pepper. Makes 4 servings.

Shallot Dressing. Stir together ¼ cup **salad oil**, 1½ tablespoons **seasoned rice vinegar** (or 1½ tablespoons white wine vinegar plus ½ teaspoon sugar), and 2 tablespoons minced **shallots.**

ASIAN PEAR PIE

Per serving: 772 calories, 8 g protein, 123 g carbohydrates, 31 g total fat, 12 mg cholesterol, 223 mg sodium

Follow directions for **Pear Pie** (page 17), but increase flour to 4½ tablespoons to compensate for the juiciness of Asian pears.

Pepinos

As the demand increases for unusual, pretty produce, fruits such as the pepino are finding a niche in U.S. markets. *(Photo on page 27.)*

To look at a pepino, you'd never guess it was a melon—only the flavor gives it away. Native to South America, this 2- to 4-inch, teardrop-shaped "bush melon" is now grown in New Zealand and California on a small-scale commercial basis. The exotic-looking skin is marked with purple and greenish yellow stripes; the flesh is pale yellow-green to yellow-orange, with a melonlike texture and a flavor like that of a cantaloupe crossed with a honeydew.

Nutrition. Like other melons, pepinos are relatively low in calories and high in vitamin C. They are also high in potassium.

■ **Season.** February through June for New Zealand fruit; August through December for the California crop.

■ **Selection.** Most pepinos are underripe when they arrive in the market; their skin is striped green and purple, and they're very firm. You'll need to ripen them at home until the green skin turns yellower.

■ **Ripening & storage.** Ripen pepinos at room temperature, uncovered, out of direct sun; turn occasionally. Refrigerate ripe fruit in a plastic or paper bag for up to 3 days.

■ **Preparation.** Cut pepinos in half lengthwise; scoop out and discard seeds. Eat from skin with a spoon, or peel and slice.

■ **Amount.** One pepino yields about ⅓ cup sliced fruit.

■ **Freezing.** Not recommended.

■ **Serving ideas.** Pepinos are the perfect size for individual servings at breakfast; sprinkle with lime or lemon juice to enhance flavor. For appetizers, wrap ½-inch pepino wedges with proscuitto. Add firm-ripe wedges to fruit or spinach salads.

■ **Cooking with pepinos.** Like most melons, pepinos are best served uncooked. However, when sautéed, they make an interesting accompaniment to meats.

Sautéing. Thinly pare peel from pepinos. Halve and seed pepinos, then cut each half in half lengthwise. Sauté (see page 124) until hot and tender when pierced (about 3 minutes).

MINTED PEPINO & CANTALOUPE SALAD

Per serving: 113 calories, 2 g protein, 29 g carbohydrates, .28 g total fat, 0 mg cholesterol, 26 mg sodium

> 1 tablespoon chopped fresh mint or 1 teaspoon dry mint
> 3 tablespoons sugar
> ¼ cup water
> 1 tablespoon orange juice
> 1½ teaspoons lemon juice
> 2 cups *each* peeled, seeded pepino pieces and cantaloupe chunks
> Mint sprigs

Place chopped mint in a bowl. In a 1- to 2-quart pan, combine sugar and water; bring to a boil over high heat, stirring until sugar is dissolved. Boil for 2 minutes; then pour over mint. Cover and refrigerate for 1 hour. Strain syrup through a wire strainer and discard mint. Stir orange juice and lemon juice into syrup.

Pile pepino and cantaloupe in a serving bowl; pour citrus-mint syrup over melon and toss gently to coat. Serve; or cover and refrigerate for up to 2 hours. Garnish with mint sprigs before serving. Makes 3 or 4 servings.

■ *See also **Fruit Sorbet** (page 41).*

Persimmons

If you've ever bitten into an underripe persimmon, you've probably had a puckery surprise. But wait until the fruit is soft and ripe, and you'll be rewarded with a powerfully sweet flavor and an extra-juicy texture.

There are basically two commercially important varieties, both bright orange in color and Asian in origin. Pointy Hachiyas (accounting for 90 percent of the U.S. commercial crop) should be ripened until squishy-soft before eating, while flat, tomato-shaped Fuyus can be enjoyed crisp, like apples.

Aside from Hachiya, other lesser-known soft persimmon varieties include Tanehashi and acorn-shaped Tamopan. Brown-streaked Chocolate and Giant Fuyu are other crisp persimmons. All soft types can be treated like Hachiyas, all crisp types like Fuyus.

About 98 percent of the persimmons sold in the United States are grown in California.

Nutrition. Persimmons contain about 77 calories in a 3½-ounce serving. They're a good source of vitamins A and C, potassium, and phosphorus.

■ **Season.** September through mid-December; peak mid-October through November.

■ **Selection.** Skin color is not an indication of ripeness, since persimmons turn bright orange before they are mature. Ripe Hachiyas are as soft as an overripe avocado; they must be shipped while still firm, though, so you're unlikely to find ripe ones in your market. Fuyus can be eaten while firm or soft.

■ **Ripening & storage.** Ripen persimmons at room temperature in a loosely closed bag to the appropriate stage for their variety; turn fruit occasionally as it ripens. Refrigerate ripe fruit, unwashed, in a plastic bag; or freeze (see page 48).

■ **Preparation.** *For Hachiya-type persimmons,* cut off top and eat pulp from skin with a spoon. *To prepare purée* for use in cooking, cut very ripe fruit in half and scoop out pulp; discard skin, seeds, and stem. In a blender or food

Two main types of persimmons are Hachiyas (right), soft when ripe, and Fuyus (lower left), which remain crisp. At upper left is Tamopan persimmon, another soft type.

processor, whirl pulp, a portion at a time, until smooth.

For Fuyu-type persimmons, rinse and eat like an apple, discarding stem end. Or cut into slices.

■ **Amount.** One large soft persimmon yields ¾ to 1 cup purée. One large crisp persimmon yields ¾ to 1 cup sliced fruit.

■ **Freezing.** Place whole Hachiya-type persimmons in a single layer on a baking sheet and freeze until solid; then package in freezer bags. Or stir 1½ teaspoons lemon juice into each cup of prepared persimmon purée; pour purée into freezer containers. Freeze whole fruit or purée for up to 6 months; use thawed fruit or purée in recipes calling for fresh persimmon pulp.

■ **Serving ideas.** For breakfast, scoop out flesh from a soft persimmon and serve with cream or milk. For appetizers, spear slices of crisp persimmon with cubes of cheese or smoked meats. Use crisp persimmon slices in fruit, poultry, fish, or smoked meat salads. For dessert, top vanilla ice cream with soft persimmon pulp or crisp persimmon slices drizzled with orange-flavored liqueur.

■ **Cooking with persimmons.** Slice unpeeled crisp persimmons and use in cooking like apples. Purée soft persimmons for use in baking.

Sautéing. Stem 2 large Fuyu-type persimmons and cut into ½-inch wedges. Discard seeds. Sauté (see page 124) until hot and tender when pierced (3 to 5 minutes).

PERSIMMON QUICK BREAD

Per loaf: 3105 calories, 61 g protein, 442 g carbohydrates, 128 g total fat, 260 mg cholesterol, 4192 mg sodium

> 1 teaspoon baking soda
> 1 cup persimmon purée (see "Preparation," page 47)
> 2½ cups all-purpose flour
> ½ cup *each* granulated sugar and firmly packed brown sugar
> 2½ teaspoons baking powder
> 1 teaspoon *each* salt, ground cinnamon, and ground nutmeg
> 1 egg
> ⅓ cup milk
> 3 tablespoons salad oil
> 1 cup chopped nuts

Stir baking soda into persimmon purée and let stand for 5 minutes. In a bowl, combine flour, granulated sugar, brown sugar, baking powder, salt, cinnamon, and nutmeg; set aside.

In a large bowl, beat together egg, milk, oil, and persimmon mixture. Add flour mixture and stir just until blended. Stir in nuts.

Spoon mixture evenly into a greased 5- by 9-inch loaf pan and bake in a 350° oven until a wooden pick inserted in center comes out clean (about 1¼ hours). Let cool for 15 minutes; then turn out of pan onto a rack and let cool completely. Makes 1 loaf.

PERSIMMON DROP COOKIES

Per cookie: 82 calories, 1 g protein, 12 g carbohydrates, 4 g total fat, 11 mg cholesterol, 60 mg sodium

> 1 teaspoon baking soda
> 1 cup persimmon purée (see "Preparation," page 47)
> 2¼ cups all-purpose flour
> ½ teaspoon *each* ground cinnamon and nutmeg
> ¼ teaspoon salt
> ½ cup (¼ lb.) butter or margarine, softened
> 1 cup sugar
> 1 egg
> 1 cup chopped nuts
> 1 cup raisins or semisweet chocolate chips

Stir baking soda into persimmon purée and let stand for 5 minutes. In

a bowl, combine flour, cinnamon, nutmeg, and salt. In large bowl of an electric mixer, cream butter and sugar; beat in egg, then stir in persimmon mixture. Stir in flour mixture to form a soft dough, then stir in nuts and raisins.

Drop batter by rounded tablespoons onto ungreased baking sheets, spacing cookies 2 inches apart. Bake in a 350° oven until edges are lightly browned and centers spring back when lightly touched (12 to 15 minutes). Transfer to racks and let cool. Makes about 4 dozen cookies.

CRISP PERSIMMON PIE

Per serving: 708 calories, 7 g protein, 108 g carbohydrates, 30 g total fat, 12 mg cholesterol, 239 mg sodium

Follow directions for **Apple Pie** (page 17), but substitute 8 cups (about 2½ lbs.) peeled, sliced **Fuyu-type persimmons** mixed with 3 tablespoons **lemon juice** for the sliced apples.

■ *See also **Autumn Kiwi Fruit Salad** (page 33), **Fruit Sorbet** (page 41).*

Pineapples

Named for its resemblance to a pine cone, the pineapple is second only to the banana as the most popular of all tropical fruits. The European love affair with this New World native began in 1493, when Christopher Columbus and his crew first came upon the fruit on the island of Guadaloupe.

In the late 18th century, pineapples were introduced to the Hawaiian Islands; today, Hawaii is the major supplier of pineapple to American markets, followed by Honduras, Mexico, the Dominican Republic, and Costa Rica.

Nutrition. Pineapple is a good source of vitamin C. It also contains the enzyme bromelin, which is an aid to digestion; this same enzyme keeps gelatin from setting, so fresh pineapple should not be used in gelatin salads or desserts (canned pineapple is fine). Each 3½-ounce serving of pineapple provides 52 calories.

■ **Season.** All year; prices tend to be lowest from April through June.

■ **Selection.** Once picked, a pineapple may get softer and juicier, but it won't get any sweeter. When choosing pineapple, look for the jet-shipped label to be guaranteed of fruit at the peak of ripeness and flavor. Don't rely on color to tell you when a pineapple is ripe—the rind may be anywhere from green to golden. Methods such as thumping or pulling a leaf from the crown don't work, either. Your best bet is to select a large, plump, fresh-looking pineapple with fresh green leaves and a sweet fragrance. Avoid fruit that has soft spots, areas of decay at the base, or an overripe (fermented) odor.

■ **Ripening & storage.** Ripe pineapples deteriorate quickly, so they should be enjoyed shortly after purchase. Store at room temperature, uncovered, out of direct sun, for up to 2 days.

■ **Preparation.** *To cut into quarters, chunks, or serve zigzag style* (see photograph below): Cut pineapple lengthwise into quarters, cutting evenly through leaves and core. Using a curved knife, cut fruit from rind and lift out, then cut away core. Cut fruit into chunks; or, for zigzag presentation, slice fruit and return to shell so slices extend alternately to one side, then the other.

To cut slices or rounds, cut off leafy top and bottom of pineapple. Cut off rind in strips from top to bottom. To remove eyes, cut grooves in fruit with a small knife, following diagonal lines made by eyes (see photograph below).

Cut fruit crosswise into slices. Cut core from each slice with a knife.

■ **Amount.** A medium-size pineapple (3 to 3½ lbs.) yields 3 cups cubed fruit.

■ **Freezing.** Cut pineapple into chunks. Freeze in light syrup (see page 125).

■ **Serving ideas.** Spear cubes of pineapple with cubes of smoked meats or other fruits to serve as appetizers. Or offer chunks plain with a hot cheese dip. Use pineapple cubes in fruit, poultry, fish, or smoked meat salads; use the hollowed shell as a "salad bowl." To serve pineapple for dessert, spoon chunks over lime, lemon, or pineapple sherbet; or drizzle with crème de menthe and serve with ice cream.

■ **Cooking with pineapple.** Versatile pineapple can be cooked in a number of different ways.

Baking. Cut pineapple into quarters; cut fruit from rind and remove core. Glaze and bake (see page 122) until hot and tender (about 20 minutes).

Grilling. Peel pineapple, then cut crosswise into ¾-inch-thick slices. Grill (see page 123) until hot and streaked with brown (6 to 8 minutes).

Poaching. Peel 1 small pineapple (2 to 2½ lbs.), then cut crosswise into ½-inch-thick slices. Simmer in poaching liquid (see page 124) until tender when pierced (about 5 minutes).

Sautéing. Cut peeled, cored pineapple into 1-inch cubes. Sauté (see page 124) until hot and tender when pierced (about 5 minutes).

MINTED CHICKEN & PINEAPPLE

Per serving: 443 calories, 40 g protein, 64 g carbohydrates, 5 g total fat, 97 mg cholesterol, 83 mg sodium

  3½ **cups shredded cooked chicken**
  ¾ **cup seasoned rice vinegar; or ¾ cup white wine vinegar plus 1½ tablespoons sugar**
  2 **tablespoons sugar**
  ¼ **cup finely chopped fresh mint**
    Salt
  1 **medium-size pineapple (3 to 3½ lbs.)**
    Butter lettuce leaves
    Mint sprigs

In a bowl, combine chicken, vinegar, sugar, and chopped mint. Season to taste with salt. Cover and refrigerate for 30 minutes to 1 hour, stirring occasionally.

Cut pineapple into quarters; cut rind and core from each quarter, then cut fruit lengthwise into thin slices. Line 4 dinner plates with lettuce; top evenly with pineapple slices. Lift chicken mixture from bowl with a slotted spoon and mound on pineapple; drizzle vinegar mixture remaining in bowl over fruit. Garnish with mint sprigs. Makes 4 servings.

SPICED PINEAPPLE SPEARS

Per pint: 927 calories, 4 g protein, 244 g carbohydrates, 2 g total fat, 0 mg cholesterol, 12 mg sodium

  3 **medium-size pineapples (3 to 3½ lbs. *each*)**
  1½ **cups distilled white vinegar**
  2 **cups sugar**
  2 **tablespoons whole cloves**
  1 **tablespoon whole cardamom, lightly crushed**
  1 **teaspoon whole allspice**
  3 **cinnamon sticks, *each* about 3 inches long**
  1 **small dried hot red chile, seeded**

Peel and core pineapples, reserving as much juice as possible. Cut pineapple into 3-inch-long, ½-inch-thick spears. Set aside.

Measure reserved pineapple juice; add enough water to make 1½ cups liquid. Pour juice mixture into a 6-quart pan; stir in vinegar, sugar, cloves, cardamom, allspice, cinnamon sticks, and chile. Bring to a boil over

For decorative effect, alternate pineapple slices to each side in the shell, zigzag style.

Remove pineapple eyes by cutting diagonal grooves in peeled fruit, then slice fruit crosswise.

high heat; reduce heat, cover, and simmer for 15 minutes. Add half the pineapple spears; cover and simmer for 5 minutes. Meanwhile, sterilize four 1-pint canning jars, lids, and rings as directed on page 28.

With a fork, lift spears from syrup and fill 2 sterilized jars. Leaving spices in pan, ladle enough hot syrup into jars to come within ½ inch of rims. Wipe rims clean; put lids and rings in place.

Add remaining pineapple spears to syrup; cover and simmer for 5 minutes. Then fill remaining 2 jars as directed above. Let jars cool; test for a good seal (see page 28). Makes 4 pints.

■ See also **Cherry Salad with Sesame Dressing** (page 20), **Autumn Kiwi Fruit Salad** (page 33), **Sweet Potato & Ginger Salad** (page 117).

Plantain   see Bananas, page 11

Plums

Plums come in a bewildering choice of varieties, with a number of skin and flesh colors and flavors ranging from quite tart to extra sweet. Yet for all their diversity, plums can be divided into two main categories: Japanese and European. The Japanese plum crop in this country comes primarily from California; European types are also grown in other parts of the country.

Of the 16 commercial varieties shown on these two pages, 15 are Japanese plums. Though produce managers prefer firm, durable varieties such as Friar, Blackamber, and Simka, *Sunset* taste testers chose Santa Rosa, Laroda, and Elephant Heart for eating fresh; Laroda, Friar, Elephant Heart, and Casselman were top choices for cooking. (Neither Elephant Heart nor Kelsey is widely available yet.)

In addition to the Japanese varieties shown in the photo, you may also find New Zealand types (in winter) and a number of other domestic varieties, including Burmosa, Wickson, Tragedy, Duarte, Mariposa, and Standard.

European plums (prune plums)

are always blue or purple and usually freestone. Smaller, firmer, sweeter, and less juicy than Japanese varieties, these are the plums that, when dried, are sold as prunes. Italian, the main commercial variety, is grown almost entirely along the Pacific slope of Washington, Oregon, and Idaho. Another commercial variety, Stanley, is grown in Michigan and western New York.

Nutrition. Pound for pound, Japanese plums are lower in calories than European plums, though one Japanese plum has 60 calories compared to just 25 for a European plum. European plums contain more vitamin A than Japanese types.

■ **Season.** Mid-May through mid-October (peak in August) for domestic plums; mid-January through mid-March for New Zealand fruit.

■ **Selection.** Plums are often picked and sold when immature. It's hard to judge maturity of dark-skinned plums by color, but try to choose fruit that's full colored for its variety. Ripe fruit is slightly soft at the tip end and gives when squeezed gently in the palm of the hand. Avoid fruit with broken or shriveled skin or brownish discoloration.

■ **Ripening & storage.** Market plums may need to ripen for a few days at room temperature. To speed ripening, group plums inside a loosely closed paper bag; check daily. Refrigerate ripe fruit, unwashed, in a plastic or paper bag for up to 3 days.

■ **Preparation.** To eat out of hand, simply wash fruit. Eat over a bowl or plate if possible; discard pit. To cut fruit, slice around seam of freestone and semi-freestone varieties, twist fruit in half, and lift or cut out pit. Cut clingstone fruit away from pit in quarters or slices.

To peel plums, dip in boiling water for 30 seconds; then lift out with a slotted spoon and cool in cold water. Slip off skins.

■ **Amount.** One pound Japanese plums (4 or 5) yields about 1½ to 2 cups sliced fruit. One pound European plums (12 to 15) yields about 2 cups.

■ **Freezing.** Halve and pit plums; or cut away from pits in quarters. Freeze in light syrup (see page 125).

Most diverse of stone fruits, plums range from purple to green in skin color, yellow to green to dark red inside.

■ **Serving ideas.** For breakfast, serve quartered or sliced plums with milk or cream. For appetizers, fill cavities of prune plums with a soft cheese such as Brie. Use firm-ripe Japanese or European plums in fruit, poultry, or fish salads.

■ **Cooking with plums.** Cooking usually brings out the best qualities in plums, smoothing the contrasting flavors of skin and flesh. (Because the skin adds so much to a plum's character, it's seldom removed before cooking.) Cooking often changes the fruit's color dramatically, too. Poaching is especially recommended as a cooking method for plums.

Poaching. Rinse 8 to 10 Japanese plums or 1½ pounds European (prune) plums. Prick skin of each plum. Simmer in poaching liquid (see page 124) until tender when pierced (7 to 10 minutes for Japanese-type plums, 3 to 5 minutes for European).

ROAST CHICKEN WITH PRUNE PLUMS

Per serving: 549 calories, 51 g protein, 21 g carbohydrates, 29 g total fat, 277 mg cholesterol, 276 mg sodium

    1 frying chicken (3½ to
       4 lbs.)
   12 large European (prune)
       plums, halved and pitted
   ½   cup port or apple juice
   ½   cup regular-strength
       chicken broth
   ¼   teaspoon ground ginger
   ⅓   cup butter or margarine

Remove chicken neck and giblets, then rinse bird inside and out and pat dry. Place chicken, breast down, on a rack in a 10- by 15-inch roasting pan. Roast in a 375° oven for 30 minutes; turn

Red Beaut

Santa Rosa

Queen Rosa

Black Beaut

breast up and roast for 20 more minutes. Add plums to pan, turning to coat with drippings. Continue to roast, turning plums once, until fruit is soft when pierced and meat near thighbone is no longer pink; cut to test (10 to 15 more minutes).

Lift chicken from rack, drain briefly, and transfer to a platter. Arrange plums around chicken. Skim and discard fat from pan drippings; then stir in port, broth, and ginger. Place pan over medium heat and stir to scrape browned particles free. Increase heat to high, bring to a boil, and boil until reduced to ½ cup. Reduce heat to low. Add butter and stir until blended. Pass sauce to spoon over chicken and plums. Makes 4 or 5 servings.

PLUM & PEACH SOUP

Per serving: 394 calories, 2 g protein, 40 g carbohydrates, 23 g total fat, 79 mg cholesterol, 24 mg sodium

- ¾ **pound Japanese plums, such as Santa Rosa**
- ¾ **pound peaches**
- 1 **cup** *each* **water and dry white wine**
- 1 **cinnamon stick, about 2 inches long**
- 1½ **tablespoons lemon juice**
- ⅓ **to ½ cup granulated sugar**
- 1 **tablespoon** *each* **cornstarch and water, stirred together**
- ¼ **cup orange- or peach-flavored liqueur**
- 1 **cup whipping cream Powdered sugar**

Peel plums and peaches. Cut fruit into chunks and discard pits. In a 3- to 4-quart pan, combine fruit, water, wine, cinnamon stick, and lemon juice. Bring to a boil; then reduce heat,

cover, and simmer until fruit mashes easily (about 15 minutes).

Remove from heat. Discard cinnamon stick. Pour fruit mixture into a blender or food processor and whirl until very smoothly puréed. Return purée to pan; stir in granulated sugar and cornstarch-water mixture. Cook over high heat, stirring, until mixture boils and thickens (about 5 minutes). Remove from heat; skim off foam. Stir in liqueur and ½ cup of the cream. Cover and refrigerate until cold, then serve (or refrigerate until next day).

To serve, beat remaining ½ cup cream until it holds soft peaks. Sweeten to taste with powdered sugar. Offer whipped cream to top soup. Makes 4 or 5 breakfast or dessert servings.

■ *See also* **Fruit Pie** *(page 17),* **Fruit Jam** *(page 28).*

Pomegranates

Spanish padres are credited with bringing pomegranates to California missions some 200 years ago. But centuries before then, the fruit was mentioned in connection with Mediterranean civilization—both in the Bible and in the writings of Homer.

Our word "pomegranate" derives from Middle French *pome garnete,* literally "seeded apple." A colorful autumn fruit about the size of an apple, the pomegranate has a leathery,

deep red to purplish red rind. When you split the hard fruit open, a mass of red seeds enclosed in a spongy white membrane is revealed. Only the seeds, with their sweet-tart flavor and juice-squirting texture, are edible.

Freeing pomegranate seeds from their membranes without making a mess or spending the whole day at the task has always been a challenge; see "Preparation" for an underwater method that works well. Once you get the seeds out, you can eat them plain, use them as a garnish on many foods, or crush them to make juice for beverages, sauces, jellies, and marinades.

Nutrition. A 3½-ounce portion of pomegranate seeds yields 60 calories and a significant amount of potassium.

■ **Season.** September through December; peak in October.

■ **Selection.** Choose large pomegranates that are heavy for their size and have a fresh-looking (not dried-out) rind.

■ **Ripening & storage.** Pomegranates are sold ripe and ready to eat. You can store them for short periods of time at room temperature, uncovered, out of direct sun—many cooks like to use them for decoration. For longer storage, refrigerate whole fruit or seeds in plastic bags or containers; or freeze the seeds separately.

■ **Preparation.** *To remove seeds,* cut crown end off pomegranate; lightly score rind lengthwise in several places. Immerse scored fruit in a bowl of cool water and let soak for 5 minutes. Then, holding fruit under water, break sections apart with your fingers, separating seeds from membranes as you

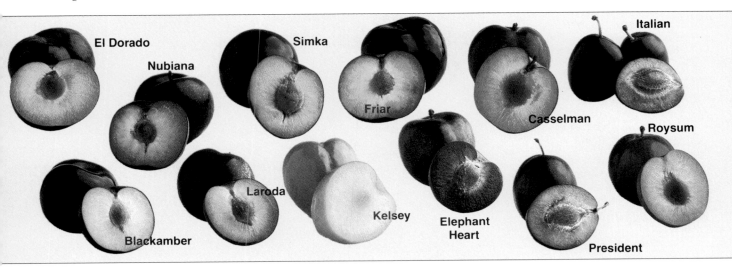

El Dorado

Nubiana

Simka

Friar

Italian

Casselman

Roysum

Blackamber

Laroda

Kelsey

Elephant Heart

President

work; seeds will sink to the bottom while rind and membranes float to the top. Skim off and discard membranes and rind. Pour seeds into a colander; let drain, then gently pat dry.

To juice pomegranates, whirl seeds in a blender or food processor, 1½ to 2 cups at a time, until liquefied. Pour through a cheesecloth-lined wire strainer and let drain. Refrigerate juice for up to 5 days; freeze for up to 6 months.

■ **Amount.** Each medium-size pomegranate yields about ¾ cup seeds or ½ cup juice.

■ **Freezing.** Scatter seeds in a rimmed pan in a single layer; freeze until firm, then pack in freezer containers. Freeze for up to 6 months. To use, spoon out desired quantity and thaw.

■ **Serving ideas.** Sprinkle pomegranate seeds on any type of fruit, poultry, fish, or green salad. Use as a garnish for grilled or roasted meats, fish, or poultry. For dessert, sprinkle on tapioca, custard, or ice cream. Pour Pomegranate Syrup (recipe follows) over ice cream, or add to sparkling water and serve as a beverage.

■ **Cooking with pomegranates.** Pomegranate juice is used in cooking; see the recipes below.

POMEGRANATE SYRUP (GRENADINE)

Per tablespoon: 29 calories, .08 g protein, 8 g carbohydrates, .05 g total fat, 0 mg cholesterol, .51 mg sodium

In a 1- to 2-quart pan, combine 1 cup **pomegranate juice** (see "Preparation," page 51) and ½ cup **sugar**. Bring to a boil over high heat, stirring until sugar is dissolved; then boil for 1 minute. Remove from heat and let cool. Cover and refrigerate for up to 2 weeks; freeze for longer storage. Makes 1¼ cups.

POMEGRANATE LAMB KEBABS

Per serving: 434 calories, 27 g protein, 5 g carbohydrates, 34 g total fat, 107 mg cholesterol, 628 mg sodium

- ½ cup **Pomegranate Syrup (above)**
- ¼ cup **salad oil**
- 1 tablespoon **lemon juice**
- 1½ teaspoons **salt**
- ¼ teaspoon **pepper**
- 2 cloves **garlic, minced or pressed**
- 2 pounds **boneless lamb shoulder or leg, cut into 1½-inch cubes**

Glistening seeds cluster inside pomegranate.

In a large bowl, stir together Pomegranate Syrup, oil, lemon juice, salt, pepper, and garlic. Add lamb and stir to coat. Cover and refrigerate for at least 6 hours or until next day.

Lift meat from marinade and drain briefly (reserve marinade). Thread meat equally on about 6 sturdy metal skewers. Place skewers on a lightly greased grill 4 to 6 inches above a solid bed of medium coals. Cook, turning often and basting with marinade, until meat is well browned on outside but still pink in center; cut to test (10 to 15 minutes). Makes about 6 servings.

Prickly Pears

Also known as cactus pears, Indian figs, or tunas, prickly pears are the rosy red fruit of a cactus plant native to Mexico. They offer good eating—if you know how to get under their thorny skin. The purple-red flesh is juicy and mildly sweet; the tiny seeds are edible.

Most of the prickly pears sold in American markets come from Washington, Oregon, and Arizona. They're usually denuded of their bristly, reddish brown spines, but you should still use tongs or wear rubber gloves when handling them.

Nutrition. Prickly pears contain about 40 calories per 3½-ounce serving. They're a fair source of vitamin C and potassium.

■ **Season.** August through December.

■ **Selection.** Ripe prickly pears are red all over and give to gentle pressure. Choose fresh-looking fruits; avoid withered ones.

■ **Ripening & storage.** Ripen at room temperature, uncovered, out of direct sun; turn occasionally. Refrigerate ripe fruit in a plastic bag for up to 5 days.

■ **Preparation.** Hold fruit with tongs or rubber-gloved hands and rinse under cold running water. Still protecting your hands, cut off both ends of fruit and split skins lengthwise. Peel skin back. Lift or scoop out pulp to make purée; or slice pulp.

To prepare purée, whirl pulp in a blender or food processor until puréed. Rub through a wire strainer to remove any seeds or strings.

■ **Amount.** One large prickly pear yields ¼ to ⅓ cup slices or purée.

■ **Freezing.** Simply scoop pulp or purée into freezer containers; freeze for up to 6 months. Thaw before using.

■ **Serving ideas.** Drizzle prickly pear slices with lemon or lime juice to accent their mellow flavor. Serve firm-ripe slices in fruit, fish, or poultry salads or alongside grilled or roasted meats. To serve prickly pears for dessert, sprinkle slices with brown sugar and lime juice; top with whipping cream.

■ **Cooking with prickly pears.** Bright-colored prickly pear purée adds a touch of drama to recipes.

Beneath thorny skin, prickly pears have juicy, purple-red flesh. Protect your hands when working with the bristly fruits.

RUBY PRICKLY PEAR DESSERT SAUCE

Per serving of sauce: 115 calories, .07 g protein, 15 g carbohydrates, 3 g total fat, 9 mg cholesterol, 102 mg sodium

- ¼ cup sugar
- 1 tablespoon cornstarch
- ⅛ teaspoon salt
- 1 cup prickly pear purée (see "Preparation," page 52)
- ⅛ teaspoon almond extract
- 2 tablespoons lemon juice
- 1 tablespoon butter or margarine
  Ice cream, sherbet, or custard

In a 2-quart pan, stir together sugar, cornstarch, salt, and prickly pear purée. Cook over medium-high heat, stirring, until sauce boils, thickens, and turns clear. Remove from heat. Add almond extract, lemon juice, and butter; stir until butter is melted. Serve hot or cooled, over ice cream, sherbet, or custard. Makes about 1¼ cups (4 to 6 servings).

■ *See also* **Fruit Sorbet** *(page 41).*

Quinces

Though quinces were once almost as familiar as apples and pears, they're seldom seen in U.S. markets today— perhaps because they're inedible unless cooked, and today's consumer doesn't spend much time making preserves.

Shaped like a fat pear with a flat bottom, this green-gold fruit often has a fuzzy, peachlike exterior. The flesh of the raw fruit is gravelly in texture and highly acidic in flavor—but after cooking, it's soft and delicately sweet, with a musky aroma and a light pink to purple color.

Nutrition. A 3½-ounce portion of quinces contains 57 calories and a fair amount of potassium.

■ **Season.** September through November; peak in October.

■ **Selection.** Quinces bruise easily, so handle them carefully. Choose firm fruit that is free of blemishes. Ripe quinces turn a pale yellow color but remain quite firm.

Quince must be cooked to be edible; cut into chunks to prepare pulp and juice for recipes.

■ **Ripening & storage.** Ripen, uncovered, in a cool, dry place, out of direct sun; turn occasionally. Refrigerate ripe fruit in a plastic or paper bag for up to 2 weeks.

■ **Preparation.** Our quince recipes call for prepared quince pulp or juice. To prepare pulp and juice, rub off outer fuzz from 8 pounds quinces; cut quinces into 1-inch chunks (do not peel or core). Place chunks in an 8- to 10-quart pan and add 5 quarts water. Bring to a boil over high heat; reduce heat, cover, and simmer until fruit mashes easily (45 to 60 minutes). Remove from heat; let cool.

Pour fruit and liquid, a portion at a time, into a colander set over a large bowl. Press fruit lightly to remove juice (reserve pressed fruit). Rinse 4 pieces of cheesecloth with cold water; wring dry and stack one atop the other to line a strainer. Pour quince juice through strainer. Use strained juice to make syrup (recipe follows).

Push reserved pressed quinces through a food mill, a portion at a time; discard residue. Use pulp to make candy (recipe follows).

■ **Amount.** One pound quinces (about 3 large quinces) yields about 1½ cups pulp and 2 cups juice.

■ **Freezing.** Not recommended.

■ **Serving ideas.** To make a quince cordial, combine equal parts Quince Syrup (recipe follows) and light rum; cover tightly and let stand at room temperature for at least a month before sipping.

■ **Cooking with quinces.** Cooked quinces have a sweet, delicate, slightly musky flavor that is especially good in syrups, jellies, and candies.

QUINCE SYRUP

Per tablespoon: 36 calories, 0 g protein, 6 g carbohydrates, 0 g total fat, 0 mg cholesterol, .06 mg sodium

- 6 cups quince juice (see "Preparation," preceding)
- 2 cups sugar
- 3 whole cloves
- 1 cinnamon stick, about 3 inches long
- 4 strips lemon peel (yellow part of peel only), *each* about ½ by 3 inches

In a 5- to 6-quart pan, combine quince juice, sugar, cloves, cinnamon stick, and lemon peel. Bring to a boil over high heat, stirring until sugar is dissolved. Then boil, uncovered, stirring occasionally, until reduced to 4 cups. Remove from heat. Remove and discard lemon peel, cloves, and cinnamon stick. Let cool; then cover and refrigerate for up to 3 months.

Serve over pancakes or ice cream. Makes 4 cups.

FRENCH QUINCE CANDY

Per piece: 81 calories, 0 g protein, 17 g carbohydrates, 0 g total fat, 0 mg cholesterol, .17 mg sodium

- 12 cups quince pulp (see "Preparation," preceding)
  About 13 cups sugar

In a heavy 8- to 10-quart pan, combine quince pulp and 12 cups of the sugar. Simmer briskly, uncovered, stirring occasionally, until mixture is thickened. Reduce heat to low. Continue to cook, stirring frequently to prevent scorching, until mixture is so thick that a clear path remains when a spoon is pulled across center of pan (2 to 3 hours). Remove from heat; let cool to room temperature.

Line two 10- by 15-inch shallow-rimmed baking pans with wax paper, letting paper extend several inches over rims. Scrape quince mixture into pans, spreading evenly. Let dry at room temperature until firm and only slightly tacky to the touch (12 to 24 hours).

Lift up ends of wax paper and turn candy over in pan. Peel off paper. Continue to dry until candy is only slightly tacky to the touch (12 to 24 more hours).

Cut candy into 1-inch squares; roll in sugar to coat. Serve, store airtight at room temperature for up to 2 months, or freeze. Makes about 12½ dozen pieces.

Raspberries *see Berries, page 13*

Rhubarb

Though rhubarb is botanically a vegetable, it's so popular in sweet pies and compotes that most of us think of it as a fruit.

Centuries ago in China, rhubarb was used only for medicinal purposes. But today, 25 to 30 million tons are grown annually for consumption in the United States, with Washington, Michigan, and California supplying the most.

You can buy two types of rhubarb—field grown or hothouse grown. In both varieties, only the stalks are edible; the leaves can be poisonous if eaten in quantity. Field-grown rhubarb stalks are large, streaked dark red and green, and very tart in flavor. Light pink hothouse stalks are smaller, less tart, and almost stringless.

Because rhubarb is so tart, it is almost always eaten cooked and sweetened with sugar.

Nutrition. Rhubarb is a good source of potassium. It is very low in calories, containing only 20 per cup of diced fruit. (But sweeten with sugar and calories soar.)

■ **Season.** February through June; peak in May.

■ **Selection.** Rhubarb is sold ripe and ready to use. Choose fresh-looking stalks that are firm and crisp; depending on the type, color should be either light pink or streaked green and cherry red. Avoid wilted, flabby stalks.

■ **Ripening & storage.** Refrigerate rhubarb, unwashed, in a plastic bag for up to 1 week.

■ **Preparation.** Remove and discard leaves; rinse stalks well. Slice crosswise as directed in individual recipes.

■ **Amount.** One pound rhubarb yields about 3 cups slices.

■ **Freezing.** Not recommended.

■ **Serving ideas.** Top cooked, sweetened rhubarb with cream for a breakfast compote; spoon over fruit salad; or offer on pound cake or ice cream for dessert.

■ **Cooking with rhubarb.** Cut rhubarb into 1-inch pieces and cook, uncovered, in just enough water to cover until soft (about 15 minutes). Then sweeten with sugar to taste (about ½ cup per pound of rhubarb); continue cooking until sugar is dissolved (about 5 minutes).

RHUBARB-STRAWBERRY PIE

Per serving: 617 calories, 6 g protein, 83 g carbohydrates, 30 g total fat, 12 mg cholesterol, 233 mg sodium

    ½ cup *each* granulated sugar
      and firmly packed brown
      sugar
    1 tablespoon cornstarch
    ¼ cup all-purpose flour
    ½ teaspoon ground nutmeg
    4 cups rhubarb, in ½-inch
      pieces
    2 cups thickly sliced
      strawberries
    1 tablespoon orange juice
      Flaky Pastry (page 17)
    2 tablespoons butter or
      margarine

In a large bowl, combine granulated sugar, brown sugar, cornstarch, flour, nutmeg, rhubarb, strawberries, and orange juice. Set aside.

Prepare pastry; roll out half the pastry and fit into a 9-inch pie pan. Pour filling into pastry shell; dot with butter. Roll out remaining pastry and add top crust as directed on page 17. (Or, if desired, roll out remaining pastry, cut into ¾-inch-wide strips, and weave a lattice top for pie.)

Bake in a 400° oven until fruit is tender and crust is well browned (about 50 minutes). If necessary, protect edges of pie with a foil strip for last 15 minutes to prevent overbrowning. Makes 6 to 8 servings.

RHUBARB-RAISIN COMPOTE

Per serving: 273 calories, 4 g protein, 68 g carbohydrates, .25 g total fat, 0 mg cholesterol, 18 mg sodium

    3 pounds rhubarb
    ¾ cup *each* water and
      granulated sugar
    1 cup golden raisins
    ¼ teaspoon *each* ground
      cinnamon and nutmeg
    ½ cup firmly packed brown
      sugar
    2 envelopes unflavored
      gelatin
      Sour cream (optional)

Trim ends off rhubarb, then cut stalks into 1-inch pieces; you should have 9 to 10 cups.

In a 5- to 6-quart pan, combine rhubarb, ¼ cup of the water, granulated sugar, raisins, cinnamon, nutmeg, and brown sugar. Bring to a simmer over medium heat; simmer, uncovered, stirring often, until rhubarb is soft (about 15 minutes). Meanwhile, sprinkle gelatin over remaining ½ cup water. Let soften for 5 minutes.

Stir softened gelatin into rhubarb; cook for 1 more minute, stirring until gelatin is dissolved. Cool to room temperature, then cover and refrigerate until cold. Top with sour cream, if desired. Makes about 6 servings.

Sapotes

Native to the highlands of Central America, subtropical white sapotes are now grown for U.S. markets in Mexico, Central America, Florida, and Southern California. The fruit is about the size and shape of a medium-size apple; the blossom end is pointed.

Though the white sapote is the only variety widely available in this country, there is a black sapote as well. The Mamay sapote, a popular Cuban fruit, is a different species entirely.

Two types of white sapotes are sold. One has slightly sour green skin that remains green when the fruit is ripe; the other has sweeter yellow-green skin that turns yellow as the fruit ripens. The skins of both varieties are thin, edible, and easily bruised.

Tart-flavored, rosy rhubarb is a favorite for baked desserts (see pie recipe, this page).

White sapote has edible skin, buttery texture.

A white sapote's cream-colored flesh is sweet and juicy like a cherimoya or a peach, but it has a buttery, avocado-like texture. The flavor is distinctive—like a blend of banana and peach.

Nutrition. Sapotes are relatively high in potassium. A medium-size fruit has about 140 calories.

■ **Season.** August through November; peak in September.

■ **Selection.** Choose firm, bruise-free sapotes with green to yellow-green skin. The fruit is ripe when it gives to gentle pressure like a ripe plum.

■ **Ripening & storage.** Ripen fruit at room temperature, uncovered, out of direct sun; turn occasionally. Refrigerate ripe fruit, unwashed, in a plastic or paper bag for up to 5 days.

■ **Preparation.** Wash sapotes and eat as you would apples, discarding seeds. Or peel fruit, cut into pieces, and discard seeds. Drizzle cut fruit with lemon or lime juice to prevent darkening.

■ **Amount.** One medium-size sapote yields ½ to ¾ cup fruit pieces.

■ **Freezing.** Not recommended.

■ **Serving ideas.** Combine sapote with citrus in fruit salads for added interest. Or purée peeled, seeded sapote and mix with orange juice or milk and a few drops of vanilla to make a refreshing drink.

■ **Cooking with sapotes.** Sapotes are best eaten uncooked; cooking makes them limp and less flavorful.

SAPOTE BREAKFAST SMOOTHIE

Per serving: 289 calories, 11 g protein, 52 g carbohydrates, 5 g total fat, 136 mg cholesterol, 98 mg sodium

>   1 cup peeled, seeded sapote pieces
>   1 cup plain yogurt
>   ½ cup cracked ice
>   1½ tablespoons frozen concentrated orange juice
>   2 to 3 tablespoons honey or sugar
>   ¼ teaspoon ground ginger
>   1 egg

In a blender or food processor, combine sapote, yogurt, ice, orange juice, honey, ginger, and egg. Whirl until smooth. Pour into glasses and serve at once. Makes 2 servings (about 10 oz. *each*).

■ See also ***Fruit Sorbet*** *(page 41).*

Starfruit see Carambolas, page 18

Strawberries see Berries, page 13

Tamarillos

The subtropical tamarillo (tam-a-*ree*-o), or tree tomato, is a smooth, egg-shaped fruit with purplish red or, less frequently, orange-yellow skin. Originally from the Peruvian Andes, the 2½- to 3-inch fruit is now grown commercially in New Zealand. *(Photo on page 27.)*

Tamarillos can be used in sweet or savory dishes as either a fruit or a vegetable. The orange-yellow flesh, studded with a swirl of edible dark red seeds, has the texture of a plum. The curious tart (almost astringent) flavor benefits from cooking and a sprinkling of sugar.

Nutrition. Tamarillos are low in calories and a good source of vitamin A.

■ **Season.** March through October; most plentiful from May through August.

■ **Selection.** Tamarillos ship and store so well that you'll almost always find them in perfect condition in markets. Ripe fruit has dark purple-red or orange-yellow skin and gives to pressure like a firm-ripe tomato.

■ **Ripening & storage.** Ripen at room temperature, uncovered, out of direct sun; turn occasionally. Refrigerate ripe fruit in a plastic bag for up to 1 month.

■ **Preparation.** To peel tamarillos, plunge into boiling water for 30 to 60 seconds; then cool in ice water. Slip off skins. Cut crosswise into slices.

■ **Amount.** One pound tamarillos (4 or 5) yields about 2 cups sliced fruit.

■ **Freezing.** Not recommended.

■ **Serving ideas.** To serve tamarillos as a savory vegetable, peel and slice, season with salt and pepper, and use in salads or sandwiches as you would tomatoes.

To serve as a sweet fruit, peel and slice, sprinkle generously with brown sugar, and serve plain or over ice cream.

■ **Cooking with tamarillos.** Cooking this fruit with sugar mellows its usually tart flavor. To serve tamarillos as a cooked vegetable, try sautéing them.

Sautéing. Peel tamarillos and cut in halves lengthwise. Sauté (see page 124) until hot and tender when pierced (about 5 minutes).

TIPSY TAMARILLOS

Per serving of fruit: 175 calories, 3 g protein, 25 g carbohydrates, 0 g total fat, 0 mg cholesterol, .36 mg sodium

>   6 tamarillos
>   ½ cup sugar
>   ¼ teaspoon ground cinnamon
>   3 tablespoons rum or brandy
>   Sweetened whipped cream or vanilla ice cream

Cut tamarillos in half lengthwise (do not peel). Arrange fruit, cut side down, in a shallow 2-quart baking dish. Combine sugar and cinnamon; sprinkle over tamarillos. Bake in a 350° oven until tamarillo skins rise and can be pulled off easily (25 to 30 minutes). Pull off and discard skins; transfer fruit to a serving bowl with a slotted spoon. Stir rum into syrup in baking dish; pour over fruit. Serve fruit warm, topped with whipped cream or spooned over ice cream. Makes about 4 servings.

■ See also ***Fruit Sorbet*** *(page 41).*

Tangerines see Citrus, page 20

*Immensely varied in form and flavor,
vegetables may be roots or tubers, leaves or
stems, flowers or seeds. Nutrition is the bonus
to their tastes and textures.*

Artichokes

Native to the Mediterranean, the artichoke has been enjoyed since the days of the ancient Greeks and Romans. It was introduced to California first by Spanish explorers, later by Italian farmers who settled along the central California coast. Today, California produces the country's entire commercial crop. Many varieties of artichokes grow throughout southern Europe, but the globe type is the only one commonly found in American markets.

Artichokes are actually thistles, and the uninitiated may need some instruction in the art of eating them. Pull off each leaf, dip in sauce or melted butter, and draw between your teeth to scrape off the tender, light green base. Discard remaining leaf tip. When you come to the fuzzy center (the "choke"), scoop it out with a spoon and discard it. The remaining "bottom" or "heart" is considered a particular delicacy; cut it into bite-size pieces to eat with a fork.

Tiny, very young artichokes—1½ inches or less in diameter—can be eaten in their entirety, since they have almost no choke.

Nutrition. The artichoke is high in potassium, phosphorus, and vitamins A and C. It's low in calories—from about 10 to 45 until sauced—but rather high in sodium.

■ **Season.** Available in some markets all year; peak March through mid-May.

■ **Selection.** Choose tight, compact heads that feel heavy for their size (overall size has no bearing on flavor).

Root vegetables hit their peak season in winter, when many other types are unavailable. Here, familiar and more unusual types mingle. In box: rutabagas and red beets. Upper right: jicama. Across center (from left): orange beets, turnips, parsnips, and Italian red radishes. Lower left: baby carrots.

Surface brown spots, caused by frost, do not affect quality.

■ **Amount.** Allow 1 medium-size to large artichoke per person.

■ **Storage.** Refrigerate, unwashed, in a plastic bag for up to 1 week.

■ **Preparation.** Prepare just before cooking. Using a stainless steel knife, slice off stem. Remove and discard coarse outer leaves, then cut off top third of artichoke. Snip off thorny tips of remaining leaves with kitchen shears. Rinse well; to prevent discoloration, plunge immediately into acidulated water (3 tablespoons vinegar or lemon juice per quart of water) or rub with a cut lemon.

Prepare tiny artichokes the same way, so that only the pale, edible interior leaves remain.

■ **Cooking methods.** For more information on the cooking methods listed here, see "A Glossary of Techniques," page 122.

Boiling. In a large, deep pan, bring about 4 quarts water, ¼ cup vinegar, 3 tablespoons salad oil, 2 bay leaves, and 10 whole black peppercorns to a boil over high heat. Add 4 to 6 artichokes and return to a boil. Cover and boil until stem end is tender when pierced: about 40 minutes for large artichokes (4-inch diameter), 25 to 35 minutes for medium-size (2½- to 3½-inch diameter), and 15 to 20 minutes for small ones (less than 2½-inch diameter). Drain.

Microwaving. Place 1 medium-size artichoke upside down in a 10-ounce custard cup; add ¼ cup water. For 2 to 4 artichokes, arrange in a 9-inch round, nonmetallic baking dish and add ½ cup water. Cover and microwave on **HIGH (100%)**: 1 medium-size artichoke for 5 to 7 minutes, 2 artichokes for 8 to 10 minutes, 3 for 9 to 11 minutes, 4 for 13 to 15 minutes. Let stand, covered, for 5 minutes. Stem end should be tender when pierced.

Steaming. Arrange on a rack and steam; cooking times will be about the same as for boiling.

■ **Serving ideas.** Use melted butter, garlic butter, or hollandaise as a dip-

ping sauce for hot artichokes. For chilled ones, offer mayonnaise, plain or seasoned to taste with tarragon, mustard, or dill weed. Stuff the hollowed-out centers of cooked artichokes with shrimp salad or other mixtures.

Cooked tiny artichokes can be quartered and quickly sautéed in olive oil, chilled and used in a salad, or served by themselves dressed with oil and vinegar.

Continued on next page

To prepare artichokes for cooking, first cut off stem even with base. Slice off top third of artichoke.

Next remove course outer leaves of artichoke; then snip off thorny tips of remaining leaves.

Using a spoon, carefully separate fuzzy choke from heart of cooked artichoke; lift out and discard.

BACON & RICE ARTICHOKE SALAD

Per serving of salad: 131 calories, 7 g protein, 21 g carbohydrates, 5 g total fat, 9 mg cholesterol, 245 mg sodium

Per tablespoon of dressing: 96 calories, .10 g protein, .29 g carbohydrates, 11 g total fat, 7 mg cholesterol, 57 mg sodium

- 6 **medium-size to large artichokes**
  Lemon juice
  Herb-Mayonnaise Dressing (recipe follows)
- 1 **small tomato, seeded and diced**
- 8 **slices bacon, crisply cooked, drained, and crumbled**
- 1 **cup cold cooked rice**
- ⅓ **cup thinly sliced green onions (including tops)**
- ½ **cup chilled cooked peas; or ½ cup frozen peas, thawed**
- 2 **tablespoons chopped parsley**

Prepare artichokes, then boil, steam, or microwave as previously directed. Drain. Pull out center leaves of each; scrape out fuzzy choke. Drizzle artichoke cavities with lemon juice; let artichokes cool, then cover and refrigerate for at least 1 hour or until next day.

Prepare dressing; spoon ½ cup into a bowl and mix in tomato, bacon, rice, onions, peas, and parsley. Evenly spoon rice mixture into artichokes. Pass remaining dressing as a dip for leaves. Makes 6 servings.

Herb-Mayonnaise Dressing. Combine ⅓ cup **olive oil** or salad oil, 2 tablespoons **white wine vinegar,** and ¼ teaspoon *each* **dry basil, oregano leaves, garlic salt,** and **paprika.** Add 1 cup **mayonnaise** and beat until well blended.

ARTICHOKES WITH CREAM CHEESE

Per serving: 259 calories, 13 g protein, 15 g carbohydrates, 20 g total fat, 63 mg cholesterol, 264 mg sodium

- 4 **medium-size to large artichokes**
- 2 **tablespoons tarragon vinegar**
- 2 **tablespoons minced green onion (including top)**
- ¼ **teaspoon dry tarragon**
- 2 **small packages (3 oz. *each*) chive-flavored cream cheese, softened**
- ⅔ **cup grated Parmesan cheese**
- 2 **tablespoons lime juice**
  Milk

Prepare artichokes, then boil, steam, or microwave as previously directed. Drain and keep hot; or let cool and serve cold.

In a small pan, combine vinegar, onion, and tarragon. Bring to a boil; boil until vinegar has evaporated. Set aside. Beat cream cheese until smooth, then add onion mixture, Parmesan cheese, and lime juice and beat until well blended. Thin to a dipping consistency by beating in milk, 1 teaspoon at a time. Serve artichokes, hot or cold, on individual plates with sauce alongside. Makes 4 servings.

Arugula see Salad Greens, page 104

Asparagus

Asparagus belongs to the lily family, which also includes onions, garlic, and leeks. It has been cultivated for centuries and also grows wild in many parts of the world. In Europe, white asparagus is prized; to prevent the spears from developing chlorophyll, the asparagus beds are covered with mulch to keep out the sun.

Nutrition. Asparagus is high in vitamin A and has fair amounts of vitamin C and iron. It's low in sodium and in calories—about 35 calories per cup of cooked slices.

■ **Season.** Almost all year, thanks to shipments from other countries; peak March through June.

■ **Selection.** Choose firm, brittle spears that are bright green almost their entire length, with tightly closed tips. Stalk thickness is pretty much a matter of personal preference.

■ **Amount.** Allow ⅓ to ½ pound per person.

■ **Storage.** Wrap ends in a damp paper towel. Refrigerate, unwashed, in a plastic bag for up to 4 days.

■ **Preparation.** Snap off and discard tough ends. If desired, peel stalks with a vegetable peeler to remove scales. Plunge into cold water to clean; lift out and drain. Leave spears whole or cut into slices.

■ **Cooking methods.** For more information on the cooking methods listed here, see "A Glossary of Techniques," page 122.

Boiling. In a wide frying pan, boil 1½ to 2 pounds asparagus spears, covered, in 1 inch water until just tender when pierced (5 to 8 minutes). Drain.

Boil 1½ to 2 pounds ½- to 1-inch slices in ½ inch water for 2 to 3 minutes. Drain.

Microwaving. Arrange 1 pound asparagus in a nonmetallic baking dish so tips are toward center. Add 2 to 3 tablespoons water; cover. Microwave on **HIGH (100%):** whole spears for 5 minutes (after 2½ minutes, bring center pieces to edge), slices for 4 to 7 minutes (stir after 3 minutes). Let stand, covered, for 4 to 5 minutes. Asparagus should be tender when pierced.

Steaming. Arrange whole spears or slices on a rack. Steam just until tender when pierced (8 to 12 minutes for spears, 5 to 7 minutes for slices). To cook spears, you may also use a special asparagus steamer (or other deep pot) that allows the spears to cook upright; the thick stalk ends stand in boiling water, while the more delicate tips are steamed.

Stir-frying. Cut asparagus into ½-inch diagonal slices. Stir-fry up to 5 cups, using 1 tablespoon salad oil, for 1 minute. Add 1 to 2 tablespoons liquid, cover, and cook until tender-crisp to bite (about 2 more minutes).

■ **Serving ideas.** Serve hot cooked asparagus with melted butter, lemon juice, or hollandaise. Serve it chilled with a simple oil and vinegar dressing, topped with grated hard-cooked egg, if desired. Add cooked slices to scrambled eggs or omelets. Wrap cooked spears in prosciutto and serve

as an appetizer, or offer raw spears
with a dip.

ASPARAGUS WITH LEMON-GINGER CREAM

Per serving: 270 calories, 12 g protein, 11 g carbohydrates, 21 g total fat, 308 mg cholesterol, 332 mg sodium

- 1 **pound asparagus**
- 1 **cup regular-strength chicken broth**
- 2 **thin, quarter-size slices fresh ginger**
- 1 **strip (½ by 4 inches) lemon peel (colored part only)**
- ⅔ **cup whipping cream**
- 4 **hot poached eggs**

Prepare asparagus, leaving spears whole; then boil, steam, or microwave as previously directed. Drain and keep warm.

In a wide frying pan, combine broth, ginger, and lemon peel. Bring to a boil; boil until reduced to ½ cup. Add cream; continue to boil until reduced to ½ cup. Remove ginger and lemon peel.

Pour sauce equally onto 4 warmed plates; top sauce on each plate with ¼ of the asparagus, then with 1 poached egg. Makes 4 servings.

ASPARAGUS WITH ORANGE BUTTER SAUCE

Per serving: 218 calories, 5 g protein, 18 g carbohydrates, 16 g total fat, 47 mg cholesterol, 205 mg sodium

- 2 **pounds asparagus**
- ½ **cup (¼ lb.) butter or margarine**
- ⅓ **cup minced shallots**
- 1¼ **teaspoons Dijon mustard**
- 1⅓ **cups orange juice**
- 6 **orange wedges**

Prepare asparagus, leaving spears whole; then boil, steam, or microwave as previously directed. Drain and keep warm.

Melt 1 tablespoon of the butter in a wide frying pan over medium heat. Add shallots; cook, stirring, until soft. Add mustard and orange juice. Bring to a boil over high heat; boil until reduced to ⅔ cup. Remove from heat. Add remaining butter in one chunk and stir until incorporated.

Arrange asparagus on 6 warmed plates and top with sauce. Garnish each serving with an orange wedge. Makes 6 servings.

An asparagus steamer is useful for cooking the tall spears; you can also use a frying pan.

WRAPPED ASPARAGUS WITH WATERCRESS MAYONNAISE

Per serving of wrapped asparagus: 128 calories, 15 g protein, 2 g carbohydrates, 6 g total fat, 41 mg cholesterol, 157 mg sodium

Per tablespoon of dressing: 85 calories, .34 g protein, .17 g carbohydrates, 9 g total fat, 11 mg cholesterol, 9 mg sodium

- **Watercress Mayonnaise (recipe follows)**
- 24 **to 36 asparagus spears**
- 12 **to 18 very thin slices smoked or roasted turkey breast (½ to ¾ lb. *total*)**
- 12 **to 18 very thin slices provolone cheese (⅓ to ½ lb. *total*)**

Prepare Watercress Mayonnaise and refrigerate.

Prepare asparagus, leaving spears whole; then boil, steam, or microwave as previously directed. Drain and plunge into cold water. When cold, drain again.

Wrap turkey slices around bottom ends of half the asparagus spears; wrap cheese slices around remaining spears. If made ahead, cover and refrigerate for up to 12 hours.

Offer mayonnaise alongside asparagus as a dip or sauce. Makes 8 to 12 servings.

Watercress Mayonnaise. In a blender or food processor, combine 1 **egg,** 1 tablespoon **white wine vinegar,** 1 teaspoon **Dijon mustard,** 1 teaspoon **anchovy paste,** 1 small clove **garlic,** and ⅓ cup lightly packed **watercress leaves.** Whirl until smooth. Add 1 cup **salad oil** in a thin, steady stream, whirling until incorporated. If made ahead, cover and refrigerate for up to 2 days. Makes about 1½ cups.

Avocados *see Fruits, page 10*

Beans

Beans are a dietary staple throughout the world, grown in a multitude of varieties and eaten at various stages of maturity. Though they belong to many different plant species, they can be divided into two broad categories—edible-pod beans and fresh-shelled beans.

Nutrition. On the whole, edible-pod beans are a good source of vitamin A and potassium and a fair source of vitamin C. They're low in calories—about 30 per cup of cooked snap beans. Fresh-shelled beans are relatively high in vitamin C, sodium, niacin, and calories (190 per cup of cooked limas).

EDIBLE-POD BEANS

Snap beans are the most popular edible-pod beans. Of these, the most familiar are green beans (such as Kentucky Wonder and Blue Lake), yellow wax beans, and purple beans that turn green when cooked. Wide-podded Romano (sometimes called Italian) beans and skinny haricots verts are two other types of snap beans. Also included in the edible-pod group are Chinese long beans, sometimes called asparagus beans or yard-long beans.

One common name for snap beans is "string beans"; until the late 19th century, the pods had tough strings along their sides that had to be removed before cooking. But thanks to American botanists who set out to build a better bean, almost all modern-day snap beans are stringless at harvest.

■ **Season.** All year; peak May through August.

■ **Selection.** Choose slender, crisp beans that are bright and blemish-free. Avoid mature beans with large seeds and swollen pods.

Continued on next page

... Beans continued

■ **Amount.** Allow about ¼ pound per person.

■ **Storage.** Refrigerate, unwashed, in a plastic bag for up to 4 days.

■ **Preparation.** Snap off and discard ends. Rinse. Leave small beans whole; cut larger beans into crosswise or diagonal slices. Or cut into long French-style slivers; this task is simplified with the use of a slicing gadget found in cookware or hardware stores.

■ **Cooking methods.** For more information on the cooking methods listed here, see "A Glossary of Techniques," page 122. Cooking time will vary depending on the type of bean and its maturity.

Boiling. In a 3-quart pan, boil whole or cut beans, covered, in 1 inch water until tender-crisp to bite (5 to 10 minutes for whole beans, 4 to 7 minutes for cut beans). Drain.

Microwaving. Cut 1 pound beans into 1-inch pieces. Place in a 1½-quart nonmetallic baking dish; add ¼ cup water. Cover and microwave on **HIGH**

Beans come in many colors, sizes, and shapes, but there are basically just two types—edible-pod and fresh-shelled. Except for fava, all the beans shown here are edible-pod types.

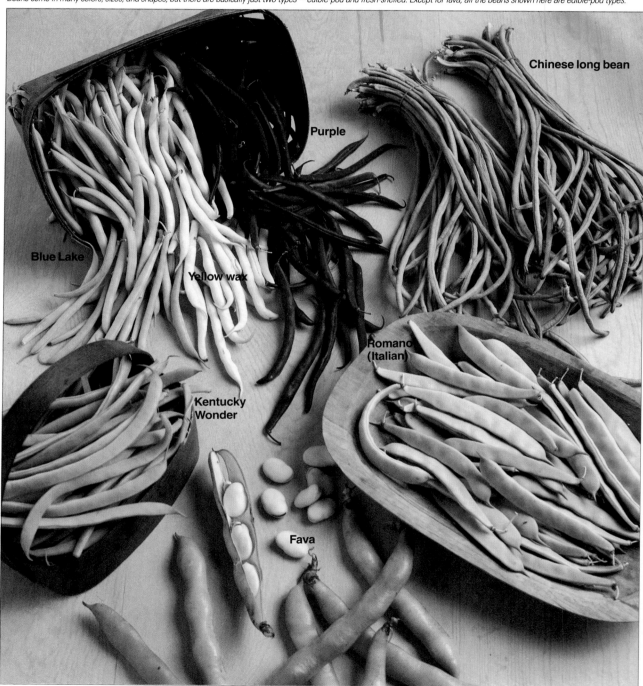

Chinese long bean

Purple

Blue Lake

Yellow wax

Romano (Italian)

Kentucky Wonder

Fava

(100%) for 7 to 12 minutes, stirring every 5 minutes. Let stand, covered, for 5 minutes. Beans should be tender-crisp to bite.

Steaming. Arrange whole or cut beans on a rack and steam until tender-crisp to bite (10 to 15 minutes for whole beans, 8 to 12 minutes for cut beans).

Stir-frying. Cut beans into 1-inch lengths. Stir-fry up to 5 cups, using 1 tablespoon salad oil, for 1 minute. Add 2 to 4 tablespoons liquid, cover, and cook until tender-crisp to bite (4 to 7 more minutes).

■ **Serving ideas.** Dress hot, cooked beans with butter, chives, dill weed, thyme, or crumbled bacon. Serve cooked beans chilled with oil and vinegar dressing. Very young, tender beans can be eaten raw with a dip as an appetizer.

BEANS & BOK CHOY WITH CHIVE BUTTER

Per serving of beans and bok choy: 32 calories, 2 g protein, 7 g carbo-hydrates, .29 g total fat, 0 mg cholesterol, 0 mg sodium
Per tablespoon chive butter: 91 calories, .21 g protein, .32 g carbohydrates, 10 g total fat, 31 mg cholesterol, 125 mg sodium

- ¾ **pound baby or regular bok choy**
- ¾ **pound Chinese long beans, haricots verts, or regular green beans, ends removed**
- ⅓ **to ½ cup butter or margarine**
- ½ **cup finely chopped, lightly packed garlic chives or regular chives**

If using baby bok choy, leave whole. If using regular bok choy, trim 2 inches off stalk ends; leave small stalks whole and cut large ones in half crosswise.

Boil or steam whole beans as previously directed. Drain well and arrange on one side of a warmed platter; keep hot.

Bring 12 cups water to a boil in a 5-quart pan. Add bok choy and boil, uncovered, until barely tender when pierced (3 to 4 minutes). Drain well and arrange on platter.

Melt butter, stir in chives, and pass to spoon over individual portions. Makes 6 servings.

GREEN BEANS WITH GARLIC

Per serving: 105 calories, 3 g protein, 11 g carbohydrates, 6 g total fat, 0 mg cholesterol, 448 mg sodium

- 4 **teaspoons soy sauce**
- 1 **teaspoon sugar**
- 1 **tablespoon dry sherry or water**
- 1 **tablespoon sesame seeds**
- 1½ **tablespoons salad oil**
- 3 **cloves garlic, minced or pressed**
- 1 **tablespoon minced fresh ginger**
- 1 **pound green beans, cut diagonally into 2-inch lengths**

Stir together soy, sugar, and sherry; set aside. In a wok or wide frying pan, toast sesame seeds over medium heat until golden (about 3 minutes), stirring often. Remove from pan and set aside.

Increase heat to medium-high and pour oil into pan. When oil is hot, stir in garlic, ginger, and beans; cook, stirring, for 1½ minutes. Stir in soy mixture; reduce heat to medium, cover, and cook until beans are tender-crisp to bite (about 7 more minutes).

Uncover, increase heat to high, and boil, stirring, until almost all liquid has evaporated (1 to 3 minutes). Pour onto a warmed platter and sprinkle with sesame seeds. Makes 4 servings.

GREEN BEANS WITH BACON DRESSING

Per serving: 107 calories, 5 g protein, 15 g carbohydrates, 4 g total fat, 7 mg cholesterol, 319 mg sodium

- 4 **slices bacon**
- 1 **pound green beans, yellow wax beans, or haricots verts, ends removed**
- 6 **tablespoons catsup**
- ¼ **cup white wine vinegar**

In a wide frying pan, cook bacon over medium heat until crisp. Lift out bacon, leaving drippings in pan; drain and crumble bacon.

Boil or steam whole beans as previously directed. Drain and keep hot; or immerse in ice water to cool quickly, then drain to serve cold.

Add catsup and vinegar to drippings in frying pan and stir over medium heat just until blended. Use hot or cold.

Arrange ¼ of the beans on each of 4 salad plates. Spoon dressing over beans; sprinkle with bacon. Makes 4 servings.

FRESH-SHELLED BEANS

Fresh-shelled beans, sometimes called shellies or shuckies in the South, are harvested when the seeds are full-sized but not yet dry. (These are the same beans that, when more mature, are dried.) All fresh-shelled beans can be used more or less interchangeably, with some adjustments in cooking time.

Particularly delicious at the fresh-shelled stage are flageolets (popular in the south of France), buttery lima beans, winged beans, red-flecked cranberry beans, and fava beans (also called horse beans, broad beans, and Windsor beans). Young winged beans may be cooked pod and all—their unusual shape adds eye appeal. Some people also like to cook and eat young fava beans complete with the pods. *One note of caution:* some people of Mediterranean descent have an enzyme deficiency that causes a mild to severe allergic reaction to eating fava beans or even inhaling the pollen.

■ **Season.** April through June for fava beans, July through September for lima beans, August through October for cranberry beans.

■ **Selection.** Look for thick, broad, tightly closed pods bulging with large beans. If purchased shelled, beans should look plump and fresh.

■ **Amount.** Allow about ¼ pound shelled or ¾ pound unshelled beans per serving. One pound unshelled beans yields about 1 cup shelled beans.

■ **Storage.** Refrigerate unwashed pods or shelled beans in a plastic bag for up to 4 days.

■ **Preparation.** Remove unshelled beans from pods; rinse shelled beans.

■ **Cooking methods.** For more information on boiling, see page 122.

Boiling. In a 3-quart pan, boil 1 pound shelled beans, covered, in 1½ inches water until tender to bite (15 to 25 minutes for cranberry or fava beans, 12 to 20 minutes for lima beans). Drain.

■ **Serving ideas.** Cook beans with pieces of ham for added flavor. Toss hot, cooked beans with butter and season with salt and freshly ground pepper; or drizzle with olive oil. Add fresh-shelled beans to soups, or combine several kinds of cooked fresh-shelled and edible-pod beans in a salad.

Continued on next page

...Beans continued

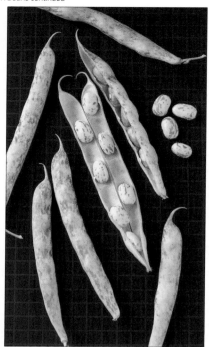

Spotted red cranberry beans, a kind of fresh-shelled bean, come to markets in August.

FAVA BEAN SAUTÉ

Per serving: 224 calories, 7 g protein, 19 g carbohydrates, 14 g total fat, 0 mg cholesterol, 4 mg sodium

- 2 cups shelled fava beans (about 2 lbs. unshelled)
- ¼ cup olive oil or salad oil
- 1 large clove garlic, minced or pressed
- 1 small onion, finely chopped
- 1 pound sunchokes (see page 115), scrubbed and finely diced
- Salt and pepper

Boil beans as previously directed, drain, and let cool. Remove bean skins with your fingers; discard. Set beans aside.

Heat oil in a wide frying pan over medium-high heat. Add garlic and onion and cook, stirring, until onion is soft. Add sunchokes and cook, turning occasionally with a wide spatula, until well browned (10 to 15 minutes). Add beans and stir gently until heated through. Season to taste with salt and pepper. Makes 4 to 6 servings.

MINESTRONE

Per cup: 310 calories, 11 g protein, 14 g carbohydrates, 23 g total fat, 34 mg cholesterol, 556 mg sodium

- 1 pound mild Italian sausages
- 3½ to 4 cups fresh-shelled beans (3½ to 4 lbs. unshelled)
- 8 cups water
- 2 tablespoons olive oil
- ¼ pound salt pork, minced
- 1 large onion, minced
- 3 cloves garlic, minced or pressed
- ¼ cup *each* minced celery leaves and minced parsley
- 1 can (about 1 lb.) pear-shaped tomatoes
- 4 cups regular-strength chicken broth
- 1 large carrot, diced
- 3 large stalks celery, thinly sliced
- 1 medium-size thin-skinned potato, peeled and diced
- 1 large zucchini, thinly sliced
- 4 cups coarsely chopped, lightly packed greens, such as cabbage, kale, or Swiss chard
- 1 cup lightly packed fresh basil leaves (optional)
- Salt and pepper
- 1 cup (about 5 oz.) grated Parmesan cheese

Pierce sausage casings with a fork. Place sausages, beans, and water in a 5-quart pan. Bring to a boil over high heat; reduce heat, cover, and simmer for 20 minutes. Remove sausages. Continue to simmer until beans mash readily (25 to 50 more minutes).

Ladle beans and 1 cup of the cooking water into a food processor; process until beans are coarsely puréed (or mash beans in a food mill or with a potato masher). Return beans to pan and set aside.

In a 6- to 8-quart pan, combine oil, salt pork, onion, garlic, celery leaves, and parsley; cook over medium heat, stirring, until onion is soft. Add puréed beans, cooking water, tomatoes (break up with a spoon) and their liquid, broth, carrot, celery, and potato. Bring to a boil; reduce heat, cover, and simmer for 15 minutes. Add zucchini and greens; simmer, uncovered, until carrot is tender to bite (about 8 more minutes). Add basil, if used. Season to taste with salt and pepper. Slice sausages, add to soup, and heat through. Stir in about ⅓ cup of the cheese; pass remaining cheese at the table. Makes about 4 quarts.

Beets

Cultivated since prehistoric times, the beet was originally grown for its leaves. Historians tell us that the early Romans ate only the tops, reserving the roots for medicinal purposes.

Today, table beets are grown commercially in 31 states for both their earthy-sweet roots and their leafy tops (see "Greens with a Bite," page 83). Root color may be red (the most common), orange, yellow, or almost white, depending on the variety, but all types taste the same. (Photo on page 56.)

Nutrition. Beets are a good source of vitamin C and potassium and a fair source of vitamin A. One cup of cooked diced beets has about 55 calories.

■ **Season.** All year; peak June through October.

■ **Selection.** Firm, smooth-skinned, small to medium beets are the most tender. Leaves should be deep green and fresh looking.

■ **Amount.** Allow ⅓ to ½ pound per person.

To prevent beets from "bleeding" during cooking, boil them unpeeled. After cooking, let cool; then trim off roots and stems and slip off skins.

■ **Storage.** Cut off tops, leaving 1 to 2 inches of stem attached. (Reserve tops and cook separately—see page 83.) Do not trim roots. Refrigerate, unwashed, in a plastic bag for up to 1 week.

■ **Preparation.** Scrub well, but do not peel. Leave roots, stems, and skin intact to prevent bleeding during cooking. Let cooked beets cool; then trim roots and stems and slip off skins under cold running water.

■ **Cooking methods.** For more information on the cooking methods listed here, see "A Glossary of Techniques," page 122. Cooking time for beets varies, depending on their size.

Baking. Wrap beets individually in heavy-duty foil. Place on oven rack in a 375° oven; bake until tender throughout when pierced (1 to 1¼ hours for medium-size beets).

Boiling. In a 4- to 5-quart pan, boil 1½ to 2 pounds beets, covered, in water to cover until tender throughout when pierced (20 to 45 minutes). Drain.

Microwaving. Place 6 medium-size beets in a 2-quart nonmetallic baking dish. Add about 1½ cups water; cover. Microwave on **HIGH (100%)** for 14 to 16 minutes. After 7 minutes, bring outside beets to center of dish. Let stand, covered, for 5 minutes. Beets should be tender throughout when pierced.

■ **Serving ideas.** Top hot cooked beets with butter, mustard butter, chives, dill weed, thyme, lemon juice, grated orange peel, or a dash of wine vinegar. Use shredded raw beets or cold cooked beets in salads.

PICKLE-PACKED BEETS

Per cup: 41 calories, 1 g protein, 11 g carbohydrates, .09 g total fat, 0 mg cholesterol, 35 mg sodium

Prepare 6 to 8 medium-size **beets,** then boil as previously directed. Drain, peel, and cut into ¼-inch-thick slices. Thinly slice 1 medium-size **mild white onion.** In a wide-mouth 1-quart jar, firmly pack beets and onion. Combine 1 cup **distilled white vinegar,** ⅔ cup **sugar,** and 1 clove **garlic,** minced or pressed (optional). Stir until sugar is dissolved, then pour over beets and onion to fill jar. Screw on lid and shake jar well. Refrigerate for at least 1 day or up to 3 months. Makes 1 quart.

SHREDDED BEETS VINAIGRETTE

Per serving: 236 calories, 3 g protein, 18 g carbohydrates, 18 g total fat, 0 mg cholesterol, 103 mg sodium

About 2¼ pounds beets
1½ tablespoons finely chopped shallot
1½ teaspoons dry mustard
1 small clove garlic, minced or pressed
3 tablespoons white wine vinegar
½ cup olive oil or salad oil
Salt and pepper
Dill sprigs (optional)

Peel beets; then coarsely shred, using a food processor or a grater. You should have about 6 cups.

Stir together shallot, mustard, garlic, vinegar, and oil. Pour over beets and mix well. Season to taste with salt and pepper. If made ahead, cover and refrigerate until next day. If desired, garnish with dill before serving. Makes 6 servings.

CHILLED BEET BORSCHT

Per cup: 86 calories, 4 g protein, 16 g carbohydrates, 2 g total fat, 63 mg cholesterol, 85 mg sodium

2 pounds beets
4 cups water
1 small onion, chopped
2 eggs, beaten
2 tablespoons sugar
3 tablespoons lemon juice
Salt and pepper
Lemon slices

Peel beets; coarsely shred, using a food processor or a grater. You should have about 5 cups. In a 4- to 5-quart pan, combine beets, water, and onion. Bring to a boil over high heat; reduce heat, cover, and simmer until beets are tender to bite (about 15 minutes). Remove from heat and let cool.

Stir eggs, sugar, and lemon juice into beet mixture. Pour mixture into a blender or food processor, a portion at a time, and whirl until puréed. Season to taste with salt and pepper. Cover and refrigerate until cold (at least 2 hours) or for up to 2 days.

Stir borscht before serving. If too thick to sip, stir in a little water. Garnish individual servings with lemon slices. Makes about 8 cups.

■ *See also **Vegetable Purée** (page 71), **Beets & Pears with Dandelion Greens** (page 84).*

Belgian Endive *see Salad Greens, page 104*

Bok Choy

Also called Chinese chard cabbage or Chinese white cabbage, bok choy has thick white stalks and dark green leaves with white veins. The raw leaves have a hint of spicy hotness; the stalks are milder, with a crunchy, slightly watery texture. When cooked, the leaves have a mild Swiss chard flavor; the stalks become sweeter and more succulent.

Bok choy heads vary in size depending on season and maturity. Mild-flavored baby bok choy is small enough to boil or steam whole. A mature bok choy head is about the size of a large bunch of celery.

Nutrition. Bok choy is very low in calories and high in vitamins A and C. It is particularly rich in calcium—a cup of the cooked vegetable provides as much calcium as 1 cup of milk.

■ **Season.** All year.

■ **Selection.** Choose heads with bright white stalks and glossy dark leaves. Avoid heads with slippery brown spots on leaves; this indicates overchilling, which robs the vegetable of flavor.

■ **Amount.** Allow ¼ to ⅓ pound per person. One small to medium head makes 4 servings.

■ **Storage.** Boy choy is best used as soon as possible but can be refrigerated, unwashed, in a plastic bag for up to 2 days.

■ **Preparation.** Wash under cold running water; drain well. Leave baby bok choy whole. To prepare mature bok choy, cut leaves from stalks (leaves cook faster). Slice stalks crosswise and coarsely shred leaves.

■ **Cooking methods.** For more information on the cooking methods listed here, see "A Glossary of Techniques," page 122. If you're using baby bok choy, you may need to adjust cooking time downward.

Boiling. In a wide frying pan, boil sliced stalks from 1¼ to 1½ pounds bok choy (1 large head), covered, in ¼ inch water for 2 minutes. Stir in leaves. Cover and cook until stalks are tender when pierced and leaves are just wilted (1 to 2 more minutes). Drain.

Continued on next page

Bok choy ranges in size from small (baby) to very large. Baby bok choy can be cooked whole. Before cooking mature heads, slice stems and leaves; add leaves after stems are partly cooked.

Microwaving. Place sliced stalks from 1¼ to 1½ pounds bok choy (1 large head) in a 2-quart nonmetallic baking dish. Add 2 tablespoons water; cover and microwave on **HIGH (100%)** for 3 minutes. Stir in leaves, cover, and microwave for 3 to 4 more minutes. Let stand, covered, for 2 minutes. Stalks should be tender when pierced; leaves should be wilted.

Steaming. Arrange sliced stalks on a rack. Steam for 3 minutes; add leaves. Steam until stalks are tender when pierced and leaves are just wilted (2 to 4 more minutes).

Stir-frying. Slice stalks and coarsely shred leaves to make a total of up to 5 cups. Stir-fry stalks, using 2 tablespoons salad oil and 1 clove garlic (minced or pressed), for 30 seconds. Add 2 tablespoons liquid, cover, and cook 2 to 4 more minutes. Add leaves and stir-fry until stalks are tender when pierced and leaves are just wilted (2 to 3 more minutes).

■ **Serving ideas.** Season hot cooked bok choy with butter, minced ginger, soy sauce, or toasted sesame seeds. Use in Chinese-style soups and mixed stir-fries, or treat like other tart greens (see page 83).

BOK CHOY WITH GINGER VINAIGRETTE

Per serving: 139 calories, 3 g protein, 6 g carbohydrates, 12 g total fat, 0 mg cholesterol, 334 mg sodium

1½ **pounds baby bok choy**
⅓ **cup salad oil**
2 **tablespoons white wine vinegar**
2 **teaspoons** *each* **Dijon mustard and soy sauce**
1 **clove garlic, minced or pressed**
1 **tablespoon finely chopped fresh ginger**
½ **teaspoon sugar**

Cut any bok choy that are thicker than 3 inches in half lengthwise; leave smaller ones whole. Arrange as many bok choy on a steaming rack as will fit without crowding. Steam (see page 122) until stalks begin to turn translucent and are soft when pierced (4 to 5 minutes). Lift out and plunge into cold water; when cool, drain well and place in a shallow dish. Repeat with remaining bok choy.

Stir together oil, vinegar, mustard, soy, garlic, ginger, and sugar. Pour over bok choy. Makes 6 to 8 servings.

■ *See also* **Beans & Bok Choy with Chive Butter** *(page 61).*

Broccoli

The modern world received broccoli from Italy, where it has been a favorite food since the days of the ancient Romans. For centuries, though, its popularity didn't extend far beyond the Mediterranean; it was introduced to France only in the 1500s, and to England about 1720.

In the United States, few besides Italians growing it in home gardens were familiar with broccoli until as recently as 1920. At that time, a group of Italian vegetable farmers in California decided to ship a trial supply to Boston. It was an instant success. Today, California produces about 95 percent of the commercial crop in this country.

Nutrition. Like other members of the cabbage family, broccoli is considered helpful in the prevention of certain types of cancer. Broccoli is an excellent source of vitamins A and C and is also high in iron, calcium, and potassium. It's low in calories—each cup of cooked broccoli has only about 40 calories.

■ **Season.** All year; peak October through April.

■ **Selection.** Look for compact clusters of tightly closed dark green flowerets. Avoid heads with yellowing flowerets and thick, woody stems.

■ **Amount.** Allow about ⅓ pound per person.

■ **Storage.** Refrigerate, unwashed, in a plastic bag for up to 5 days.

■ **Preparation.** Rinse. Cut off and discard base of stalks, leaving about 3½ inches of stalks below flowerets. Peel bottom few inches of stalks, if desired. Cut stalk and flowerets lengthwise into spears. Leave spears whole and cut a slash upward through bottom inch of stalks to ensure even cooking; or slice stalks crosswise, leaving flowerets whole.

■ **Cooking methods.** For more information on the cooking methods listed here, see "A Glossary of Techniques," page 122.

Boiling. In a wide frying pan, boil 1 to 1½ pounds broccoli spears, covered, in 1 inch water until tender when pierced (7 to 10 minutes). Drain.

Boil 1 to 1½ pounds broccoli pieces, covered, in ½ inch water for 3 to 6 minutes. Drain.

Microwaving. Arrange about 1¼ pounds broccoli spears in a single layer in a nonmetallic baking dish, with flowerets toward center of dish. Add 2 tablespoons water; cover. Or arrange 1¼ pounds broccoli pieces in dish; sprinkle with 1 tablespoon water. Cover. Microwave spears on **HIGH (100%)** for 8 to 10 minutes, rotating dish ¼ turn halfway through microwaving. Microwave pieces for 5 to 6 minutes, stirring after 3 minutes. Let stand, covered, for 4 minutes. Broccoli should be tender when pierced.

Steaming. Arrange spears or pieces on a rack. Steam until tender when pierced (15 to 20 minutes for spears, 8 to 10 minutes for pieces).

Stir-frying. Cut broccoli stalks and flowerets into ¼-inch slices. Stir-fry up to 5 cups, using 1 tablespoon salad oil, for 1 minute. Add 3 tablespoons liquid, cover, and cook until tender-crisp to bite (about 3 more minutes).

■ **Serving ideas.** Top hot cooked broccoli with melted butter seasoned with dill weed, rosemary, or lemon juice. Or top with hollandaise or cheese sauce. Serve raw broccoli spears or flowerets with a dip for an appetizer.

To prepare broccoli, cut off tough stalk bases; peel stalks. Cut broccoli lengthwise into spears; slit each stem. Or cut off flowerets, then thinly slice stems crosswise.

CAPELLINI WITH BROCCOLI CREAM SAUCE

Per serving: 697 calories, 21 g protein, 46 g carbohydrates, 49 g total fat, 167 mg cholesterol, 397 mg sodium

1½	**pounds broccoli**
1	**package (10 oz.) capellini or coil vermicelli**
6	**tablespoons butter or margarine**
⅓	**cup water**
2	**cups whipping cream**
¼	**teaspoon ground nutmeg**
	About 2 cups (10 oz.) grated Parmesan cheese

Prepare broccoli as previously directed. Peel stalks. Reserve a few whole flowerets for garnish; finely chop remaining broccoli.

Following package directions, cook pasta until *al dente*. Drain, rinse under cold running water, and drain again.

While pasta is cooking, melt butter in a wide frying pan over medium-high heat. Add broccoli (including reserved flowerets) and water. Cover and cook until broccoli is tender when pierced (about 5 minutes). Lift out whole flowerets; set aside. Add cream and nutmeg to pan; bring to a boil, then add cooked pasta and toss gently until mixture is hot and cream clings to pasta. Remove from heat. Sprinkle with 1¼ cups of the cheese; mix with 2 forks.

Transfer pasta to a hot platter; top with 3 or 4 more tablespoons cheese and reserved flowerets. Serve at once. Pass remaining cheese at the table to sprinkle over individual servings. Makes 6 servings.

MARINATED BROCCOLI & MUSHROOMS

Per serving of vegetables: 216 calories, 5 g protein, 14 g carbohydrates, 17 g total fat, 0 mg cholesterol, 51 mg sodium

Per tablespoon of marinade: 89 calories, 0 g protein, 2 g carbohydrates, 9 g total fat, 0 mg cholesterol, .17 mg sodium

	About 1½ pounds broccoli
¾	**pound mushrooms, thinly sliced**
1	**cup thinly sliced green onions (including tops)**
1	**cup thinly sliced celery**
¼	**cup sugar**
⅓	**cup cider vinegar**
1	**teaspoon paprika**
1	**teaspoon celery seeds**
1	**cup salad oil**
	Salt and pepper

Prepare broccoli as previously directed. Cut flowerets into bite-size pieces; peel stalks, then cut diagonally into ¼-inch-thick slices. Steam (see "Cooking methods") until barely tender-crisp to bite (2 to 3 minutes). Immerse in cold water; when cold, drain well. In a large bowl, combine broccoli, mushrooms, onions, and celery.

Stir together sugar and vinegar until sugar is dissolved. Stir in paprika, celery seeds, and oil. Pour over vegetable mixture; stir to coat. Cover and refrigerate for 1 to 2 hours, stirring occasionally. Season to taste with salt and pepper. Makes 6 to 8 servings.

BROCCOLI ORIENTAL

Per serving: 41 calories, 3 g protein, 9 g carbohydrates, .27 g total fat, 0 mg cholesterol, 68 mg sodium

¾	**to 1 pound broccoli**
½	**cup unseasoned rice vinegar or ¼ cup *each* cider vinegar and water**
1	**tablespoon sugar**
½	**teaspoon soy sauce**

Prepare broccoli as previously directed; cut off stalks and reserve for another use. Steam flowerets (see "Cooking methods") just until tender when pierced (5 to 8 minutes). Turn into a bowl.

Stir together vinegar, sugar, and soy; pour over warm broccoli and mix well. Drain immediately and serve. Makes 4 servings.

Brussels Sprouts

Though Brussels sprouts were developed somewhere in Europe, it is not on record whether their place of origin was really Brussels. A relatively modern vegetable, this member of the cabbage family was first cultivated in the 1600s or 1700s and didn't become widely known in this country until the 1920s. Most of today's U.S. crop is grown in California.

Brussels sprouts tend to arouse strong emotions—people either love or hate them. Opinion probably hinges on the age of the sprouts first

DRESSING UP VEGETABLES

From classically simple vinaigrette to a rich hollandaise or béarnaise, the right dressing or sauce can cloak a vegetable with an elegance befitting the most festive occasion. Don't limit the use of vinaigrette to salad greens—it enhances many vegetables, both cooked and raw.

Seasoned butters offer an especially easy way to give hot vegetables extra flavor, and they can be stored in the refrigerator for several weeks. For longer storage, shape the prepared butter into a log, wrap it in foil, and freeze; then cut off slices of the frozen log to melt over hot vegetables.

VINAIGRETTE DRESSING

In a small bowl or jar, combine 1 tablespoon finely chopped **shallot** or mild red onion, 1 tablespoon **Dijon mustard**, 3 tablespoons **wine vinegar**, and ½ cup **olive oil** or salad oil. Mix well. If made ahead, cover and refrigerate for up to 2 weeks. Makes ¾ cup.

GARLIC BUTTER

Mix ½ cup (¼ lb.) **butter** or margarine (softened), 2 or 3 cloves **garlic** (minced or pressed), and 2 tablespoons minced **parsley**. Makes ½ cup.

HERB-CHEESE BUTTER

Mix ½ cup (¼ lb.) **butter** or margarine (softened), 1 tablespoon minced **parsley**, ½ teaspoon **Italian herb seasoning**, ¼ teaspoon **garlic salt**, ⅛ teaspoon **pepper**, and 3 tablespoons grated **Parmesan cheese**. Makes about ½ cup.

LEMON BUTTER

Mix ½ cup (¼ lb.) **butter** or margarine (softened), ¾ teaspoon grated **lemon peel**, 4 teaspoons **lemon juice**, and ¼ cup minced **parsley**. Makes about ½ cup.

SPICED BUTTER

Mix ½ cup (¼ lb.) **butter** or margarine (softened), 3 tablespoons firmly packed **brown sugar**, ¼ teaspoon *each* **ground cinnamon** and **ground allspice**, and ⅛ teaspoon **ground nutmeg**. Makes about ½ cup.

BÉCHAMEL SAUCE

> 2 tablespoons butter or margarine
> 2 tablespoons all-purpose flour
> ½ cup regular-strength chicken or beef broth
> ½ cup half-and-half or light cream
> Salt
> Freshly grated or ground nutmeg

Melt butter in a small pan over medium heat. Blend in flour and cook, stirring, until bubbly. Remove from heat and gradually stir in broth and half-and-half. Return to heat and cook, stirring, until sauce boils and thickens. Season to taste with salt and nutmeg. Use hot. Or let cool, then cover and refrigerate until next day. To serve, reheat over medium heat, stirring constantly. Makes about 1 cup.

MORNAY SAUCE

Follow directions for **Béchamel Sauce**, but when sauce comes to a boil, reduce heat and stir in 2 tablespoons shredded **Gruyère or Swiss cheese** and 2 tablespoons grated **Parmesan cheese**. Remove from heat and season to taste with **salt** and **ground red pepper** (cayenne); omit nutmeg. Thin with additional half-and-half, if desired. Makes about 1 cup.

CURRY SAUCE

Follow directions for **Béchamel Sauce**, but stir 2 teaspoons **curry powder** and ⅛ teaspoon **ground ginger** into melted butter along with flour. Season to taste with **salt** and **pepper;** omit nutmeg. Makes about 1 cup.

HOLLANDAISE SAUCE

> 1 egg or 3 egg yolks*
> 1 teaspoon Dijon or other prepared mustard
> 1 tablespoon lemon juice or white wine vinegar
> 1 cup (½ lb.) butter or margarine, melted and hot

In a blender or food processor, whirl egg, mustard, and lemon juice until well blended. With motor running, add butter, a few drops at a time at first, increasing to a slow, steady stream about 1/16 inch wide as mixture begins to thicken. Serve immediately. Or let stand at room temperature for up to several hours; or cover and refrigerate for up to 1 week.

To reheat, bring refrigerated sauce to room temperature. Place container of sauce in water that's just warm to the touch; stir constantly with a whisk for about 1 minute. Transfer to water that's hot to the touch; stir until sauce is warm. Makes 1 to 1½ cups.

An all-yolk hollandaise is thicker and richer tasting than a whole-egg sauce, with a more golden color.

BÉARNAISE SAUCE

In a small pan, combine 1 tablespoon minced **shallot** or onion, ½ teaspoon **dry tarragon,** and 2 tablespoons **white wine vinegar.** Cook over medium heat, stirring, until liquid has evaporated. Then follow directions for **Hollandaise Sauce,** adding shallot mixture (hot or cold) along with egg, mustard, and lemon juice. Makes 1 to 1½ cups.

...Brussels Sprouts continued

tasted: young sprouts are sweet and delicate, but older ones have a strong, cabbagy flavor and odor and a coarse texture.

Brussels sprouts are peculiar-looking plants that resemble miniature palm trees with lumps—sprouts—growing on the trunk. The sprouts mature from the bottom of the stem to the top, so harvesting each plant is a continuous process over the space of a month or two.

Nutrition. High in vitamin C, Brussels sprouts also contain significant amounts of vitamin A, thiamin, iron, potassium, and phosphorus. Like other members of the cabbage family, Brussels sprouts are considered helpful in the prevention of certain types of cancer. One cup of cooked Brussels sprouts (about ⅓ lb.) has 56 calories.

■ **Season.** All year; peak September through February.

■ **Selection.** Good sprouts are firm, compact, and fresh looking, with a bright green color; they feel heavy for their size. The smallest, youngest sprouts taste the best.

■ **Amount.** Allow ¼ to ⅓ pound per person.

■ **Storage.** Pull off and discard any limp or discolored leaves. Refrigerate, unwashed, in a plastic bag for up to 3 days.

■ **Preparation.** Trim stem ends; rinse sprouts. To ensure even cooking, cut a shallow "X" into each stem end.

■ **Cooking methods.** For more information on the cooking methods listed here, see "A Glossary of Techniques," page 122.

Boiling. In a 3-quart pan, boil 1 to 1½ pounds sprouts in 1 inch water just until stem ends are tender when pierced (7 to 10 minutes). Cover during last half of cooking time. Drain.

Butter-steaming. Cut 1 to 1½ pounds sprouts in half lengthwise. Butter-steam, using 2 tablespoons butter or margarine. Cook, stirring, for 1 minute. Add 3 to 5 tablespoons liquid; cover and cook until stem end is tender when pierced (3 to 5 more minutes).

Microwaving. Arrange 1 pound medium-size sprouts in a 1½-quart nonmetallic baking dish. Add 2 tablespoons water; cover. Microwave on **HIGH (100%)** for 6 to 7 minutes, stirring after 3 minutes. Let stand,

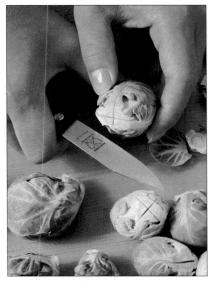

To ensure even cooking, cut a shallow "x" in stem end of each Brussels sprout.

covered, for 3 minutes. Stem end should be tender when pierced.

Steaming. Arrange sprouts on a rack. Steam just until stem end is tender when pierced (15 to 25 minutes).

■ **Serving ideas.** Top hot cooked sprouts with melted butter seasoned with basil, chives, dill weed, minced parsley, rosemary, or thyme. Offer lightly cooked and chilled sprouts with a dip for an appetizer, or marinate them in an oil and vinegar dressing for a flavorful salad.

BRUSSELS SPROUTS & RED BELL PEPPERS

Per serving: 137 calories, 6 g protein, 11 g carbohydrates, 9 g total fat, 27 mg cholesterol, 134 mg sodium

> 2 **pounds Brussels sprouts**
> 6 **tablespoons butter or margarine**
> 2 **large red bell peppers, seeded and cut into ¾-inch-wide strips**
> 1 **teaspoon** *each* **dry basil and prepared mustard**
> **Salt and pepper**

Prepare and boil or steam sprouts as previously directed. Set aside.

Melt butter in a 4- to 5-quart pan over medium-high heat; add bell peppers, cover, and cook until slightly soft (about 3 minutes). Stir in basil, mustard, and sprouts. Cook, stirring frequently, until sprouts are heated through (about 3 more minutes). Season to taste with salt and pepper. Makes 8 to 10 servings.

SOUTHERN SPROUTS

Per serving: 186 calories, 8 g protein, 15 g carbohydrates, 12 g total fat, 32 mg cholesterol, 183 mg sodium

> **About 1 pound Brussels sprouts**
> 3 **slices bacon**
> 1 **tablespoon butter or margarine**
> 1 **medium-size onion, chopped**
> 2 **small tomatoes, seeded and diced**
> **Salt and pepper**
> **Sour cream**

Prepare and boil or steam sprouts as previously directed.

Meanwhile, cook bacon in a wide frying pan over medium heat until crisp. Lift out, drain, crumble, and set aside. Discard all but 2 tablespoons drippings. Add butter and onion to drippings and cook, stirring, until onion is soft. Stir in tomatoes, bacon, and sprouts; heat through, then season to taste with salt and pepper.

Pass sour cream at the table to spoon over individual portions. Makes about 4 servings.

MARINATED BRUSSELS SPROUTS

Per serving: 279 calories, 9 g protein, 18 g carbohydrates, 21 g total fat, 8 mg cholesterol, 33 mg sodium

> **About 1¼ pounds Brussels sprouts**
> ⅓ **cup salad oil**
> 3 **tablespoons white wine vinegar**
> 2 **tablespoons thinly sliced green onion (including top)**
> ¼ **cup finely chopped cooked ham**
> 1 **jar (2 oz.) sliced pimentos, drained**
> ½ **cup thinly sliced water chestnuts**
> **Salt and pepper**

Prepare sprouts and steam as previously directed. Drain well; cut in half lengthwise. Add oil and vinegar; toss to mix. Stir in onion, ham, pimentos, and water chestnuts. Season to taste with salt and pepper. Serve hot. Or let cool, then cover and refrigerate until next day; serve as a salad. Makes 4 to 6 servings.

■ *See also* **Bean & Celery Root Soup** *(page 75).*

Cabbage

One of the oldest vegetables known, cabbage has been cultivated for at least 4,000 years. Its original home was probably along the temperate northern European coast; today, it is also grown throughout much of the United States.

In addition to the many types of head cabbages, the cabbage family includes broccoli, Brussels sprouts, cauliflower, collards, kale, and kohlrabi. All are covered elsewhere in this book.

Here we discuss the head cabbages —green, red, and Savoy—and their close relative napa cabbage (also called celery cabbage or Chinese cabbage). Salad Savoy is basically ornamental kale.

Green (white) cabbage is probably the most commonly available type. The heads are firm, compact, and spherical, with smooth, very pale green leaves that tightly overlap one another. Green cabbage is often served raw as cole slaw; it's also used in cooked dishes and for making sauerkraut.

Except for its color, red cabbage is nearly identical to the green type. It, too, is served both raw and in cooked dishes, and is often pickled.

Savoy cabbage's crinkly, flexible green leaves grow in a loosely packed head. More tender than green cabbage and milder in flavor, Savoy may be used interchangeably with green and red cabbage. Salad Savoy's frilly leaves have the heavy texture of kale in variegated colors of white, green, and red. The stems are slightly bitter, the leaves sweet. Use leaves raw in salads, or cook salad Savoy as you would kale (see page 83).

Napa cabbage has pale green, oblong leaves. Somewhat sweeter than the head cabbages, it has a slight zestiness and moist crispness. Napa cabbage is tasty both raw and cooked; it combines well with many foods.

Nutrition. Health experts recommend eating cabbage and its close relatives on a regular basis, since they are thought to help prevent certain types of cancer.

Raw cabbage is rich in vitamin C, has a fair amount of vitamin B_1, and is a good source of several minerals. It's also low in calories—about 20 per cup for shredded head cabbage, even less for napa.

■ **Season.** All year.

■ **Selection.** Choose firm heads that feel heavy for their size. Outer leaves should look fresh, have good color, and be free of blemishes.

■ **Amount.** Allow about ¼ pound per person. A 1½-pound cabbage yields 6 to 8 cups shredded raw cabbage.

■ **Storage.** Refrigerate, unwashed, in a plastic bag for up to 1 week (up to 4 days for napa cabbage).

■ **Preparation.** For head cabbages, pull off and discard any wilted outer leaves. Rinse head, cut in half lengthwise, and cut out core. Cut into wedges or shred.

For napa cabbage, pull off and discard any wilted outer leaves; rinse. Cut off base and cut cabbage in half lengthwise; then slice crosswise.

■ **Cooking methods.** Head cabbage can be cooked by all the following methods; napa cabbage is best when cooked quickly, either by microwaving or stir-frying. For more information on these cooking methods, see "A Glossary of Techniques," page 122.

Boiling. Cut 1 to 1½ pounds head cabbage into wedges; do not use napa cabbage. In a wide frying pan, boil in 1 inch water just until tender when pierced (5 to 7 minutes); cover after 2 minutes. Drain.

Microwaving. *For 1 pound of head cabbage wedges,* arrange in a 9- to 10-inch nonmetallic baking dish with wide ends toward outside of dish. Add 2 tablespoons water; cover. Microwave on **HIGH (100%)** for 6 to 8 minutes, rotating dish ¼ turn after 3 minutes. Let stand, covered, for 2 to 3 minutes. Wedges should be tender when pierced.

For 1 pound shredded head or napa cabbage, arrange in a 3-quart nonmetallic baking dish. Add 2 tablespoons water; cover. Microwave on **HIGH (100%)** for 4 to 6 minutes, stirring after 3 minutes. Let stand, covered, for 3 minutes. Cabbage should be tender-crisp to bite.

Steaming. Arrange head cabbage wedges on a rack (do not use napa cabbage). Steam just until tender when pierced (9 to 14 minutes).

Stir-frying. Shred head or napa cabbage. Stir-fry up to 5 cups, using 1 tablespoon salad oil, for 1 minute. Add 2 tablespoons liquid, cover, and cook until tender-crisp to bite (3 to 5 more minutes).

■ **Serving ideas.** Use melted butter and caraway seeds, dill weed, ginger, or soy sauce to season hot cooked cabbage. Serve plain cooked cabbage wedges with roast pork, ham, or beef pot roast. Combine shredded red cabbage with other greens for a colorful tossed salad. Stir shredded green cabbage into hearty soups; combine napa cabbage with other vegetables in stir-fry dishes.

CRISP CABBAGE SLAW

Per serving: 294 calories, 2 g protein, 12 g carbohydrates, 28 g total fat, 24 mg cholesterol, 305 mg sodium

12	cups shredded cabbage (green, red, or some of each)
¾	cup *each* sliced celery and green onions (including tops)
1¼	cups mayonnaise
1	tablespoon mustard seeds
2	teaspoons *each* prepared horseradish and Worcestershire
3	tablespoons sweet pickle relish, drained
	Salt and pepper

In a large bowl, mix cabbage, celery, and onions. In another bowl, stir together mayonnaise, mustard seeds, horseradish, Worcestershire, and relish. Spoon dressing over cabbage mixture and mix well. Season to taste with salt and pepper. If made ahead, cover and refrigerate for 4 to 6 hours. Makes 8 to 10 servings.

STIR-FRIED NAPA CABBAGE

Per serving: 137 calories, 2 g protein, 11 g carbohydrates, 10 g total fat, 0 mg cholesterol, 362 mg sodium

2	tablespoons unseasoned rice vinegar or white wine vinegar
2	tablespoons sugar
1	tablespoon soy sauce
¼	teaspoon ground red pepper (cayenne)
1	medium-size head napa cabbage (1¼ to 1½ lbs.)
3	tablespoons salad oil

In a small bowl, stir together vinegar, sugar, soy, and red pepper; set aside.

Cut cabbage into 2-inch squares.

Heat a wok or wide frying pan over high heat; add oil. When oil is hot, add cabbage and stir-fry until it begins to wilt (2 to 3 minutes). Add vinegar mixture and mix well. Pour into a serving dish. Serve warm or at room temperature. Makes 4 to 6 servings.

Carrots

Cabbages range in color from pale green to shocking purple.

Native to Afghanistan, carrots were cultivated in the Mediterranean region as early as 500 B.C. Their cultivation spread from there throughout Europe; by about 1600 they were found in England, where stylish ladies of the court used the feathery leaves to adorn their hair and hats. *(Photo on page 56.)*

Though cultivated carrots come in many shapes and sizes—globular, short and stubby, long and thin, with blunt or pointed ends—the variety most widely available in U.S. markets is the long, pointed Imperator type. Recently, however, there has been a great increase in market supplies of the miniature carrots commonly found in Europe—often called Belgian or French carrots.

Nutrition. The carrot owes its nutritional fame to its extraordinarily high content of vitamin A, which improves vision (particularly night vision). A medium-size raw carrot contains about 30 calories.

■ **Season.** All year.

■ **Selection.** Choose firm, clean, well-shaped carrots with bright orange-gold color. Carrots with their tops still attached are likely to be freshest; look for fresh-looking, bright green leaves.

■ **Amount.** Allow about ¼ pound per person, or 1 medium-size bunch for 4 servings. One large carrot (about ⅓ lb.) yields about 1 cup shredded.

■ **Storage.** Cut off and discard green tops, leaving 1 to 2 inches attached to carrots. Refrigerate, unwashed, in a plastic bag for up to 2 weeks.

■ **Preparation.** Trim top and root ends. Scrub well; if desired, peel with a vegetable peeler and rinse. Cook whole; or slice, dice, shred, or cut into julienne strips.

■ **Cooking methods.** For more information on the cooking methods listed here, see "A Glossary of Techniques," page 122.

Baking. Cut carrots into 1-inch diagonal slices. Arrange in a shallow layer

TOASTED CABBAGE WITH NOODLES

Per serving: 491 calories, 10 g protein, 57 g carbohydrates, 26 g total fat, 124 mg cholesterol, 310 mg sodium

- 1 **small head green cabbage (about 1½ lbs.)**
- ½ **cup (¼ lb.) butter or margarine**
- 1 **large onion, chopped**
- 1 **clove garlic, minced or pressed**
- 2 **tablespoons sugar**
- 8 **ounces wide egg noodles**
  Salt and pepper

Finely shred cabbage, discarding core; you should have 6 to 8 cups. Set aside.

Melt butter in a wide frying pan over medium heat. Add onion and garlic and cook, stirring often, until onion is soft. Add cabbage and cook, stirring frequently, until cabbage is limp and turns a brighter green (about 5 minutes). Sprinkle on sugar and continue to cook, stirring often, until cabbage takes on an amber color and begins to brown lightly (about 25 more minutes).

Meanwhile, following package direction, cook noodles until *al dente*. Drain. In a shallow serving bowl, combine noodles and cabbage mixture. Lift with 2 forks to mix thoroughly. Season to taste with salt and pepper. Makes 4 servings.

■ *See also **Minestrone** (page 62).*

in a baking dish; generously dot with butter or margarine. Cover and bake in a 325° oven until tender when pierced (40 to 50 minutes). Stir several times.

Boiling. In a wide frying pan, boil 1 pound whole carrots, covered, in 1 inch water until tender when pierced (10 to 20 minutes). Drain.

Boil 1 pound ¼-inch slices or whole miniature carrots, covered, in ½ inch water for 5 to 10 minutes. Drain.

Microwaving. Arrange 1 pound whole regular carrots or sliced carrots (about 1 inch in diameter) in a 1½-quart nonmetallic baking dish. Add 3 tablespoons water; cover. Microwave on **HIGH (100%)**—whole carrots for 6 to 7 minutes, slices for 6 to 8 minutes. Stir after 3 minutes. Let stand, covered, for 5 minutes. Carrots should be tender when pierced.

Steaming. Arrange slices or whole regular or miniature carrots on a rack. Steam until tender when pierced (5 to 10 minutes for slices, 12 to 20 minutes for whole regular carrots, 8 to 12 minutes for whole miniature carrots).

Stir-frying. Cut carrots into ¼-inch-thick slices. Stir-fry up to 5 cups, using 1 tablespoon salad oil, for 1 minute. Add 2 tablespoons liquid, cover, and cook until tender-crisp to bite (3 to 5 more minutes).

■ **Serving ideas.** Top hot cooked carrots with melted butter seasoned with basil, chives, dill weed, ginger, mint, nutmeg, minced parsley, lemon juice, or brown sugar. Offer chilled cooked carrots in a vinaigrette dressing. Serve raw carrot sticks with a dip for an appetizer. Shred raw carrots and add to cole slaw, or toss with an oil and vinegar dressing for a salad. Add carrots to soups, stews, pot roasts, and other one-dish meals.

GINGERED CARROTS & APPLES

Per serving: 216 calories, 1 g protein, 18 g carbohydrates, 16 g total fat, 53 mg cholesterol, 138 mg sodium

> 3 tablespoons butter or margarine
> ¼ cup slivered fresh ginger
> 2 cups very thinly sliced carrots
> 2 large Golden Delicious apples, peeled, cored, and cut into ½-inch-thick slices
> ⅓ cup water
> ¼ cup whipping cream
> 1½ teaspoons sugar

Melt butter in a wide frying pan over medium-high heat. Add ginger, car-

rots, apples, and water. Cover and cook, stirring occasionally, until carrots are tender when pierced (about 5 minutes). Add cream and sugar; bring to a boil, stirring. Continue to boil until cream thickens and glazes carrots and apples (about 1 more minute). Makes 4 servings.

SPICED CARROT BISQUE

Per serving: 409 calories, 13 g protein, 20 g carbohydrates, 32 g total fat, 118 mg cholesterol, 828 mg sodium

> 1¼ pounds carrots
> 3 cups regular-strength chicken broth
> 1 large onion, sliced
> ¼ teaspoon white pepper
> ¾ teaspoon ground ginger
> 1 cup whipping cream, half-and-half, or light cream
> Salt
> Freshly grated nutmeg
> 1 cup (4 oz.) shredded Cheddar cheese

Peel carrots and slice about ¼ inch thick; you should have about 4 cups.

In a 4- to 5-quart pan, combine carrots, broth, and onion. Bring to a boil over high heat; reduce heat, cover, and simmer until carrots are tender when pierced (8 to 10 minutes).

Pour mixture into a blender or food processor, about half at a time, and whirl until puréed. Return purée to pan and add white pepper, ginger, and cream. Season to taste with salt. If made ahead, let cool, then cover and refrigerate for up to 2 days.

To serve, stir over low heat until hot. Pour into bowls and sprinkle with nutmeg. Offer cheese at the table to spoon into individual portions. Makes 4 to 6 servings.

CARROT CAKE

Per serving: 598 calories, 8 g protein, 78 g carbohydrates, 30 g total fat, 84 mg cholesterol, 230 mg sodium

> 3 cups all-purpose flour
> 2 cups sugar
> 1½ cups chopped walnuts
> 1½ teaspoons ground cinnamon
> 1 teaspoon *each* baking powder and baking soda
> ½ teaspoon salt
> 2 cans (8 oz. *each*) crushed pineapple
> 2 cups coarsely shredded carrots
> 1 cup salad oil
> 4 eggs
> 2 teaspoons vanilla
> Glaze (recipe follows)

In a large bowl, combine flour, sugar, walnuts, cinnamon, baking powder, baking soda, and salt. Drain pineapple, reserving 2 tablespoons juice for Glaze; place pineapple in another bowl and beat in carrots, oil, eggs, and vanilla. Add to flour mixture and stir until evenly moistened. Spoon batter into a well-greased 10-inch or 12-cup tube pan.

Bake in 350° oven until a wooden pick inserted in center comes out clean (about 1 hour). Let cool in pan for 15 minutes. Loosen edges; invert from pan onto a rack and let cool. Prepare Glaze and drizzle over cooled cake. Makes about 12 servings.

Glaze. Stir together 1 cup **powdered sugar** and 2 tablespoons **reserved pineapple juice** until smoothly blended.

■ *See also* ***Vegetable Purée*** *(page 71),* ***Sprout & Vegetable Medley*** *(page 110).*

Cauliflower

The word "cauliflower" comes from two Latin terms and literally means "cabbage flower." Though cultivated in Asia Minor and the Mediterranean for more than 2,000 years and known throughout Western Europe by the 16th century, this vegetable has only been an important American crop since the 1920s. New York and California are the major growing areas in the United States today.

Growing a perfect head of cauliflower requires a lot of work, so cauliflower usually commands a higher price than other members of the cabbage family. The head, technically known as the "curd," must be protected from the sun to remain snowy white. When the bud forms in the center of the plant, the outer leaves are gathered into a tent over the developing curd to shield it from sunlight.

Commercial growers have recently begun to market a new, purplish green variety of cauliflower. A cross between broccoli and conventional white cauliflower, it requires no hand

VERSATILE VEGETABLE PURÉES

For cooks seeking an imaginative and convenient way to present the flavors of fresh vegetables, purées may be the answer. Lightly cooked and puréed vegetables make a flavorful base for dips, soups, and sauces. They take up relatively little space in the freezer, and since they can be prepared well ahead of time, they're especially helpful if you need a head start on dinner party menus.

Here, we tell you how to prepare beet, carrot, tomato, and zucchini purées; you might experiment with other vegetables as well. To freeze any of these, spoon the cooled purée into ice cube trays or 1-cup freezer containers. Freeze until solid, then transfer cubes to freezer bags. Store in the freezer for up to a year, ready to use in any of the recipes below.

VEGETABLE PURÉE

Beets, carrots, tomatoes, and zucchini are all quickly puréed in a food processor. You can also use a blender for tomatoes and zucchini. A food chopper is a more time-consuming alternative for firm vegetables, producing a coarser purée.

Beet Purée. Cut off all but 1 inch of tops from about 5 pounds **beets;** do not cut off roots. Scrub beets well. In a 6- to 8-quart pan, bring about 2 quarts **water** to a boil; add beets and boil, covered, until tender when pierced (20 to 50 minutes, depending on size and maturity). Drain; when cool, trim stem and root ends and slip off skins. Cut beets into 1-inch chunks. Whirl, a portion at a time, in a food processor until smooth; or put through a food chopper fitted with a fine or medium blade. Makes 8 cups.

Carrot Purée. Peel about 5 pounds **carrots** and cut into 1-inch pieces. In a 6- to 8-quart pan, bring 1 to 2 quarts **water** to a boil; add carrots, cover, and boil until tender when pierced (10 to 12 minutes). Drain. Whirl, a portion at a time, in a food processor until smooth; or put through a food chopper fitted with a fine or medium blade. Makes 8 cups.

Tomato Purée. Wash about 5 pounds **tomatoes;** remove stem ends, then cut in half crosswise and squeeze out seeds. Cut into 1-inch chunks and whirl, a portion at a time, in a food processor or blender until puréed. Pour into a 5- to 6-quart pan and boil, uncovered, stirring occasionally, until reduced by half. As tomatoes thicken, reduce heat and stir more often. Makes 4 cups.

Zucchini Purée. Wash about 5 pounds **zucchini,** trim off ends, and cut into ½-inch slices. In a 6- to 8-quart pan, bring 1 to 2 quarts **water** to a boil. Add zucchini; boil, covered, until barely tender when pierced (5 to 7 minutes). Drain well. Whirl, a portion at a time, in a food processor or blender until puréed. Makes 7 cups.

For cool dips, stir intensely flavored fresh vegetable purée into herb-seasoned sour cream; serve with crisp vegetables.

VEGETABLE PURÉE DIP

Mix ½ cup **sour cream** or mayonnaise, 1 tablespoon minced **shallot** or green onion (white part only), and ¼ teaspoon *each* **dry mustard, thyme leaves,** and **dry tarragon.** Add ½ cup **vegetable purée** (thawed if frozen). Mix to blend. Season to taste with **salt.** Serve as a dip for **raw vegetables.** Makes about 1 cup.

COOL VEGETABLE BUTTERMILK SOUP

Stir together 2 cups **vegetable purée** (thawed if frozen), 1 cup *each* **regular-strength chicken broth** and **buttermilk,** and ¼ teaspoon **dill weed.** Season to taste with **salt.** Serve chilled. Makes 3 or 4 servings.

HOT VEGETABLE PURÉE

Melt 2 tablespoons **butter** or margarine in a 10- to 12-inch frying pan over medium heat. Add 1 large **onion,** finely chopped; cook, stirring often, until onion is very soft and pale golden. Add ⅓ cup **whipping cream** and 1 cup **vegetable purée** (thawed if frozen). Boil gently, uncovered, stirring constantly, until hot and thick. Season to taste with **salt** and **pepper.** Makes 2 or 3 servings.

VEGETABLE-SAUCED PASTA

Follow directions for **Hot Vegetable Purée,** but increase whipping cream to 1½ cups and add ½ teaspoon **dry basil** and ½ cup **regular-strength chicken broth.** Boil gently, uncovered, stirring constantly, until sauce is slightly thickened. Pour into a serving dish. Top with 6 cups **hot cooked pasta** (about 8 oz. dry pasta). Mix pasta and sauce; sprinkle with grated **Parmesan cheese.** Makes 4 servings.

tying in the field. This new variety remains green when cooked; it also cooks faster than regular cauliflower.

Nutrition. Like other members of the cabbage family, cauliflower is considered helpful in the prevention of certain kinds of cancer. It is a good source of vitamin C and potassium. One cup of cooked cauliflower contains 28 calories.

■ **Season.** All year; peak late autumn through spring.

■ **Selection.** Choose firm, compact, creamy white (or bright purplish green) heads with flowerets pressed tightly together. A yellow tinge and spreading flowerets indicate over-maturity. Any leaves should be crisp and bright green.

■ **Amount.** Allow about ⅓ pound per person. One medium-size head serves 4.

■ **Storage.** Refrigerate, unwashed, in a plastic bag for up to 1 week.

■ **Preparation.** Remove and discard outer leaves and cut out core; rinse. Leave head whole or break into flowerets; cut flowerets into slices, if desired.

■ **Cooking methods.** For more information on the cooking methods listed here, see "A Glossary of Techniques," page 122.

Boiling. Place 1 medium-size head, stem side down, in a 4- to 5-quart pan. Boil, covered, in 1 inch water until stem end is tender when pierced (15 to 20 minutes). Drain.

Place 1 to 1½ pounds flowerets in a wide frying pan. Boil, covered, in ½ inch water until tender when pierced (5 to 9 minutes). Drain.

Place about 1 pound ¼-inch slices in a wide frying pan. Boil, covered, in ½ inch water until tender when pierced (3 to 5 minutes). Drain.

Microwaving. Place a 1¼- to 1½-pound whole head, stem side down, or about 1¼ pounds flowerets in a deep 2-quart nonmetallic baking dish. Add 2 tablespoons water. Cover. Microwave on **HIGH (100%)**—whole head for 10 to 11 minutes (turn over after 7 minutes), flowerets for 6 to 8 minutes (stir after 4 minutes). Let stand, covered, for 4 to 5 minutes. Cauliflower should be tender when pierced.

Steaming. Place whole head, flowerets, or ¼-inch slices on a rack.

Steam until tender when pierced (20 to 25 minutes for a whole head, 10 to 18 minutes for flowerets, 7 to 12 minutes for slices).

Stir-frying. Cut flowerets into ¼-inch slices. Stir-fry up to 5 cups, using 1 tablespoon salad oil, for 1 minute. Add 3 to 4 tablespoons liquid, cover, and cook until tender-crisp to bite (4 to 5 more minutes).

■ **Serving ideas.** Top hot cooked cauliflower with melted butter seasoned with chives, dill weed, nutmeg, minced parsley, or lemon juice. Or serve with mornay or hollandaise sauce (page 66). Raw cauliflower is delicious on a crudité platter and makes a crunchy addition to a tossed salad. Add chopped cooked cauliflower to a quiche, or stir it into scrambled eggs.

GOLDEN CAULIFLOWER FRITTERS

Per serving of fritters: 161 calories, 6 g protein, 9 g carbohydrates, 12 g total fat, 137 g cholesterol, 52 mg sodium
Per tablespoon of sauce: 5 calories, .24 g protein, 1 g carbohydrates, .07 g total fat, 0 mg cholesterol, 272 mg sodium

    Lemon Dipping Sauce (recipe follows)
1 medium-size head cauliflower
3 eggs
3 tablespoons all-purpose flour
    Salad oil

Prepare Lemon Dripping Sauce; set aside.

Cut cauliflower into flowerets, then cut each floweret lengthwise into ¼-inch slices. Set aside.

In large bowl of an electric mixer, beat eggs on high speed until foamy. Add flour and beat until about doubled in volume.

Pour about ⅛ inch of oil into a wide frying pan over medium-high heat. Stir cauliflower into batter. When oil is hot, lift cauliflower pieces, one at a time, from batter; drain briefly. Arrange in a single layer in oil; do not crowd. Cook until golden brown on all sides, turning as needed. As pieces are browned, lift from oil and arrange in a single layer in a paper-towel-lined baking pan; keep hot. Or, if made ahead, let cool, then cover and refrigerate until next day. To reheat, uncover and remove paper towels; arrange cauliflower evenly in pan and bake in a 350° oven until hot (7 to 10 minutes).

To serve, arrange hot fritters in a napkin-lined basket; offer dipping

Tender spinach leaves contrast with cauliflower and avocado in this tricolor salad (recipe below).

sauce in a small bowl. Makes 6 to 8 appetizer servings.

Lemon Dipping Sauce. Stir together ¼ cup **lemon juice,** 1 tablespoon **soy sauce,** and 6 to 8 drops **liquid hot pepper seasoning.**

CAULIFLOWER-SPINACH TOSS

Per serving: 302 calories, 10 g protein, 12 g carbohydrates, 27 g total fat, 0 mg cholesterol, 243 mg sodium

½ cup pine nuts or slivered almonds
    About 1 pound spinach
½ medium-size head cauliflower, broken into flowerets, then cut into ¼-inch-thick slices
1 large avocado
    Lemon juice
6 tablespoons salad oil
3 tablespoons white wine vinegar
1 large clove garlic, minced or pressed
½ teaspoon *each* salt, dry mustard, and dry basil
¼ teaspoon pepper
    Dash of ground nutmeg

Spread nuts in a shallow pan and toast in a 350° oven until golden (about 8 minutes). Set aside.

Discard tough stems from spinach. Plunge leaves into cold water to clean; lift out, pat dry, and tear into bite-size pieces. Place in a bowl and add cauliflower. Pit, peel, and slice avocado. Dip avocado slices in lemon juice to coat, then add to spinach and cauliflower.

Combine oil, vinegar, garlic, salt, mustard, basil, pepper, and nutmeg; blend well. Pour over salad; add nuts and gently mix to coat thoroughly. Makes 6 servings.

CAULIFLOWER & PEA STIR-FRY

Per serving: 398 calories, 32 g protein, 22 g carbohydrates, 21 total fat, 78 mg cholesterol, 1174 mg sodium

- 1 medium-size head cauliflower
- 1 pound lean boneless beef steak, such as top round or flank steak
- 2 tablespoons salad oil
- 2 cloves garlic, minced or pressed
- 1 small onion, sliced
   About 1¼ cups water
- 1 beef bouillon cube
- 5 teaspoons cornstarch
- 2½ tablespoons soy sauce
- 1¼ teaspoons ground ginger
- 1 cup cooked fresh peas; or 1 cup frozen peas, thawed
   Hot cooked rice

Cut cauliflower into small flowerets; cut flowerets in half lengthwise if thicker than 1 inch. Set aside. Trim excess fat from beef, then cut beef across the grain into ⅛-inch-thick strips about 3 inches long.

Heat a wide frying pan or wok over high heat. Add oil. When oil is hot, add garlic and meat; stir-fry until lightly browned (about 3 minutes). Remove from pan. Add cauliflower, onion, 1 cup of the water, and bouillon cube. Reduce heat, cover, and boil gently until cauliflower is barely tender when pierced (4 to 5 minutes). Stir together remaining ¼ cup water, cornstarch, soy, and ginger; add to vegetable mixture. Cook, stirring, until sauce boils and thickens. Stir in a little additional water if sauce is too thick. Stir in meat and peas; heat through. Serve over rice. Makes 4 servings.

■ *See also **Maltese Soup** (page 95).*

Celery

Celery, a member of the carrot family, has been known for thousands of years. The ancient Greeks and Romans, however, viewed wild celery as a medicine rather than a food; it wasn't until the 16th century that celery was widely cultivated in Europe to eat at the table.

There are two distinct types of celery—Golden Heart, bleached white and most often found as packaged celery hearts, and Pascal, which is bright green. In today's markets, Pascal celery has practically replaced the white variety because of its pronounced flavor and crisp, meaty texture.

Nutrition. Celery is low in calories—one large stalk has only 7. It's high in fiber, moderately rich in minerals, and a fair source of vitamins A and B.

■ **Season.** All year.

■ **Selection.** Look for crisp, rigid, green stalks with fresh-looking leaves. Avoid celery with limp, rubbery stalks.

■ **Amount.** Allow ¼ to ⅓ pound per person. One large stalk (about ¼ lb.) yields about 1 cup sliced or diced celery.

■ **Storage.** Refrigerate, unwashed, in a plastic bag for up to 2 weeks.

■ **Preparation.** Separate stalks and rinse thoroughly. Trim off leaves (reserve for soups and stock) and base; cut out brown spots. To remove strings from outer stalks, pull strings with a knife from top of stalk down to base; discard. Dice stalks; or cut into slices or julienne strips.

For celery hearts, simply rinse and cut in half lengthwise.

■ **Cooking methods.** Pascal and Golden Heart types of celery can be used interchangeably in cooking. For more information on the cooking methods listed here, see "A Glossary of Techniques," page 122.

Boiling. In a wide frying pan, boil 1¼ to 1½ pounds of celery (cut into 1-inch slices) or halved celery hearts, covered, in ½ inch water until just tender when pierced (slices for 5 to 10 minutes, hearts for 8 to 12 minutes). Drain.

Butter-steaming. Cut celery into ¼-inch slices. Butter-steam up to 5 cups, using 2 tablespoons butter or margarine. Cook, stirring, for 1 minute. Add 1 to 2 tablespoons liquid, cover, and cook until just tender-crisp to bite (1 to 3 more minutes).

Steaming. Arrange celery (cut into 1-inch slices) or halved celery hearts on a rack. Steam until just tender when pierced (8 to 10 minutes for slices, 10 to 14 minutes for hearts.)

Stir-frying. Cut celery into ¼-inch slices. Stir-fry up to 5 cups, using 1 tablespoon salad oil, for 1 minute. Add 1 to 2 tablespoons liquid, cover, and cook until just tender-crisp to bite (1 to 3 more minutes).

■ **Serving ideas.** Top hot cooked celery with melted butter seasoned with tarragon or thyme. Offer raw celery sticks as an appetizer or on a relish tray, or stuff with cream cheese spreads, peanut butter, or egg salad. Add sliced or diced raw celery to potato, pasta, meat, poultry, shellfish, or egg salads; or add to vegetable and bread stuffings for poultry. Use as a basic ingredient in stocks, stews, soups, and casseroles.

LAMB & CELERY STEW

Per serving: 768 calories 33 g protein, 17 g carbohydrates, 64 g total fat, 134 mg cholesterol, 460 mg sodium

- ½ cup salad oil
- 1 large onion, thinly sliced
- 2½ pounds boneless lamb shoulder, cut into 1½-inch cubes
- 1¼ cups water
- 2 bunches celery (about 3 lbs. *total*)
- 4 cups *each* finely chopped, lightly packed fresh mint and parsley
- ½ cup lime juice

Heat 2 tablespoons of the oil in a 5- to 6-quart pan over medium-high heat. Add onion and cook, stirring, until lightly browned. Add lamb and ¼ cup of the water. Reduce heat to medium-low, cover, and cook for 30 minutes,

For a cool first course, cut long celery hearts into quarters, cook in bundles, and coat with a piquant caper dressing (recipe on page 74).

stirring occasionally. Uncover and continue to cook until liquid has evaporated; stir to brown meat evenly. Add remaining 1 cup water and stir to loosen browned particles. Cover and simmer until meat is just tender when pierced (about 30 minutes); stir occasionally.

Meanwhile, prepare celery as previously directed, removing any strings. Cut stalks into 2- to 3-inch lengths.

Heat remaining 6 tablespoons oil in a wide frying pan over medium-high heat. Add about half the celery, making a single layer in pan; cook, turning, until pieces are tinged with gold (about 4 minutes). Lift out celery; drain. Repeat with remaining celery.

Discard all but 2 tablespoons oil from pan; add mint and parsley to pan and stir just until wilted. Add mint, parsley, and celery to meat; stir in more water if meat is dry. Cover and simmer until meat is very tender when pierced (about 30 more minutes), stirring occasionally. Stir in lime juice and heat through. Makes 6 to 8 servings.

CELERY HEARTS WITH CAPER DRESSING

Per serving: 218 calories, 2 g protein, 5 g carbohydrates, 22 g total fat, 3 mg cholesterol, 217 mg sodium

> 1 **large celery heart (about 1 lb.) Caper Dressing (recipe follows)**
> 4 to 8 **canned anchovy fillets, drained**
> 4 to 8 **pitted ripe olives**

Cut celery heart lengthwise into quarters. Rinse well. Tie each quarter together with string. Boil as previously directed, but cook for only 5 minutes. Remove from pan and plunge into ice water. When cool, drain well.

Prepare Caper Dressing. Arrange celery in a serving dish; pour dressing over top. Cover and refrigerate for at least 1 hour or until next day. Before serving, garnish with anchovies and olives. Makes 4 servings.

Caper Dressing. Stir together 6 tablespoons **salad oil**, 3 tablespoons **white wine vinegar**, 1 clove **garlic** (minced or pressed), 1 tablespoon drained **capers**, ¼ teaspoon **dry basil**, and a dash of **pepper**.

Celery Root

Upstairs, downstairs is the relationship between celery and celery root. When cultivated, wild celery yielded two separate plants: celery, grown for its fat stalks, and celery root (also called celeriac or celery knob), cultivated for its enlarged root.

On first encounter, you may be put off by the appearance of celery root. It really is rather ugly—knobby and hairy, its top just a cluster of scrawny stems. But peel away that rough exterior and you'll find creamy white flesh with a mild flavor and an intriguing texture that combines the crunch of celery with the smoothness of potatoes.

Nutrition. Celery root is high in phosphorus and a good source of potassium. A 3½-ounce portion of raw celery root contains 40 calories.

■ **Season.** October through April.

■ **Selection.** Pick small to medium roots that are firm and relatively clean. Any tops should be bright green and fresh looking.

■ **Amount.** Allow ¼ to ⅓ pound per person.

■ **Storage.** Refrigerate roots, unwashed, in a plastic bag for up to 1 week.

■ **Preparation.** Scrub with a vegetable brush; cut off and discard top and root ends. Peel away thick outer skin with a stainless steel knife. Cut out spots where vegetable is pitted. Slice,

To prepare celery root, trim off ends; then peel and shred, dice, or cut into julienne strips.

dice, shred, or cut into julienne strips. To keep peeled or cut surfaces of raw celery root white, submerge immediately in a bowl of acidulated water (3 tablespoons vinegar or lemon juice per quart water).

■ **Cooking methods.** For more information on the cooking methods listed here, see "A Glossary of Techniques," page 122.

Boiling. In a 3-quart pan, boil 1 unpeeled medium-size celery root (¾ to 1 lb.), covered, in water to cover until tender when pierced (40 to 60 minutes). Drain and peel.

Butter-steaming. Cut celery root into ¼-inch slices; cut larger slices in half. Butter-steam up to 5 cups, using 2 tablespoons butter or margarine. Cook, stirring, for 1 minute. Add 3 to 4 tablespoons liquid, cover, and cook until tender-crisp to bite (2 to 4 more minutes).

■ **Serving ideas.** Melted butter with a hint of dill weed or tarragon goes well on hot cooked celery root. Chilled raw or lightly cooked celery root makes a delicious salad when dressed with a flavorful vinaigrette or mayonnaise; serve as a first course or as an accompaniment to simply cooked meat.

CELERY ROOT SALAD

Per serving: 249 calories, 2 g protein, 15 g carbohydrates, 21 g total fat, 8 mg cholesterol, 225 mg sodium

> 6 **tablespoons olive oil**
> 3 **tablespoons white wine vinegar**
> 1 teaspoon *each* **sugar and caraway seeds**
> 1 clove **garlic, minced or pressed**
> 2 **medium-size celery roots (about 1½ lbs. *total*), peeled and cut into julienne strips Salt**
> ¼ cup **mayonnaise**

In a bowl, combine oil, vinegar, sugar, caraway seeds, and garlic. Stir in celery root; season to taste with salt. Cover and let marinate at room temperature, stirring occasionally, for about 2 hours.

Just before serving, pour salad into a wire strainer and drain off marinade; reserve marinade to use on green salads, if desired. Stir mayonnaise into celery root. Makes 4 to 6 servings.

HIGH-POTENCY PRODUCE— GINGER & HORSERADISH

Two of the homeliest items in produce markets are also two of the most powerful: fresh ginger and horseradish root. Each enlivens other foods with its own distinctive bite.

Knobby ginger root (actually a rhizome, or underground stem) has dull brown skin, fibrous flesh, and spicy-hot flavor when mature. Young ginger (available from July through September) is milder, more tender, and especially aromatic; you'll recognize it by its thin, translucent, pink-tinged skin.

Refrigerate mature ginger in a plastic bag for up to 2 weeks; refrigerate young ginger uncovered. To use ginger, rinse and scrub; peel mature ginger with a paring knife (it's not necessary to peel young ginger). Thinly slice, sliver, grate, or chop to use in stir-fries, marinades, salad dressings, preserves, or wherever your taste dictates.

Horseradish, unlike ginger, is a true root. Look for firm horseradish without soft spots or sprouts. To store, wrap in a damp paper towel, place in a plastic bag, and refrigerate. To use, scrub and peel horseradish, then grate it directly onto any food that benefits from its zip. Or make what aficionados consider the perfect prepared horseradish—the kind that brings tears to the eyes. The following recipe is tempered with grated turnip, but it's still hot; for a milder flavor, add more turnip.

FRESH HORSERADISH

 1 horseradish root (about 1 lb.)
 1 cup distilled white vinegar
 1 teaspoon salt
 ½ teaspoon sugar
 1 small turnip, peeled and cubed

Scrub and peel horseradish, cutting away any dark parts. Cut into cubes.

If using a blender, place vinegar, salt, and sugar in container. Add about ⅓ *each* of the horseradish and turnip. Process until evenly grated—coarse or fine, as you prefer. Stop motor occasionally and scrape down sides of container. Gradually add remaining horseradish and turnip, blending until uniform in texture.

If using a food processor, place horseradish, salt, sugar, and turnip in work bowl; whirl until finely chopped, adding vinegar with motor running.

Place in a glass or plastic container, cover tightly, and refrigerate for up to 3 months. Makes about 3 cups.

Add bite to foods with fresh-grated horseradish root (right), ginger.

BEAN & CELERY ROOT SOUP

Per serving: 282 calories, 14 g protein, 34 g carbohydrates, 12 g total fat, 44 mg cholesterol, 738 mg sodium

 1 medium-size celery root (¾ to 1 lb.)
 2 tablespoons salad oil
 1 medium-size onion, chopped
 ½ cup all-purpose flour
 3½ cans (14½ oz. *each*) or 6½ cups regular-strength beef broth
 3 cups cooked or 2 cans (about 1 lb. *each*) Great Northern beans, drained
 2 medium-size carrots, thinly sliced
 ¾ pound Brussels sprouts, halved lengthwise
 ½ cup whipping cream

Prepare celery root as previously directed, cutting it into ½-inch cubes and submerging immediately in acidulated water.

Heat oil in a 6- to 8-quart pan over medium-high heat; add onion and cook, stirring often, until soft. Stir in flour; cook, stirring, until bubbly. Gradually stir in broth; bring to a boil, stirring. Drain celery root; add to broth mixture along with beans and carrots. Return to a boil; then reduce heat, cover, and simmer until celery root is tender when pierced (about 10 minutes). Add Brussels sprouts and cream; cook, uncovered, until sprouts are tender when pierced (about 10 more minutes). Makes 6 to 8 servings.

Chard   *see Swiss Chard, page 117*

Chayote

A tropical summer squash, chayote is a Latin American native that was grown by the Aztecs and Mayans centuries ago. Sometimes referred to as vegetable pear, it has a deeply ridged surface and a single flat seed in the center—which may explain why South Americans call the chayote "mango squash."

Chayotes may be either female or male. The female fruit, with its smooth skin and corrugated, slightly lumpy surface, is preferable to the less meaty male fruit, often covered with spines.

Continued on next page

Nutrition. Chayote provides some vitamin A and potassium. A 3½-ounce portion of raw chayote has 28 calories.

■ **Season.** October through March.

■ **Selection.** Choose firm, young chayotes that are free of blemishes. The harder and darker green the chayote, the better.

■ **Amount.** Allow ½ medium-size to large chayote per person.

■ **Storage.** Store, unwrapped, in a cool (50°F), dry, dark place with good ventilation for up to 1 month. Or refrigerate, unwashed, in a plastic bag for up to 1 week.

■ **Preparation.** If the chayote's skin isn't tough or spiny, there's no need to peel before cooking. Just rinse well, then cut lengthwise into halves or quarters; or slice crosswise or lengthwise. Cut through the seed; when cooked, it's edible.

■ **Cooking methods.** For more information on the cooking methods listed here, see "A Glossary of Techniques," page 122.

Boiling. In a wide frying pan, boil 2 medium-size to large chayotes, halved lengthwise, covered, in 2 inches water until tender when pierced (25 to 35 minutes). Drain.

Boil 1½ to 2 pounds ¼-inch-thick slices in ½ inch water for 7 to 9 minutes. Drain.

Butter-steaming. Cut chayote crosswise into ¼-inch-thick slices. Butter-steam up to 5 cups, using 2 to 3 tablespoons butter or margarine. Cook, stirring, for 1 minute. Add 4 to 6 tablespoons liquid, cover, and cook until tender-crisp to bite (6 to 8 minutes).

Steaming. Cut chayotes in half lengthwise; or cut crosswise into ¼-inch-thick slices. Arrange on rack. Steam until tender when pierced (35 to 40 minutes for halves, 18 to 22 minutes for slices).

■ **Serving ideas.** Top hot cooked chayote with melted butter seasoned with basil, thyme, marjoram, or oregano. Or add sliced sautéed mushrooms, crumbled cooked bacon, shredded Cheddar cheese, or grated Parmesan cheese. For a tasty salad, combine marinated cooked chayote with other vegetables or fruits; serve chilled.

Unusual-looking chayote is really just a summer squash. Cut into slices for cooking.

CARIBBEAN STUFFED CHAYOTES

Per serving: 360 calories, 17 g protein, 19 g carbohydrates, 25 g total fat, 59 mg cholesterol, 165 mg sodium

- 3 **large chayotes, halved lengthwise**
- 1 **tablespoon salad oil**
- ¾ **pound lean ground pork**
- ¼ **pound ground ham**
- ½ **cup finely chopped onion**
- 1 **clove garlic, minced or pressed**
- ¼ **cup raisins**
- 10 **pitted prunes, finely chopped**
- ¼ **cup tomato sauce**
- 1 **teaspoon oregano leaves**
- ½ **teaspoon vinegar**
   Salt
- 6 **tablespoons shredded Cheddar cheese**

Boil chayotes as previously directed. Set aside.

While chayotes are cooking, heat oil in a wide frying pan over medium heat; add pork, ham, onion, and garlic. Cook, stirring often, until meat is browned and onion is soft. Scoop pulp from each chayote half, leaving a ¼-inch-thick shell. Dice pulp and seed; add to meat mixture with raisins, prunes, tomato sauce, oregano, and vinegar. Season to taste with salt.

Place chayote shells in a greased shallow baking pan: evenly fill with meat mixture and top with cheese. Bake, uncovered, in a 400° oven until cheese is melted (about 10 minutes). Makes 6 servings.

Chicory *see Salad Greens, page 104*

Chiles *see Peppers, page 97*

Collards *see Greens with a Bite, page 83*

Corn

Strictly speaking, corn is not a vegetable—it's actually a grain native to the Americas. Aztecs, Mayans, Incas, and North American tribes cultivated corn (maize) for thousands of years before the Pilgrims arrived. The sweet or sugar corn we enjoy today is a mutation of Indian field corn.

Sweet corn first appeared in the mid-1800s, but the major advances in its evolution have occurred since 1920. Sweet corn differs from other types of corn in its ability to produce and retain greater quantities of sugar. Very recent research has led to the development of "sweet gene" corn hybrids, which keep their sweetness for several days. Prior to this breakthrough, sweet corn didn't stay sweet for long—the sugar began turning to starch within minutes of picking.

More than 200 varieties of sweet corn are grown in the United States today. The majority are yellow, though white corn (such as Silver Queen) is preferred in some areas. You may also find baby corn, edible cob and all.

Nutrition. Cooked sweet yellow corn on the cob has about 70 calories per small ear. It is a good source of vitamin A.

■ **Season.** May through September.

■ **Selection.** If possible, always buy and cook fresh corn on the very day it's picked. Choose fresh-looking ears with green husks, moist stems, and silk ends that are free of decay and worm injury. When pierced with a thumbnail, the kernels should give a spurt of milky juice. Tough skin indicates overmaturity.

■ **Amount.** Allow 1 large or 2 small ears per person. One small ear yields about ½ cup kernels.

■ **Storage.** Wrap unhusked ears in damp paper towels. If necessary, refrigerate in a plastic bag for up to 2 days.

■ **Preparation.** Remove and discard husk and silk; trim stem end. To cut corn from cob, stand cooked or raw ear on end and slice straight down, leaving kernel bases attached to cob. If desired, scrape cob with back of knife to remove remaining corn pulp and "milk."

■ **Cooking methods.** For more information on the cooking methods listed here, see "A Glossary of Techniques," page 122.

Boiling. In a 5-quart pan, boil 1 to 6 ears of corn, covered, in 2 to 3 quarts water until kernels are tender when pierced (3 to 5 minutes).

Grilling. *To grill corn in husks,* pull off dry outside husks; tear several into ¼-inch-wide strips to use as ties. Gently peel back inner husks, remove silk, and spread corn with oil, butter, or basting sauce. Lay inner husks back in place around corn; tie at top with husk strips. Immerse in cold water to cover for 15 to 30 minutes. Drain well. Grill for 15 to 20 minutes, turning often.

To grill corn out of husks, peel off and discard all husks and silk. Grill for about 8 minutes, turning often.

Microwaving. To microwave in the husk, peel husk back and remove silk, then replace husk to enclose kernels completely. Secure ends with string. Or wrap husked corn ears individually in plastic wrap. If microwaving only one ear, place in center of oven. Place 2 ears side by side; 3 in a triangle; 4 in a square; 5 in a line of 4 with one

at the top; and 6 in a line of 4 with one across the top and one across the bottom. Microwave on **HIGH (100%)** for 3 to 4 minutes per ear. Turn ears halfway through cooking. Let stand for 2 to 3 minutes. Kernels should be tender when pierced.

Roasting (baking). Rub husked ears with butter or margarine. Wrap each in heavy-duty foil. Roast in 375° oven until kernels are tender when pierced (about 30 minutes).

Steaming. Arrange ears on a rack. Steam until kernels are tender when pierced (8 to 10 minutes).

■ **Serving ideas.** Spread hot corn on the cob with butter and season as desired; or first season butter with chili powder, curry powder, or chopped chives; or pass lime wedges to squeeze over corn. Add cooked corn kernels to pancakes, muffins, or cornbread. Use raw corn kernels in soups, stews, and casseroles, and in stir-fries with other vegetables.

REFRIGERATOR CORN RELISH

Per ¼ cup: 56 calories, 1 g protein, 13 g carbohydrates, .45 g total fat, 0 mg cholesterol, 168 mg sodium

> 1¼ **cups distilled white vinegar**
> ¾ **cup sugar**
> 2½ **teaspoons salt**
> 1¼ **teaspoons celery seeds**
> ¾ **teaspoon mustard seeds**
> ½ **teaspoon liquid hot pepper seasoning**
> 8 **cups cooked corn kernels**
> 1 **small green bell pepper, seeded and chopped**
> 1 **jar (4 oz.) diced pimentos, drained**
> 3 **green onions (including tops), chopped**

In a 3-quart pan, combine vinegar, sugar, salt, celery seeds, mustard seeds, and hot pepper seasoning. Bring to a simmer over medium heat. Simmer, uncovered, for 5 minutes; then remove from heat and let cool.

Stir in corn, bell pepper, pimentos, and green onions. Ladle into 1-pint jars and screw on lids. Refrigerate for up to 1 month. Makes about 4 pints.

CORN & ONION SAUTÉ

Per serving: 166 calories, 4 g protein, 22 g carbohydrates, 9 g total fat, 24 mg cholesterol, 101 mg sodium

Melt ¼ cup **butter** or margarine in a wide frying pan over medium heat. Add 4 large **onions,** thinly sliced; cook, stirring occasionally, until soft

and golden (about 20 minutes). Add 3 cups **corn kernels** and cook, stirring, just until corn is hot and turns a darker gold color (3 to 5 more minutes). Season to taste with **ground nutmeg, salt,** and **white pepper.** Makes 6 to 8 servings.

OLD-FASHIONED CORN FRITTERS

Per serving: 384 calories, 8 g protein, 23 g carbohydrates, 30 g total fat, 225 mg cholesterol, 186 mg sodium

> 3 **eggs**
> 2 **cups corn kernels**
> ¼ **cup all-purpose flour**
> 1 **teaspoon sugar**
> ¼ **cup butter or margarine, melted**
>   **Salt**
> ¼ **cup salad oil**
>   **Maple syrup**

In a bowl, beat together eggs, corn, flour, sugar, and 1 tablespoon of the butter. Season to taste with salt.

Pour 1½ tablespoons of the butter and 2 tablespoons of the oil into a wide frying pan over medium-high heat. When fat is hot, drop batter into pan in 1½-tablespoon portions. Cook until bottoms are well browned and tops look slightly dry (about 3 minutes); turn over and cook until bottoms are well browned (2 to 3 more minutes). Lift from pan and keep warm. Heat remaining butter and oil in pan and cook remaining batter. Serve hot, with syrup. Makes 4 to 6 servings.

Cucumbers

"**C**ool as a cucumber" isn't just a catchy phrase—it's one figure of speech that actually has some basis in fact. A cucumber's pulp temperature may be up to 20° cooler than the outside air.

Cucumbers are about 96 percent water. Because their skin holds in moisture like a jug, these vegetables have been used to quench thirst since ancient times. They originated in India more than 3,000 years ago and were soon favored by desert inhabitants for their cool, refreshing taste.

Cucumbers are divided into three classes: the field-grown slicing or table cukes, characterized by small white

Sweet corn hybrids likely to show up in your market include yellow and white types, as well as tender, all-edible baby corn (you can even eat the cob).

spines on the skin; the much smaller pickling varieties, also field grown; and the greenhouse varieties adapted to culture under artificial heat. Long, slender, nearly seedless European or English cucumbers fall into the third category. Mild-flavored Armenian cucumbers, similar in shape to Europeans but paler in color, are grouped with slicing cucumbers, as are Japanese and Sfran (from the Persian Gulf) varieties.

In a category of their own are oval-shaped lemon cucumbers. You may find locally grown lemon cukes in your market, but they don't ship well.

Nutrition. If eaten unpeeled, cucumbers are a fair source of vitamin A. One large, unpeeled cucumber (10 to 12 oz.) has about 45 calories.

■ **Season.** All year; peak June through September.

■ **Selection.** Choose firm, dark green slicing, pickling, or greenhouse cucumbers that are slender and well shaped. Soft, yellowing cucumbers are overmature. Lemon cucumbers should be small (2 to 3 inches in diameter), with pale yellow-green skin.

■ **Amount.** Allow about half a small slicing cucumber per person.

■ **Storage.** Refrigerate whole or cut cucumbers in a plastic bag for up to 1 week.

■ **Preparation.** Cucumbers are often commercially waxed to preserve their moisture content. Peel waxed cucumbers (or those with bitter skin) with a vegetable peeler. If you're going to leave your cucumbers unpeeled, wash them well in cold water.

To seed cucumbers, cut in half lengthwise and scrape out seeds with a spoon. To use in salads or sandwiches, slice crosswise; for a decorative effect, score cucumber lengthwise with the tines of a fork before slicing.

■ **Cooking methods.** Cucumbers should be cooked briefly—just until tender-crisp to bite. (Because of their high seed content, lemon cucumbers are best served raw.)

Butter-steaming. Peel and seed cucumbers; cut crosswise into ¼-inch-thick slices. Butter-steam up to 5 cups (see page 123), using 1 to 2 tablespoons butter or margarine. Cook, stirring, for 1 minute. Add 1 tablespoon liquid, cover, and cook just until tender-crisp to bite (2 to 2½ more minutes).

Many new cucumber varieties are coming to market today. Our photo shows (from left) pickling, pale green Armenian, long, dark green English, stubby Sfran, slim Japanese, yellow lemon, and familiar market cucumbers.

■ **Serving ideas.** Top hot cooked cucumbers with melted butter seasoned with chervil, chives, dill weed, or minced parsley. Raw cucumbers are excellent sliced in salads, cut into spears and served with a dip, or used in sandwiches in place of lettuce. Cut lengthwise and seeded, they make crunchy edible containers for chicken or seafood salads.

CUCUMBER CREAM SOUP

Per serving: 139 calories, 5 g protein, 10 g carbohydrates, 9 g total fat, 25 mg cholesterol, 186 mg sodium

> 3 **medium-size cucumbers,** peeled and cut into cubes
> 1 **clove garlic,** halved
> 3 **tablespoons** *each* **chopped parsley and chopped onion**
> 1 **cup regular-strength chicken broth**
> 3 **tablespoons white wine vinegar**
> 2 **cups plain yogurt**
> 1 **cup sour cream**
> **Salt and pepper**
> **Condiments (suggestions follow)**

In a blender, combine cucumbers, garlic, parsley, onion, broth, and vinegar; whirl until well blended. Pour about half the mixture into a 1-quart container; set aside.

Add about half the yogurt and half the sour cream to cucumber mixture remaining in blender. Whirl until smooth; pour into a 3-quart bowl. Repeat with reserved cucumber mixture and remaining yogurt and sour cream. Season soup to taste with salt and pepper. Cover and refrigerate for at least 4 hours or until next day.

Stir well, then pour into small bowls. Place condiments in separate bowls; pass at the table to sprinkle over soup. Makes about 6 servings.

Condiments. Choose 3 or 4 of the following: seeded, chopped **tomatoes;** thinly sliced **green onions** (including tops); chopped **fresh mint** or parsley; crisply cooked, crumbled **bacon; sunflower seeds; seasoned croutons.**

QUICK REFRIGERATOR CUCUMBER CHIPS

Per ¼ cup: 24 calories, .26 g protein, 6 g carbohydrates, .04 g total fat, 0 mg cholesterol, 209 mg sodium

> 3 **large regular cucumbers or 2 long English or Armenian cucumbers**
> 1 **large red bell pepper,** seeded and cut into ½-inch-wide strips
> 1 **medium-size onion, thinly sliced**
> 1 **tablespoon salt**
> 2 **teaspoons dill seeds**
> ¾ **cup sugar**
> ½ **cup white wine vinegar**

Wash cucumbers well, but do not peel. Cut off and discard ends; cut cucumbers crosswise into ¼-inch-thick slices. You should have about 6 cups. In a large bowl, combine cucumbers, bell pepper, and onion. Sprinkle in salt and dill seeds; stir well. Let stand, uncovered, for 1 to 2 hours; stir occasionally.

Stir together sugar and vinegar until sugar is dissolved, then pour over vegetables and mix gently. Spoon into glass or ceramic containers. Cover and refrigerate for at least 1 day or up to 3 weeks. Makes about 2 quarts.

■ *See also **Cucumber & Radish Salad** (page 103).*

Daikon *see Radishes, page 102*

Dandelions *see Greens with a Bite, page 83*

Eggplant

Eggplant belongs to the night-shade family, along with tomatoes, potatoes—and some poisonous plants. Perhaps because of this family tie, eggplant was called "mad apple" when it was first introduced into northern Europe; botanists of the region believed that eating the vegetable caused insanity.

Today, eggplant is found in many cuisines. Its subtle flavor and meaty texture make it especially versatile in cooking; it absorbs the flavor of whatever it's cooked with, while adding a creamy bulkiness.

As shown in the photograph on page 80, eggplant may be white, purple, purple-black, green, orange, or even striped. The dark purple, egg-shaped to nearly globular type is the most common in U.S. markets, but smaller and elongated varieties are more familiar in many countries—and becoming increasingly available here, as well.

In general, the long Oriental kinds have smoother flesh, fewer and smaller seeds, and thinner skin. Under the skin, however, most varieties are pretty much alike—interchangeable in many recipes. Exceptions are tiny green Thai bunch eggplants, which add crunch to certain Asian dishes, and a bitter orange Thai eggplant used in sweet-sour dishes (Thai eggplants are sold mainly in Asian markets). Among the other varieties shown in the photograph, Easter Egg is tough skinned and somewhat bitter, but other egg-shaped varieties have creamy texture and fine flavor.

Nutrition. Eggplant is not especially rich in any one vitamin or mineral. A 1-cup portion of cooked eggplant has about 38 calories.

■ **Season.** All year; peak July through October.

■ **Selection.** Look for firm eggplant that's heavy for its size, with taut, glossy, deeply colored skin. The stem should be bright green. Dull skin and rust-colored spots are signs of old age.

■ **Amount.** Allow about ⅓ pound per person. One large eggplant (about 1½ lbs.) serves 4.

■ **Storage.** Refrigerate, unwashed, in a plastic bag for up to 5 days.

■ **Preparation.** Rinse and pat dry. Cut off and discard stem end; peel, if desired. Cut into cubes or ½-inch-thick slices. Halve or slice miniature eggplants lengthwise.

To reduce the amount of oil absorbed by eggplant during cooking, sprinkle cut sides of raw eggplant with salt and let drain in a colander for 30 minutes. Then rinse and pat dry with paper towels.

■ **Cooking methods.** Miniature eggplants can be cooked by the same methods as regular eggplants, though you'll probably need to cut them differently and, in recipes, make some adjustments in amounts. For more information on the cooking methods listed here, see "A Glossary of Techniques," page 122.

Baking. Cut eggplant into ½-inch-thick slices; brush all sides with salad oil. Arrange in a single layer in a shallow baking pan. Bake, uncovered, in a 450° oven until well browned and soft when pierced (20 to 30 minutes).

Grilling. Use miniature or small regular eggplants. Cut off stem end, then cut miniature eggplants in half lengthwise or regular eggplants in 1½-inch-thick wedges. Grill until streaked with brown and tender when pierced (12 to 15 minutes).

Pan-frying. Prepare 1 to 1¼ pounds eggplant, cutting it into ½-inch-thick slices and salting it as previously directed. Heat 2 tablespoons salad oil in a wide frying pan over medium-high heat. Add a single layer of eggplant, without crowding; cook, turning as needed, until browned on both sides and soft throughout when pierced (8 to 10 minutes). Add oil as needed until all eggplant is cooked. Lower heat to medium if eggplant browns too quickly.

■ **Serving ideas.** Top hot cooked eggplant with garlic butter, basil, oregano, marjoram, or minced parsley. Top baked slices with sliced tomato and shredded Cheddar cheese; return to oven until cheese is melted. Sauté cubed eggplant in olive oil with garlic, onions, and mushrooms until soft. Spoon sautéed eggplant into pocket bread and top with shredded jack or Cheddar cheese and sliced ripe olives. Add raw or sautéed cubes to soups or stews.

EGGPLANT WITH SESAME SAUCE

Per serving: 323 calories, 4 g protein, 16 g carbohydrates, 29 g total fat, 0 mg cholesterol, 1336 mg sodium

> ¼ **cup** *each* **regular-strength chicken broth and soy sauce**
> ½ **teaspoon grated fresh ginger**
> 1 **tablespoon toasted sesame seeds**
> 8 **Japanese-type eggplants,** *each* **about 6 inches long Salad oil**

In a small bowl, stir together broth, soy, ginger, and toasted sesame seeds. Set aside.

Trim and discard ends from eggplant; rinse and pat dry. Cut 4 equidistant slashes, about ⅓ inch deep, lengthwise to within about ½ inch of each end.

Pour oil into a wide frying pan to a depth of about ¾ inch. Heat over medium-high heat to 350°F on a deep-frying thermometer. Slip several eggplant at a time into oil and cook, turning occasionally, until soft when pressed (about 4 minutes). Lift out, drain, and keep warm until all are cooked.

Arrange eggplant on a platter. Pass sesame sauce to spoon over individual servings. Makes 4 servings.

ROASTED EGGPLANT SOUP

Per serving: 62 calories, 5 g protein, 12 g carbohydrates, .40 g total fat, 11 mg cholesterol, 548 mg sodium

> 1 **large eggplant (about 1½ lbs.)**
> 1 **small onion**
> 3 **cups regular-strength chicken broth**
> 2 **tablespoons lemon juice Salt and pepper Finely chopped parsley**
> 12 **thin red bell pepper strips**

Pierce unpeeled eggplant in several places with a fork, then place with unpeeled onion in a shallow baking

French,
Ronde de Valence

Casper

Chinese, white

Puerto Rican, Rayada

Commercial
varieties,
globe-shaped

Asian, bitter orange

Thai, round, pale green and white

Italian,
Rosa Bianco

Japanese,
mature and
immature sizes

Green
egg-shaped

Easter Egg

Thai, round, purple

Thai,
round,
green-streaked

White Egg

Italian, small
globe-shaped

Thai, round,
white (turtle egg

Applegreen

Thai, green,
bunch

...Eggplant continued

pan. Bake in a 400° oven until vegetables are very soft when squeezed (about 1¼ hours). Let cool, then peel. Whirl eggplant and onion in a food processor or blender until puréed.

In a 2- to 3-quart pan, combine purée and broth; mix well. Bring to a boil over medium heat; add lemon juice. Season to taste with salt and pepper. Pour into 4 individual bowls; garnish each serving with parsley and 3 bell pepper strips. Makes 4 servings.

BAKED MARINATED EGGPLANT

Per serving: 152 calories, 3 g protein, 11 g carbohydrates, 11 g total fat, 3 mg cholesterol, 139 mg sodium

- 2 small eggplants (about 1 lb. *each*), cut into 1-inch cubes
- 1 can (about 1 lb.) pear-shaped tomatoes, drained
- 3 slices bacon
- ¼ cup minced onion
- 2 cloves garlic, minced or pressed
- 1 teaspoon chopped fresh rosemary or ¾ teaspoon dry rosemary
- ¼ teaspoon black pepper
- ⅛ teaspoon ground red pepper (cayenne)
- ¼ cup *each* red wine vinegar and olive oil
- Lettuce leaves (optional)

Place eggplant in a shallow 2½- to 3-quart casserole. Cut tomatoes in half crosswise; cut bacon into ½-inch pieces. Add tomatoes and bacon to eggplant along with onion, garlic, rosemary, black pepper, red pepper, vinegar, and oil. Stir well.

Bake, uncovered, in a 350° oven for 30 minutes. Stir well; then continue to bake, uncovered, until eggplant mashes easily (20 to 25 more minutes).

Serve hot, with barbecued meats; or cover and refrigerate for up to 3 days and serve cold on lettuce leaves as a salad or appetizer. Makes 6 servings.

Endive *see Salad Greens, page 104*

Escarole *see Salad Greens, page 104*

The 18 varieties of eggplant at left are only a sampling of hundreds of types grown around the world. Look for the less common ones in Asian and farmers' markets.

Fennel

Also called Florence fennel and finocchio, fennel has been a Mediterranean favorite since the time of the ancient Romans. Though planted in California as early as the 1800s, it has only recently become readily available in American markets.

A fennel plant looks like a flattened bunch of celery with a large, white, bulbous base and feathery green leaves. The raw bulb is crunchy and celery-like in texture; both bulb and leaves have a slightly sweet, licorice-like taste. The licorice flavor is pronounced in raw fennel bulbs, milder when the vegetable is cooked.

Nutrition. Fennel is rich in vitamin A, calcium, and potassium. A 3½-ounce portion has only 28 calories.

■ **Season.** October through April.

■ **Selection.** Look for firm, white bulbs with rigid, crisp stalks and feathery, bright green leaves.

■ **Amount.** Allow about half of a 4-inch bulb per serving.

■ **Storage.** Refrigerate, unwashed, in a plastic bag for up to 1 week.

■ **Preparation.** Rinse thoroughly. Trim stalks to within ¾ to 1 inch of bulb; discard hard outside stalks and reserve leaves for seasoning and garnish. Cut away and discard bulb base. Cut bulb lengthwise into halves or quarters, cut into julienne strips or crosswise slices, or dice.

■ **Cooking methods.** For more information on the cooking methods listed here, see "A Glossary of Techniques," page 122.

Boiling. Cut fennel bulbs in half lengthwise. In a wide frying pan, boil 4 to 6 fennel halves, covered, in ½ inch water until tender when pierced (8 to 10 minutes).

Butter-steaming. Cut crosswise into ¼-inch-thick slices. Butter-steam up to 5 cups, using 1 to 2 tablespoons butter or margarine. Cook, stirring, until just tender-crisp to bite (2 to 3 minutes).

Grilling. Cut each fennel bulb lengthwise into 4 equal slices. Grill until streaked with brown and tender when pierced (about 20 minutes).

To prepare fennel bulbs, trim off stalks and bulb base. Then cut lengthwise into halves or quarters, dice, slice, or cut into julienne strips.

Steaming. Cut fennel bulbs in half lengthwise; arrange on a rack. Steam until tender when pierced (18 to 22 minutes).

■ **Serving ideas.** Top hot cooked fennel with butter, a little whipping cream, or Parmesan cheese; or sprinkle with shredded Swiss cheese and grated orange peel. Garnish with fennel leaves. Serve raw fennel as a dipper for melted butter seasoned with anchovies or garlic, or add thinly sliced fennel to green salads.

FENNEL SALAD VINAIGRETTE

Per serving: 304 calories, 4 g protein, 1 g carbohydrates, 32 g total fat, 15 mg cholesterol, 118 mg sodium

- 2 or 3 fennel bulbs
- ½ cup olive oil
- 2 tablespoons *each* lemon juice and white wine vinegar
- Salt and pepper
- Lettuce leaves
- About ½ cup crumbled blue-veined cheese

Prepare fennel as previously directed; reserve feathery leaves, covered, in refrigerator. Cut bulbs in half lengthwise, then thinly slice crosswise. In a bowl, combine oil, lemon juice, and vinegar. Stir in fennel and season to

...Fennel continued

taste with salt and pepper. Cover and refrigerate for at least 8 hours or until next day.

To serve, line 4 plates with lettuce; mound fennel mixture on top. Chop enough fennel leaves to make ½ cup, and sprinkle each serving with about 2 tablespoons of the chopped leaves and 2 tablespoons of the cheese. Makes 4 servings.

GLAZED FENNEL & ONIONS

Per serving: 144 calories, .67 g protein, 2 g carbohydrates, 15 g total fat, 48 mg cholesterol, 224 mg sodium

2 pounds fennel bulbs
⅓ cup butter, margarine, or olive oil
1 medium-size onion, sliced
3 tablespoons regular-strength beef broth
Salt

Prepare fennel as previously directed, reserving feathery leaves. Thinly slice fennel crosswise.

Melt butter in a 5- to 6-quart pan over medium-low heat. Add fennel and onion; cover and cook until vegetables are soft (about 15 minutes). Uncover; continue to cook, stirring occasionally, until juices have evaporated and vegetables are golden (about 40 more minutes). Add broth and cook, stirring, until vegetables are evenly moist. Season to taste with salt. Chop fennel leaves; sprinkle over fennel-onion mixture. Makes 4 servings.

Garlic

The virtues credited to garlic go far beyond its culinary value. Garlic has been cultivated in almost every part of the world for centuries and is reputed to do everything from warding off evil spirits to curing a variety of ailments. The ancient Egyptians forced their slaves to eat garlic to give them strength, the Romans believed it gave soldiers courage, and the Greeks fed it to convicted criminals as a soul-cleansing agent. (*Photo on page 88.*)

In fact, there's good evidence that garlic does possess certain medicinal properties. The Food and Drug Research Laboratories in New York issued this statement in 1959: "For some time, it has been known that compounds derived from garlic have a pronounced bactericidal effect, which has been attributed to their reactivity for sulfhydryl groups essential for the action of enzymes." In other words, garlic actually does seem to have a healing effect.

Garlic's personality changes dramatically depending on how it's treated. Whole raw garlic is relatively mild; when minced or chopped, it's somewhat stronger. When the cloves are mashed or pressed, even more of the potent juices are released.

Upon cooking, though, the harshness of raw garlic in any form is softened considerably. Heat brings out the mellow, sweet side of garlic; and when roasted whole, the cloves become deliciously soft and spreadable.

Besides the familiar white- or purple-skinned garlic found in most markets, you may come across giant-size elephant garlic. This type is much milder in flavor than regular garlic but can be used in the same ways.

Nutrition. Garlic is about 75 percent water and contains just 4 calories per average-size clove. It has very small amounts of most vitamins and minerals.

■ **Season.** All year; heaviest supply July through September.

■ **Selection.** Choose firm, dry heads with tightly closed cloves and smooth skin. Avoid garlic with sprouting green shoots.

■ **Amount.** For roasted garlic, allow about ¼ large head of regular garlic per person. To use garlic as a seasoning, let your taste buds be your guide—the taste for garlic is a highly individual matter.

■ **Storage.** Store, unwrapped, in a cool (50°F), dry, dark place with good ventilation for 2 to 3 months. Some cooks like to store peeled cloves in oil, then use either the oil or the garlic for flavoring; replenish the oil to keep the jar full and cloves submerged.

■ **Preparation.** To peel individual cloves, cut off root ends and crush cloves with side of a heavy knife blade; then pull skin away. Mince or press through a garlic press to use as a seasoning.

■ **Cooking methods.** Be careful when sautéing garlic as a seasoning, since it quickly scorches and turns bitter.

Roasting. Place large, whole, unpeeled heads in a greased baking dish. Roast, uncovered, in a 325° oven until tender when pierced (about 1 hour). Let cool slightly before serving. To eat, pluck off individual cloves and squeeze the contents over meats, vegetables, crackers, or bread.

■ **Serving ideas.** Sauté minced or pressed garlic in olive oil, salad oil, butter, or margarine to use as a seasoning for soups, stews, meat mixtures, and sauces. Or simply add sautéed garlic to butter to spread on breads or to enhance cooked vegetables. Rub peeled, cut raw cloves over roasts and poultry before cooking; rub them over the inside of your salad bowl before adding greens.

GARLIC SOUP

Per serving: 215 calories, 5 g protein, 23 g carbohydrates, 12 g total fat, 42 mg cholesterol, 1138 mg sodium

¼ cup butter or margarine
2 large onions, coarsely chopped
1 large carrot, sliced
1 small thin-skinned potato, cubed
10 to 14 cloves garlic, peeled
4 cups water
4 chicken bouillon cubes
½ cup milk
2 tablespoons cornstarch
Condiments (suggestions follow)

Melt butter in a 3- to 4-quart pan over medium heat. Add onions and carrot; cook, stirring often, until onions are soft. Stir in potato and 10 cloves of the garlic. Cook, stirring, until garlic begins to soften (don't let it brown)—about 5 minutes. Add water and bouillon cubes and bring to a boil; then reduce heat, cover, and simmer, stirring occasionally, until potato is tender when pierced (about 20 more minutes).

Meanwhile, in a small bowl, blend milk and cornstarch until smooth. Stir into soup and bring to a boil; boil, stirring, until thickened.

Whirl soup, a portion at a time, in a blender until smooth. Return to pan. Bring to a simmer over medium heat. If you're a garlic fan, mince or press up to 4 more cloves garlic and stir into soup. Ladle into individual bowls.

Place condiments in separate small bowls and pass at the table to sprinkle over soup. Makes 4 to 6 servings.

Condiments. Choose 2 or 3 of the following: **seasoned croutons;** grated **Parmesan cheese;** thinly sliced **green onions** (including tops); **sour cream;** crisply cooked, crumbled **bacon.**

GARLIC PICKLES

Per tablespoon: 14 calories, .25 g protein, 4 g carbohydrates, 0 g total fat, 0 mg cholesterol, 23 mg sodium

    3 cups large garlic cloves,
      peeled
 1½ cups distilled white
      vinegar
    ½ cup sugar
    ½ teaspoon salt

Cut any garlic cloves thicker than ¾ inch in half lengthwise. In a 3-quart pan, combine vinegar, sugar, and salt. Bring to a boil over high heat, stirring until sugar is dissolved. Drop in garlic; cook, uncovered, stirring several times, for 1 minute. Remove from heat and let cool. Pour into jars, cover tightly, and refrigerate for at least 1 day or up to 2 months. Serve as a condiment with cold meats and cheeses; or use in salads. Makes about 3 cups.

Greens with a Bite

Low in calories and loaded with vitamins and minerals, the dark leafy vegetables we refer to as "greens with a bite" range from earthy to peppery in flavor. Though we group these greens together because of their texture, pronounced flavor, and general uses, they actually come from several vegetable families. Some are cabbage-like, while others are simply the tops of root vegetables such as beets and turnips. (For the more tender, milder flavored greens and lettuces, see "Salad Greens," page 104; see also individual listings for bok choy, cabbage, sorrel, spinach, and Swiss chard.)

In general, these tart greens are cooked before eating. But immature, very tender home-grown greens are an exception to the rule; these can be eaten raw, as a spirited addition to tossed salads.

Nutrition. Most of the tart greens are excellent sources of calcium and vitamins A and C, as well as being low in calories. See individual listings for specifics.

■ **Greens choices.** Here we discuss six of the greens you're most likely to find in produce markets.

Beet greens. Sold still attached to the beets or cut and bunched, these have an earthy flavor and provide plenty of vitamin A and potassium. A 3½-ounce portion of the cooked greens contains 18 calories.

Collards. Collards are full-bodied in flavor, yet somewhat milder than either mustard or turnip greens. Their large, smooth leaves are high in vitamins A and C, calcium, and potassium. A 3½-ounce cooked portion has about 30 calories.

Dandelion greens. Long, slender leaves with an authoritative, slightly bitter taste, these are high in vitamins A and C, iron, calcium, and potassium. A 3½-ounce portion contains about 33 calories.

Kale. Kale has a sprightly flavor and beautiful, curly leaves—and, unlike other greens, it holds its texture when cooked. It's high in calcium, phosphorus, potassium, iron, and vitamins A and C. A 3½-ounce cooked portion has 39 calories.

Mustard greens. You'll find regular as well as Oriental or Chinese mustard greens in many supermarkets. Regular mustard greens pack a strong bite; the Oriental greens are milder but still have a pleasant pungency. In general, the Oriental type has much larger, rounder leaves.

All mustard greens are high in vitamins A and C, calcium, phosphorus, and potassium. A 3½-ounce cooked portion contains 23 calories.

Turnip greens. Noted for their bite, turnip greens are high in calcium and vitamins A and C. A 3½-ounce cooked portion provides 20 calories.

■ **Season.** January through April for collards, dandelion greens, kale, and mustard greens; June through October for beet greens; October through March for turnip greens.

■ **Selection.** Look for fresh, tender, deep green leaves that are free of blemishes. Avoid bunches with thick, coarse-veined leaves.

■ **Amount.** Allow about ½ pound per person. (Remember that greens cook down to ¼ to ⅛ of their original volume, depending on type.)

■ **Storage.** Remove and discard damaged, yellowed, or wilted leaves. Rinse greens well under cold running water, shake off excess water, and pat dry. Wrap in paper towels and refrigerate in a plastic bag. Use as soon as possible—leafy greens toughen as they age. If necessary, store beet and turnip greens for up to 2 days, collards, dandelion greens, kale, and mustard greens for up to 4 days.

■ **Preparation.** Tear out and discard tough stems and center ribs. Use leaves whole; or cut or tear into bite-size pieces, or shred.

■ **Cooking methods.** Boil collards, kale, mustard greens, and turnip greens; microwave collards, kale, and mustard greens; butter-steam beet and turnip greens. Dandelion greens are best served raw. For more information on the cooking methods listed here, see "A Glossary of Techniques," page 122.

Boiling. Coarsely chop or shred collards, kale, mustard greens, or turnip greens. In a 4- to 5-quart pan, boil about 1¼ pounds greens, covered, in 1 inch water until tender to bite (5 to 15 minutes). Drain.

Butter-steaming. Coarsely chop or shred beet or turnip greens. Butter-steam up to 5 cups, using 2 tablespoons butter or margarine. Cook, stirring, for 1 minute. Add 1 to 2 tablespoons liquid, cover, and cook until greens are just tender to bite (2 to 5 more minutes).

Microwaving. Rinse and coarsely chop collards, kale, or mustard greens. Place 1¼ pounds (with water that clings to leaves) in a 3-quart nonmetallic baking dish. Cover. Microwave on **HIGH (100%)** for 7 to 10 minutes, stirring after 3 minutes. Let stand, covered, for 2 minutes. Greens should be just tender to bite.

■ **Serving ideas.** Season hot cooked greens with butter, oregano, lemon juice, wine vinegar, or crisply cooked and crumbled bacon. Cook greens Southern-style, with salt pork or

Mustard greens

Kale

Beet greens

Dandelion greens

Collards

Turnip greens

To soften the earthy to peppery flavor of some greens, cut or tear into bite-size pieces, then sauté in butter or olive oil, add water, and cook as directed for butter-steaming. Use dandelion greens raw in salads.

smoked ham hocks. Add greens to soups and stews; top cooked greens with poached eggs for a light brunch or supper entrée; or add cooked greens to an omelet or frittata. Try tossing raw dandelion or other very young greens with a bacon and vinegar dressing.

BEETS & PEARS WITH DANDELION GREENS

Per serving: 244 calories, 3 g protein, 16 g carbohydrates, 20 g total fat, 0 mg cholesterol, 109 mg sodium

    Mustard Vinaigrette (recipe follows)
1 **medium-size pear**
3 **cups slivered dandelion greens**
2 **medium-size beets, cooked, peeled, and cut into ⅛-inch julienne strips**
1 **to 2 tablespoons finely chopped walnuts**

Prepare Mustard Vinaigrette; set aside. Peel and core pear; cut into ⅛-inch julienne strips and immediately mix with vinaigrette to prevent darkening.

Arrange dandelion greens evenly on 4 salad plates. Make 2 or 3 alternating layers of beets and pears on each plate; drizzle with any remaining vinaigrette, then sprinkle with walnuts. Makes 4 servings.

Mustard Vinaigrette. Stir together 2 teaspoons *each* **Dijon mustard** and finely chopped **mild red onion,** 2 tablespoons **distilled white vinegar,** and ⅓ cup **salad oil.**

WILTED GREENS

Per serving: 446 calories, 11 g protein, 37 g carbohydrates, 29 g total fat, 13 mg cholesterol, 282 mg sodium

¼ **cup *each* salad oil and wine vinegar**
2 **teaspoons Dijon mustard**
4 **small thin-skinned potatoes, cooked, peeled, and sliced**
    Garlic Croutons (recipe follows)
8 **slices bacon, cut into ½-inch pieces**
5 **cups mustard or turnip greens, cut into bite-size pieces**
    Salt and pepper

Stir together oil, vinegar, and mustard. Mix half the dressing with potatoes; cover and refrigerate for 2 to 4 hours. Meanwhile, prepare croutons; set aside.

Shortly before serving, cook bacon in a wide frying pan over medium heat until crisp. While bacon is cooking, combine greens and potatoes in a salad bowl. Lift out bacon; add to salad. Discard all but 3 tablespoons drippings; add remaining dressing to drippings and bring to a boil. Pour hot dressing over salad, inverting pan over greens for a few seconds to wilt greens. Season to taste with salt and pepper; add croutons and mix well. Makes 4 servings.

Garlic Croutons. In a wide frying pan, combine 2 tablespoons **olive oil**, 2 cloves **garlic** (minced or pressed), and 1½ cups **French bread cubes.** Cook over medium-low to medium heat, stirring often, until bread is toasted (about 10 minutes).

STUFFED BEET LEAVES

Per serving: 286 calories, 30 g protein, 21 g carbohydrates, 9 g total fat, 84 mg cholesterol, 932 mg sodium

- About 25 medium-size to large beet leaves, *each* 4 to 5 inches long
- 1 pound lean ground beef
- 1 medium-size onion, chopped
- 1 cup cooked white or brown rice
- 1 tablespoon finely chopped fresh dill or 1½ teaspoons dry dill weed
- 3 cups regular-strength chicken broth
- 2 cloves garlic, minced or pressed
- 1 teaspoon lemon juice
- Plain yogurt

Cut off and discard stems from beet leaves. Rinse leaves well, then pour boiling water over them to cover. Let stand until limp (3 to 5 minutes). Drain well.

Combine beef, onion, rice, and dill. Shape meat mixture into about 25 logs, each about 1½ inches long and ¾ inch in diameter. Place each log on stem end of a beet leaf. Fold stem end of leaf over meat, then fold in sides and roll to enclose. Arrange, seam side down, in a wide frying pan. Add broth, garlic, and lemon juice. Bring to a boil over high heat. Reduce heat, cover, and simmer until meat is no longer pink in center; cut to test (about 20 minutes).

With a slotted spoon, lift stuffed leaves to a platter. Reserve broth for soup, if desired. Offer yogurt to spoon onto individual portions. Makes 4 to 6 servings.

■ *See also* **Minestrone** *(page 62),* **Turnips with Mustard Greens** *(page 121).*

Jerusalem Artichokes
see Sunchokes, page 115

Jicama

Jicama (HEE-cah-mah) is a popular Mexican root vegetable that looks like a giant-size brown turnip—one tuber weighs from 1 to 6 pounds. Underneath its thick-skinned, almost ugly exterior, you'll find crisp, slightly sweet white flesh that resembles water chestnuts in texture and flavor. In fact, Asian cooks often use jicama as an economical substitute for water chestnuts in stir-fry dishes. *(Photo on page 56.)*

Nutrition. Jicama is high in potassium and a fair source of vitamin C. One cup of shredded raw jicama contains about 50 calories.

■ **Season.** All year; peak October through June.

■ **Selection.** Choose firm, well-formed tubers, free of blemishes. Size usually doesn't affect flavor, but larger roots do tend to be coarser in texture.

■ **Amount.** Depends on use. For appetizers and salads, allow about ¼ pound per person.

■ **Storage.** Store whole jicama, unwashed, in a cool (50°F), dark, dry place for up to 3 weeks. Wrap cut pieces in plastic wrap and refrigerate for up to 1 week.

■ **Preparation.** Scrub well and peel with a knife. Slice, dice, cut into julienne strips, or shred. To keep peeled or cut surfaces of raw jicama white, submerge in a bowl of acidulated water (3 tablespoons vinegar or lemon juice per quart water).

■ **Cooking methods.** Jicama is frequently cooked in combination with other foods, though it isn't generally served alone as a cooked vegetable. Cooked jicama becomes mellower and sweeter in flavor, yet it retains its distinctive crunch.

■ **Serving ideas.** Offer peeled, thinly sliced raw jicama, drizzled with lime juice and sprinkled with chili-seasoned salt, for a crunchy appetizer. Add diced raw jicama to seafood, poultry, mixed green, or orange and onion salads. Combine diced or julienne-cut jicama with other similarly cut vegetables in a stir-fry dish.

JICAMA WITH FRIED POTATOES

Per serving: 254 calories, 3 g protein, 23 g carbohydrates, 17 g total fat, 54 mg cholesterol, 217 mg sodium

- 2 large russet potatoes (about 1 lb. *total*)
- 1 pound jicama
- 6 tablespoons butter or margarine
- 1 large onion, thinly sliced and separated into rings
- Salt and pepper
- ½ cup thinly sliced green onions (including tops)

Peel potatoes and cut into ¼-inch-thick slices. Peel jicama and cut into ¼-inch-thick, 1½-inch-square slices; you should have about 3 cups.

Melt butter in a wide frying pan over medium heat. Add potatoes, onion rings, and jicama. Cook, turning as needed with a wide spatula, until potatoes are tender and golden (25 to 30 minutes). Season to taste with salt and pepper, then stir in green onions. Makes about 4 servings.

JICAMA TABBOULEH

Per appetizer serving: 115 calories, 1 g protein, 10 g carbohydrates, 8 g total fat, .22 mg cholesterol, 63 mg sodium

- 1 cup bulgur
- 2 cups boiling water
- 2 teaspoons beef bouillon granules
- Mint Dressing (page 86)
- 3 cups peeled, shredded jicama
- 1 cup chopped mild red onion
- 2 large carrots, shredded
- ½ cup chopped celery
- Salt
- Romaine lettuce leaves

In a large bowl, combine bulgur, boiling water, and bouillon granules; mix and let stand until water is absorbed (about 1 hour). Place in a fine wire strainer to drain. Meanwhile, prepare Mint Dressing and set aside.

Mix bulgur, jicama, onion, carrots, celery, and dressing. Season to taste with salt. Mound salad on a platter.

Continued on next page

…Jicama continued

Arrange lettuce around tabbouleh. To eat as an appetizer, spoon onto lettuce leaves; to eat as a salad, eat alongside lettuce.

Makes 18 appetizer servings or 10 side-dish servings.

Mint Dressing. Stir together ⅔ cup **salad oil**, ⅓ cup **white wine vinegar**, ⅓ cup *each* chopped **fresh mint** and chopped **parsley**, and 2 cloves **garlic,** minced or pressed.

■ *See also* **Pea-Jicama Salad** *(page 96),* **Sweet Potato & Ginger Salad** *(page 117).*

Kale *see Greens with a Bite, page 83*

Kohlrabi

Kohlrabi doesn't look like a culinary treat, but this homely vegetable is well worth discovering. A native of northern Europe, it's a member of the cabbage family but has a delicate, turnip-like flavor—in fact, the name means "cabbage turnip" in German.

Though kohlrabi looks like a root vegetable, the bulb-shaped section is actually a swollen stem (the base of the leaf stalks), formed above the ground.

The true root extends from below the "bulb" down into the soil. Leaves and stems, including the bulb, are all good to eat.

Nutrition. Kohlrabi is a fair source of calcium, phosphorus, potassium, and vitamin C. It is also low in calories, providing about 40 per cup (uncooked).

■ **Season.** June through October.

■ **Selection.** Choose young, tender bulbs with fresh, green leaves; avoid those with scars and blemishes. The smaller the bulb, the more delicate the flavor and texture.

■ **Amount.** Allow 1 small to medium-size bulb per person.

PRODUCE EXOTICA

New fruits and vegetables keep showing up in U.S. markets, and what's exotic today may become common tomorrow. The American consumer's increased willingness to try new foods—and to pay premium prices for them—has encouraged importers and growers to make many more types of produce available. Recent Asian and Hispanic immigrants have also had a strong influence, since their native cuisines use many of these "exotics."

Depending on where you live, you may find some of the following foods in local produce markets or ethnic food stores.

Bitter melon, winter melon. Despite their names, these two vegetables are really squashes, not melons. Both are used in a variety of Asian dishes. Bitter melon looks like a bumpy cucumber and has a sour-bland squash flavor. Mild-tasting winter melon looks like a big green melon with a waxy white coating.

Breadfruit, jackfruit. A good-sized yellow-green fruit (5 lbs. or more), breadfruit is cooked as a starchy vegetable in parts of the Caribbean, many Pacific islands, and Brazil. Jackfruit is a close relative; it's bigger and covered with fleshy spikes.

Burdock (gobo). A long, thin, brownish root, burdock is widely used in Japanese cooking as an earthy-sweet flavor accent.

Cactus pads (nopales). The big, round pads of the prickly pear cactus, or *nopal*, are utilized in Mexican

One of the strangest-looking of the new exotic fruits, the kiwano has seedy, cucumber-flavored flesh.

cooking. Once they've been despined, peeled, and cooked, they offer a crisp texture and fresh flavor something like green beans. The prickly pear's tart-sweet fruit is good to eat, too; see page 52.

Cardoon. This thistlelike artichoke relative is favored in parts of southern Europe for its mild-flavored stalk and midrib. Cardoon resembles an extra-large celery head.

Fiddlehead ferns. These tightly coiled, bright green baby ferns have come into favor as a cooked vegetable or a decorative garnish.

Kiwano. One of the newest New Zealand creations, the kiwano is a spiky golden cucumber-melon cross with bright green flesh and a mild flavor.

Lotus root. A pattern of holes inside the lotus root gives it the look of a flower when cut in cross-section. Lotus root is used in Asian cooking.

Loquat. The bright golden Chinese loquat looks like an elongated apricot. It's a small, fragile fruit with acid-sweet flesh and three or four pits.

Taro. In many parts of the tropics, this starchy root is as important a staple as the potato is in other areas of the world. The flesh of some varieties turns from white or grayish to bright purple when cooked.

Ugli fruit. A Jamaica native, this citrus fruit looks like a greenish yellow, loose-skinned grapefruit. It's tart-sweet and juicy.

Water chestnut. Familiar to almost everyone in canned form, the crunchy and mildly sweet water chestnut may also be found fresh in markets catering largely to an Asian clientele.

Red or green kohlrabi are hollowed out to fill with a savory pork and veal stuffing for entrée (recipe below).

■ **Storage.** Cut off leaves and stems; reserve for seasoning soups or cooked kohlrabi bulbs, if desired. Refrigerate kohlrabi, unwashed, in a plastic bag for up to 1 week.

■ **Preparation.** Scrub well. Peel if bulbs are to be sliced or diced before cooking.

■ **Cooking methods.** For more information on the cooking methods listed here, see "A Glossary of Techniques," page 122.

Boiling. In a 3-quart pan, boil 4 medium-size whole, unpeeled kohlrabi, covered, in 1 inch water until tender when pierced (30 to 40 minutes). Drain.

Peel and slice 4 medium-size kohlrabi and place in a wide frying pan; boil, covered, in ½ inch water for 12 to 25 minutes. Drain.

Butter-steaming. Cut kohlrabi into ⅛-inch-thick slices. Butter-steam up to 5 cups, using 2 to 3 tablespoons butter or margarine. Cook, stirring, for 1 minute. Add 7 tablespoons liquid, cover, and cook until just tender-crisp to bite (6 to 8 more minutes).

Steaming. Place 4 medium-size whole, unpeeled kohlrabi on a rack. Steam until tender when pierced (45 to 50 minutes).

■ **Serving ideas.** Serve sliced small raw kohlrabi with a dip for an appetizer, or without the dip for a low-calorie snack. Add diced raw kohlrabi to stews and hearty soups during the last 20 to 30 minutes of cooking; or stir-fry it with other vegetables and meats. Shredded and mixed with your favorite dressing, kohlrabi makes an unusual crunchy salad.

MEAT-STUFFED KOHLRABI

Per serving: 455 calories, 27 g protein, 18 g carbohydrates, 31 g total fat, 158 mg cholesterol, 953 mg sodium

  6 to 8 kohlrabi, *each* 2½ to 3
    inches in diameter, with
    leaves and stems attached
  1 tablespoon salad oil
  1 small onion, chopped
  2 cloves garlic, minced or
    pressed
  ½ pound *each* ground veal
    and lean ground pork
  3 tablespoons fine dry bread
    crumbs
  1 egg
  ½ teaspoon salt
    Dash of pepper
  ⅛ teaspoon ground mace
  2 chicken bouillon cubes
  1½ cups boiling water
    Milk
  2 tablespoons butter or
    margarine
  2 tablespoons all-purpose
    flour

Cut kohlrabi leaves and stems from bulbs. Chop enough tender inner leaves to make 1 cup; discard stems and remaining leaves. Peel bulbs. Then, using a spoon and a small, sharp knife, scrape out center of each, leaving a ¼-inch-thick shell. Chop flesh, combine with leaves, and set aside.

Heat oil in a wide frying pan over medium heat. Add onion and garlic and cook, stirring, until onion is soft; transfer to a bowl and mix in veal, pork, bread crumbs, egg, salt, pepper, and mace. Fill kohlrabi shells with meat mixture and place in frying pan; scatter chopped leaves and flesh around filled shells. Dissolve bouillon cubes in boiling water and pour into pan. Bring to a boil over high heat; then reduce heat, cover, and simmer until kohlrabi shells are tender when pierced (about 50 minutes).

Transfer kohlrabi shells to a platter; keep warm. Strain pan liquid; discard leaves and flesh. Add enough milk to strained liquid to make 1¼ cups; set aside. Wipe frying pan clean, then add butter and melt over medium heat. Add flour and cook, stirring, until bubbly. Gradually stir in milk mixture; cook, stirring constantly, until sauce boils and thickens. Spoon over kohlrabi. Makes 3 or 4 servings.

BUTTER-STEAMED KOHLRABI & MUSHROOMS

Per serving: 123 calories, 4 g protein, 9 g carbohydrates, 9 g total fat, 27 mg cholesterol, 122 mg sodium

  4 medium-size kohlrabi
  3 tablespoons butter or
    margarine
  7 tablespoons water
  ½ teaspoon dry basil or
    oregano leaves
  ½ pound mushrooms, sliced
    Salt and pepper
    Grated Parmesan cheese

Peel and thinly slice kohlrabi; you should have 3 cups. Melt butter in a wide frying pan over high heat. Add kohlrabi; cook, stirring, for 1 minute. Add water and basil; cover and cook, stirring often, for 4 minutes. Add mushrooms, cover, and cook, stirring often, until kohlrabi is tender when pierced (about 4 more minutes). Season to taste with salt and pepper, pour into a serving dish, and sprinkle with cheese. Makes 4 to 6 servings.

■ *See also **Maltese Soup** (page 95).*

Leeks

There's some question about the leek's place of origin—it may have come from the eastern Mediterranean, Egypt, China, or any number of other places. But the one fact we're sure of is that this mild-mannered member of the onion family has been cultivated since the start of recorded history.

The leek is special to the Welsh people. It is the national emblem of Wales, symbolizing the victory of King Cadwallader over the Saxons in the year 640. To avoid attacking one another

Red onions

Yellow onions

Vidalia Sweet

White onions

Vidalia Sweet Onions
NET WT. 48 OZ. (3 lb)

Leeks

Boiling onions

Italian torpedo

Shallots

Green onions

Chives

Garlic

...Leeks continued

during the battle, the Welsh wore leek leaves in their hats as an identifying symbol. On St. David's Day each year, Welshmen still wear bits of leeks, generally in their buttonholes, in memory of the victory.

Nutrition. Leeks are a fair source of a variety of vitamins and minerals. Trimmed raw leeks contain about 125 calories per pound.

■ **Season.** October through May.

■ **Selection.** Select leeks with clean white bottoms and crisp, fresh-looking green tops. Small to medium-size leeks (less than 1½ inches in diameter) are the most tender, with a mild, delicate flavor.

■ **Amount.** About 1½ pounds of untrimmed leeks serves 4.

■ **Storage.** Refrigerate, unwashed, in a plastic bag for up to 1 week.

■ **Preparation.** Cut off and discard root ends. Trim tops, leaving about 3 inches of green leaves. Strip away and discard coarse outer leaves, leaving tender inner ones. Beginning at the green end, cut leeks in half lengthwise. Cut to within ½ inch of root end if leeks are to be cooked whole; otherwise, cut all the way through. Hold under cold running water, separating layers carefully to rinse out any dirt.

■ **Cooking methods.** Overcooking ruins leeks—they become mushy (almost slimy) and fall apart easily. Test for doneness after the minimum suggested cooking time.

For more information on the cooking methods listed here, see "A Glossary of Techniques," page 122.

Boiling. In a wide frying pan, boil about 1½ pounds halved leeks, covered, in ½ inch water until just tender when pierced (4 to 7 minutes). Drain.

Butter-steaming. Cut white part crosswise into ¼-inch-thick slices. (Reserve green tops for other uses.) Butter-steam up to 5 cups, using 2 tablespoons butter or margarine. Cook, stirring, for 1 minute. Add 3 tablespoons liquid, cover, and cook until tender-crisp to bite (about 3 more minutes).

Steaming. Arrange halved leeks on a rack. Steam until tender when pierced (5 to 8 minutes).

Microwaving. Arrange about 1½ pounds halved leeks in a single layer

Introducing the onion and garlic family—with flavors ranging from sweet and mild to strong and loud.

in a nonmetallic baking dish with just the water that clings after rinsing. Cover. Microwave on **HIGH (100%)** for 4 to 5 minutes, rotating dish ¼ turn after 2 to 2½ minutes. Let stand, covered, for 5 minutes.

Stir-frying. Cut white part crosswise into ¼-inch-thick slices. (Reserve green tops for other uses.) Stir-fry up to 5 cups, using 1 tablespoon salad oil, for 1 minute. Add 3 tablespoons liquid, cover, and cook until tender-crisp to bite (about 3 more minutes).

■ **Serving ideas.** Dress hot cooked leeks with butter seasoned with chervil, minced parsley, or tarragon. Or top leeks with crisply cooked and crumbled bacon or grated lemon peel. To serve chilled, plunge leeks into ice water immediately after cooking; when cool, drain well and marinate in an oil and vinegar dressing. Add sliced leeks to soups and stews during the last 5 to 8 minutes of cooking.

ADD-ON VICHYSSOISE

Per serving: 269 calories, 8 g protein, 20 g carbohydrates, 18 g total fat, 67 mg cholesterol, 713 mg sodium

> 5 medium-size leeks
> ½ cup (¼ lb.) butter or margarine
> 1 medium-size onion, coarsely chopped
> 4 medium-size thin-skinned potatoes, peeled and cut into chunks
> 5½ cups regular-strength beef broth
> 1 cucumber, peeled, seeded, and cut into chunks
> 1 cup *each* plain yogurt and sour cream
> Whole chives
> 1 pound cooked ham, slivered (optional)
> Ground nutmeg (optional)

Prepare leeks as previously directed, then coarsely chop.

Melt butter in a 5- to 6-quart pan over medium heat. Add leeks and onion; cook, stirring often, until leeks are very soft and slightly tinged with brown (about 30 minutes). Add potatoes, broth, and cucumber. Bring to a boil over high heat; reduce heat, cover, and simmer until potatoes mash easily (about 25 more minutes). Remove from heat and let cool to lukewarm.

Whirl leek mixture, yogurt, and sour cream, a portion at a time, in a blender until smooth. Cover and refrigerate until well chilled. Garnish each serving with chives; if desired, sprinkle with ham slivers and nutmeg. Makes 8 to 10 servings.

LEEKS AU GRATIN

Per serving: 129 calories, 6 g protein, 12 g carbohydrates, 6 g total fat, 23 mg cholesterol, 259 mg sodium

> About 2 pounds leeks
> 2 tablespoons butter or margarine
> 2 tablespoons all-purpose flour
> ½ cup half-and-half or light cream
> ½ cup regular-strength chicken broth
> ¼ teaspoon ground nutmeg
> 1 cup (4 oz.) shredded Swiss cheese
> 3 tablespoons crushed seasoned croutons

Prepare leeks for cooking whole as previously directed. Divide into 2 portions and tie each into a bunch, securing it with string near both ends. Boil or steam as previously directed. Drain well and snip off string; arrange leeks in a shallow baking dish. Set aside.

Melt butter in a small pan over medium heat. Add flour and cook, stirring, until bubbly. Gradually stir in half-and-half and broth. Cook, stirring constantly, until sauce boils and thickens. Blend in nutmeg and ¾ cup of the cheese; stir until cheese is melted. Pour sauce evenly over leeks, then top with remaining ¼ cup cheese and croutons. Bake, uncovered, in a 375° oven until heated through and lightly browned (15 to 20 minutes). Makes about 6 servings.

Lettuce *see Salad Greens, page 104*

Mushrooms

Mushrooms have no roots, leaves, flowers, or seeds—and strictly speaking, they're not vegetables. They actually belong to a broad plant group called *fungi*, as do truffles, yeast, and even bread mold.

Despite their humble heritage, mushrooms have been considered a delicacy for thousands of years. They appear in Egyptian hieroglyphic writings as food for the Pharaohs; in ancient Greek and Roman times, they were reserved for the upper classes.

The French were the first to produce cultivated mushrooms on a commer-

White button

Shiitake

Butter

Lobster

Angel trumpets

Morel

Brown
(Italian field)

Wood-ear

Enoki

Oyster

Look in fancy produce stores for mushrooms in colorful variety. Here are 10 of the most common types.

cial scale, starting in the late 19th century. By 1920, mushroom farming was underway in the United States; today, Pennsylvania produces half the American crop. Mushrooms are cultivated in special windowless buildings where temperature, humidity, and ventilation are precisely controlled.

Nutrition. Commercial mushrooms are low in sodium and relatively high in potassium. One cup (raw) contains about 20 calories.

■ **Mushroom varieties.** Though some 2,000 species of mushrooms are eaten throughout the world, here we discuss only those most commonly sold in American markets. Cost is related to ease of cultivation; those that can't be domesticated are most expensive. (Of the many mushroom varieties, a few are poisonous, so it's best to leave wild mushroom gathering to the experts.)

Button or commercial. This is the mushroom cultivated on a large scale in the United States. Plump and dome-shaped, with a smooth texture and mild flavor, it may be white, cream, or tan in color.

Chanterelle. Chanterelles grow wild in the forests of the Pacific Northwest and are also cultivated to some extent. Most common among them is the yellow chanterelle, which resembles a curving trumpet. It has an apricotlike aroma and a delicate flavor.

Enoki. With their long stems and tiny caps, these small, white mushrooms resemble bean sprouts. They're very delicate and should be eaten raw (as a garnish or in a salad) or briefly heated in a flavorful broth. Enoki mushrooms are cultivated in California and Malaysia as well as their native Japan.

Morel. Rich and intensely earthy in flavor, these wild mushrooms are among the least adaptable to cultivation. Because their elongated dome has a spongelike appearance, they're sometimes called sponge mushrooms.

Oyster. Oyster mushrooms grow both wild and under cultivation on straw and wood fiber products. Cultivated mushrooms may be either white or almost black. The flesh of an oyster mushroom has a smooth texture and a flavor something like seafood.

Angel trumpets, an earthier-tasting oyster hybrid, are larger and whiter.

Shiitake. Large, flat shiitake mushrooms have a woody odor and a rich mushroom flavor. Commercially, they're grown by injecting mushroom spores into oak or composite logs (the Japanese have been growing them this way for 2,000 years).

Others. In fancy produce markets, you're also likely to find brown or Italian field mushrooms, darker-skinned button mushroom look-alikes with slightly sweeter, more intense flavor; wood-ears, with brown, jellylike tops and dry tan undersides; large, meaty lobster mushrooms; woodsy-flavored, bright yellow-gold butter mushrooms; and sweet-tasting pompons blancs.

■ **Season.** All year; sporadic availability for specialty mushrooms.

■ **Selection.** For all types, look for fresh mushrooms that are blemish-free, without slimy spots or signs of decay. For button (commercial) mushrooms, choose smooth, plump mushrooms with caps closed around stems; avoid spotted mushrooms and those that have open caps with dark gills exposed.

■ **Amount.** Allow about ¼ pound per person when served as a vegetable.

■ **Storage.** Wrap in paper towels and refrigerate, unwashed, in a plastic or paper bag for up to 4 days.

■ **Preparation.** Wipe with a damp cloth or mushroom brush; or rinse briefly under cold running water and pat dry. Trim and discard stem base; discard shiitake stems. Use whole, slice lengthwise through stem, or chop.

■ **Cooking methods.** For more information on the cooking methods listed here, see "A Glossary of Techniques," page 122.

Butter-steaming. Cut mushrooms lengthwise into ¼-inch slices. Butter-steam up to 5 cups, using 2 tablespoons butter or margarine. Cook, stirring, for 3 to 4 minutes.

Grilling. Use button, brown, or shiitake mushrooms. Cut off tough stem ends. Thread smaller mushrooms on skewers. Brush with plain or seasoned salad oil or melted butter or margarine. Grill for about 10 minutes.

Microwaving. Cut 1 pound mushrooms lengthwise into ¼-inch slices. Place in a 2-quart nonmetallic baking dish; dot with 2 tablespoons butter or margarine, cut into 6 pieces. Cover. Microwave on **HIGH (100%)** for 4 to 6 minutes, stirring after 2 minutes. Let stand, covered, for 2 minutes.

Stir-frying. Cut mushrooms lengthwise into ¼-inch slices. Stir-fry up to 5 cups, using 1 tablespoon salad oil, for 3 to 4 minutes.

■ **Serving ideas.** Offer whole raw medium-size mushrooms with a dip for an appetizer, or slice and add to green salads or soups. Butter-steam mushroom slices to tuck into omelets or serve atop steaks and hamburgers. Dress cooked mushrooms with a cheese sauce or melted butter seasoned with parsley, tarragon, thyme, or dry sherry. Stuff large mushroom caps (2 to 3 inches in diameter) to bake as a side dish or entrée. Add minced morels to a red wine sauce to serve with hearty meats.

ENOKI WITH SOY-MUSTARD DIP

Per serving: 25 calories, .99 g protein, 3 g carbohydrates, .25 g total fat, 0 mg cholesterol, 662 mg sodium

Stir together 2 tablespoons *each* **soy sauce** and **dry sherry**, ½ teaspoon **dry mustard**, and 1 tablespoon minced **green onion** (including top). Trim limp stem ends from 1 or 2 bags (3½ oz. *each*) **enoki mushrooms;** rinse mushrooms, then shake off excess water.

To eat, dip mushrooms in soy mixture. Makes 4 to 6 servings.

MARINATED MUSHROOMS

Per ¼ cup: 79 calories, 2 g protein, 3 g carbohydrates, 7 g total fat, 0 mg cholesterol, 9 mg sodium

    4 cups water
    6 tablespoons white wine
       vinegar
    2 pounds small mushrooms
    4 or 5 small shallots, cut in
       half lengthwise
    2 large cloves garlic, cut in
       half lengthwise
    3 or 4 fresh tarragon sprigs
       or ½ teaspoon dry tarragon
    1 bay leaf
    ½ cup olive oil or salad oil
    ¼ teaspoon salt (optional)

In a 4- to 5-quart pan, bring water and 2 tablespoons of the vinegar to a rolling boil over high heat. Add mushrooms, cover, return to a boil, and boil for 5 minutes. Remove from heat and let cool, then cover and refrigerate in cooking liquid until next day.

Drain mushrooms and pack into a 1-quart glass jar. Poke shallots, garlic, tarragon, and bay leaf down among mushrooms. Stir together remaining ¼ cup vinegar, oil, and salt, if desired; pour over mushrooms. Cover and let stand at room temperature until next day, then serve. Or refrigerate, covered, for up to 3 weeks; if oil thickens, bring to room temperature before serving. Makes about 1 quart.

HEAVENLY MUSHROOMS

Per serving: 159 calories, 5 g protein, 3 g carbohydrates, 14 g total fat, 60 mg cholesterol, 277 mg sodium

    18 to 20 mushrooms,
       each about 1½ inches
       in diameter
    3 tablespoons butter
       or margarine
    2 tablespoons black
       lumpfish caviar
    1 large package (8 oz.) cream
       cheese, softened
    1 teaspoon dill weed
    2 tablespoons minced mild
       red or white onion
    ⅓ cup minced parsley

Rinse mushrooms well, then carefully remove stems from caps. Reserve stems for other uses, if desired.

Place butter in an 8- by 12-inch baking dish; place in oven while it preheats to 350°. When butter is melted, remove dish from oven. Swirl mushroom caps in butter to coat evenly, then arrange in dish in a single layer, cup side up.

Put caviar in a fine wire strainer and rinse under a gentle stream of cold water until water runs clear; drain.

Beat cream cheese, dill weed, and onion until well combined; stir in caviar. Evenly mound cheese mixture in mushroom caps. Bake, uncovered, until cheese mixture is very lightly browned (about 15 minutes). Sprinkle with parsley and serve hot. Makes 18 to 20 appetizers (5 or 6 servings).

SHIITAKE & EGG SOUP

Per serving: 53 calories, 3 g protein, 6 g carbohydrates, 2 g total fat, 66 mg cholesterol, 1196 mg sodium

In a 2-quart pan, combine 4 cups **water,** 4 **chicken bouillon cubes,** 2 teaspoons **soy sauce,** and ⅛ teaspoon **ground ginger;** bring to a boil over high heat. Rinse ¼ pound **fresh shiitake mushrooms,** pat dry, and cut into ¼-inch strips. Stir together 2 tablespoons *each* **cornstarch** and **water.** Add mushrooms and cornstarch mixture to broth; stir until soup boils and thickens. Lightly beat 1 **egg;** stir into soup. Remove from heat and stir until egg separates into shreds. Sprinkle with 3 tablespoons thinly sliced **green onions** (including tops). Season to taste with **salt** and **white pepper.** Makes 4 servings.

■ *See also* ***Marinated Broccoli & Mushrooms*** *(page 65),* ***Butter-Steamed Kohlrabi & Mushrooms*** *(page 87).*

Mustard Greens *see Greens with a Bite, page 83*

Okra

Okra is believed to have originated in northern Africa, in the area encompassing present-day Ethiopia. Slaves very likely brought okra to America's South, where it is still a staple in Louisiana's famed Creole cooking.

Outside the South, though, okra is not widely consumed. Many people object to the slippery quality—referred to as "roping"—that this vegetable can develop when cooked. But roping can be virtually eliminated if the conical pods are left whole (keeping the mucilaginous juices inside) and cooked just until tender-crisp. On the other hand, when okra is sliced and cooked longer, its stickiness makes it a good thickener in soups and stews.

Nutrition. Okra is a good source of vitamin C and potassium. One cup of cooked okra has about 45 calories.

■ **Season.** All year; peak June through August.

■ **Selection.** Select small to medium-size pods (2 to 3 inches long) that are deep green, firm, and free of blemishes. Pods should snap easily; you should be able to puncture them with slight pressure.

■ **Amount.** Allow ¼ pound per person.

■ **Storage.** Refrigerate, unwashed, in a plastic bag for up to 3 days.

■ **Preparation.** *For quickly cooked dishes,* trim stems carefully to avoid piercing pods. Rinse, using a vegetable brush to remove the very thin layer of fuzz on the skin. Leave whole.

For long, slow cooking, rinse pods; cut off and discard stem ends, then slice crosswise.

■ **Cooking methods.** Do not cook okra in iron, tin, copper, or brass pans. These metals react with the pods, causing them to discolor (they're still perfectly safe to eat).

For more information on the cooking methods listed here, see "A Glossary of Techniques," page 122.

Boiling. In a wide frying pan, boil 1 pound okra, covered, in 1 inch water until just tender when pierced (5 to 10 minutes). Drain.

To prepare okra, trim stems without piercing pods.

Steaming. Arrange whole okra on a rack. Steam until just tender when pierced (15 to 20 minutes).

■ **Serving ideas.** Top hot, cooked okra with melted butter, a squeeze of lemon, chopped chives, or parsley. Add cooked sliced okra to an omelet along with chopped tomatoes and slivered ham; or add it to a stewed vegetable medley such as ratatouille.

CURRIED OKRA

Per serving: 354 calories, 31 g protein, 24 g carbohydrates, 16 g total fat, 74 mg cholesterol, 351 mg sodium

- 2 tablespoons salad oil
- 1 medium-size onion, chopped
- 4 to 6 teaspoons curry powder
- 1 pound lean ground beef
- 1 large can (28 oz.) tomatoes
- 1½ pounds okra
  Salt and pepper
  Hot cooked rice
  Condiments (suggestions follow)

Heat oil in a wide frying pan over medium heat; add onion and cook, stirring often, until soft. Stir in curry powder and cook, stirring, for 2 to 3 more minutes. Crumble in beef; cook, stirring, until browned. Add tomatoes (break up with a spoon) and their liquid.

Prepare okra as previously directed for quickly cooked dishes, then stir into beef mixture. Bring to a boil over high heat; reduce heat, cover, and simmer until okra is very tender to bite (about 30 minutes). Season to taste with salt and pepper.

Spoon okra mixture over hot cooked rice; place condiments in separate bowls and pass to sprinkle over individual servings. Makes 4 servings.

Condiments. Choose 3 or more of the following: **plain yogurt, shredded coconut, raisins, salted peanuts,** and chopped **Major Grey's chutney.**

LAMB STEW WITH OKRA & FRUIT

Per serving: 379 calories, 30 g protein, 33 g carbohydrates, 15 g total fat, 100 mg cholesterol, 336 mg sodium

- 2 tablespoons butter or margarine
- 2 tablespoons salad oil
- 2 pounds lean boneless lamb stew meat, cut into about 1½-inch cubes
- 1 large onion, cut lengthwise into thin slices
- ¼ cup catsup or tomato-based chili sauce
- 1 can (about 1 lb.) tomatoes
- 1½ pounds okra
- 1 green or red bell pepper, seeded and cut into 1-inch squares
- ½ cup *each* moist-pack pitted prunes and dried apricots
  Salt and pepper

Melt butter in oil in a 5- to 6-quart pan over medium heat. Add lamb and cook, turning, until browned on all sides. Add onion; cook, stirring often, until onion is soft. Stir in catsup; then add tomatoes (break up with a spoon) and their liquid. Bring to a boil over high heat; reduce heat, cover, and simmer until meat is tender when pierced (40 to 50 minutes).

Meanwhile, prepare okra as previously directed for quickly cooked dishes. Add okra, bell pepper, prunes, and apricots to lamb mixture. Cover and cook until okra is just tender-crisp to bite (10 to 15 more minutes); gently push okra under surface of cooking liquid several times. Skim fat, if necessary; season to taste with salt and pepper. Makes 6 servings.

Chicken Stew with Okra & Fruit. Follow directions for **Lamb Stew with Okra & Fruit,** but substitute 6 **whole chicken legs,** thighs attached, for lamb stew meat.

Onions

The onion group, part of the lily family, is a broad one. Most of its members are bulbs or bulblike, but they differ greatly in appearance. Their flavors vary just as much, from the meek, sweet piquancy of chives to the commanding authority of pungent garlic. In between you'll find green onions (sometimes called scallions), leeks, shallots, and the familiar yellow, red, or white type often referred to as "dry" onions. *(Photo on page 88.)*

Nutrition. Dry onions are a fair source of vitamin C, green onions a fair source of vitamin A. Shallots are high in iron. One cup of cooked dry onions has about 36 calories. One tablespoon of chopped green onion has only 2 calories; 1 tablespoon of chopped raw shallot has 7 calories.

■ **Family members.** Garlic and leeks are discussed in separate listings (see pages 82 and 87).

Chives. Generally used as a fresh herb, the slender spikes or leaves of these little onions can be snipped to add to salads, sandwiches, and spreads, or to use as a garnish on soups and vegetables.

Green onions. These are merely onions that are harvested green; they have a definite bulb formation. Though the terms "green onion" and "scallion" are often used interchangeably, scallions are, strictly speaking, different from green onions—they're any shoots from the white onion varieties that are pulled *before* the bulb has formed.

Often served raw as part of a relish tray or sliced and added to salads or egg dishes, green onions are also a colorful, tasty addition to stir-fries.

Shallots. In contrast to green onions and chives, shallots are distinct small bulbs made up of cloves, like garlic. They're quick-cooking, with a mild, delicate flavor and a tender texture—characteristics that make them a good choice for sauces and salad dressings.

Dry onions. Dry onions fall into two general categories. First come the early spring onions, grown during short winter days in mild climates and therefore referred to as "short day" onions. The Bermuda-Granex-Grano type are in this group. Short day onions are flattened or shaped like tops; they may be red, yellow, or white in color. The crisp, medium-firm flesh is exceptionally mild in flavor. Due to their high moisture content, short day onions have a short storage life.

Late or main crop onions, harvested in autumn, are mostly of the globe type and have distinctly yellow, white, or red skins. Grown during long summer days, they are often called "long day" onions. Their flesh is firm and strong-flavored; their outer skin is thinner and dryer than that of short-day onions, with more layers. Their moisture content is lower, too, so they store well.

Some onion varieties (often named for the place they're grown) combine the characteristics of both short day and long day onions. For example, Walla Walla, Maui, Vidalia, and Texas Sweet onions are large and globe-shaped—but their flesh is mild, sweet, and medium-firm, and their storage life is short.

Dry onions 1 to 1½ inches in diameter are often called "boilers"; even smaller ones are known as "picklers" or "pearls."

■ **Season.** All year.

■ **Selection.** Choose *chives* with all-over green color; select *green onions* with crisp, bright green tops and clean, white bottoms. *Shallots* and *dry onions* should be firm, with characteristically brittle outer skin; avoid those with sprouting green shoots and dark spots.

■ **Amount.** One pound of dry onions served as a vegetable will serve 4; smaller amounts are needed for seasoning.

■ **Storage.** *For chives:* Rinse under cold running water; shake dry. Wrap in paper towels and refrigerate in a plastic bag for up to 4 days.

For green onions: Refrigerate, unwashed, in a plastic bag for up to 1 week.

For shallots and dry onions: Store whole onions, unwrapped, in a cool (50°F), dry, dark place with good ventilation for up to 2 months. Wrap cut pieces in plastic wrap and refrigerate for up to 4 days.

■ **Preparation.** *For chives:* Leave whole, chop, or mince.

For green onions: Rinse and pat dry. Trim root ends; strip off and discard wilted outer leaves. Trim brown or dried areas from tops. Leave whole, slice, or cut into julienne strips.

For shallots and dry onions: Trim stem and root ends, then peel off outer skin. Leave whole, cut into quarters, slice, or chop.

To peel small boiling onions, pour boiling water over onions; let stand for 2 to 3 minutes, then drain. Trim stem and root ends; peel off outer skin. Cut a shallow "X" into stem end to ensure even cooking and keep onion layers from separating.

■ **Cooking methods.** Chives and green onions are generally served raw, though they can be stir-fried with other foods. Shallots are usually minced and used as a seasoning, either raw or sautéed.

For more information on the cooking methods listed here, see "A Glossary of Techniques," page 122.

Baking. Peel medium-size dry onions; stand upright in a close-fitting baking dish. Drizzle with melted butter or margarine. Bake, uncovered, in a 350° oven until tender when pierced (30 to 45 minutes). Baste several times with more melted butter or margarine.

Boiling. This method is recommended only for small white boiling onions (1 to 1½ inches in diameter). In a 3-quart pan, boil 1 pound onions, uncovered, in water to cover until tender when pierced (15 to 20 minutes). Drain.

Butter-steaming. Cut dry onions into ¼-inch slices. Butter-steam up to 5 cups, using 2 tablespoons butter or margarine. Cook, stirring, for 1 minute. Then cover and continue to cook until tender-crisp to bite (3 to 4 more minutes).

Grilling. Cut unpeeled small dry onions in halves; cut larger ones into quarters and thread on skewers, making sure pieces lie flat. Grill until tender when pierced and streaked with brown (15 to 20 minutes).

To grill green onions, trim off roots and 2 inches of tops. Grill until tender and streaked with brown (6 to 8 minutes).

Microwaving. Peel 8 to 12 small white boiling onions (1 to 1½ inches in diameter) as previously directed. Or peel 1 pound medium-size dry onions and cut into quarters or slices. Place in a 1-quart nonmetallic baking dish. Cover. Microwave on **HIGH (100%)** for 4 to 5 minutes, stirring after 2 minutes. Let stand, covered, for 5 minutes. Onions should be tender when pierced.

Steaming. Arrange small white boiling onions (1 to 1½ inches in diameter) on a rack. Steam until tender when pierced (20 to 25 minutes).

Continued on next page

Stir-frying. Cut dry onions into ¼-inch slices. Stir-fry up to 5 cups, using 1 tablespoon salad oil, until tender-crisp to bite (3 to 4 minutes).

■ **Serving ideas.** Top hot cooked boiling onions with butter, cream sauce, cheese sauce, or an orange-honey glaze. You can include chopped chives or sliced or chopped dry onions, shallots, or green onions in almost all dishes except desserts. Add them to salads, soups, stews, quiches, and casseroles. Slice raw onions to top hamburgers; chop them to sprinkle on frankfurters and other sausages.

ONION KNOTS WITH PEANUT SAUCE

Per serving: 65 calories, 2 g protein, 9 g carbohydrates, 3 g total fat, 0 mg cholesterol, 145 mg sodium

> 24 to 36 green onions (including tops)
> 12 cups water
> Peanut Sauce (recipe follows)

Rinse onions and cut off roots. Bring water to a boil in a 5- to 6-quart pan over high heat. Add onions, a few at a time, and cook just until green ends appear limp (about 20 seconds). Lift out and plunge immediately into cold water; when cool, place on a cloth and let drain.

Pull off and discard tough outside layers of each onion. Tie each onion in a loose knot so that white end protrudes about 1 inch; trim green end about 1 inch from knot. (At this point, you may cover and refrigerate for up to 6 hours.)

Prepare Peanut Sauce. Arrange onions on a tray; dip white ends into sauce. Makes 2 to 3 dozen appetizers (about 12 servings).

Peanut Sauce. In a small bowl, combine ¼ cup *each* **crunchy peanut butter** and **plum jam** and 1 tablespoon *each* **lemon juice** and **soy sauce.** Season to taste with **liquid hot pepper seasoning.**

CRISP-FRIED ONIONS

Per ½ cup: 92 calories, .98 g protein, 7 g carbohydrates, 7 g total fat, 0 mg cholesterol, .85 mg sodium

> 2 large onions (about 1 lb. total)
> ½ cup all-purpose flour
> Salad oil
> Salt

Thinly slice onions, then separate into rings. Place flour in a bag, add onions, and shake to coat.

Pliable blanched green onions are tied in knots and dipped in peanut sauce (recipe at left).

In a deep 2½- to 3-quart pan, heat 1½ inches of oil to 300°F on a deep-frying thermometer. Add onions, about ¼ at a time; cook, stirring often, until golden (about 5 minutes). Oil temperature will drop at first but rise again as onions brown; regulate heat to maintain temperature at 300°F.

Remove onions with a slotted spoon and drain on paper towels; discard any scorched bits. Pile in a napkin-lined basket or on a plate; sprinkle with salt and serve warm.

If made ahead, let cool completely, package airtight, and refrigerate for up to 3 days. To reheat, spread in a single layer in a shallow baking pan; heat in a 350° oven for 2 to 3 minutes. Makes about 6 cups.

PUB ONIONS

Per serving: 240 calories, 3 g protein, 46 g carbohydrates, 7 g total fat, 0 mg cholesterol, 27 mg sodium

> 1½ cups Madeira or port
> ¾ cup distilled white vinegar
> ½ cup firmly packed brown sugar
> ½ cup currants or raisins
> ⅛ teaspoon ground red pepper (cayenne)
> 2 pounds small white boiling onions, *each* 1 to 1½ inches in diameter
> 3 tablespoons salad oil
> Salt

In a 3- to 4-quart pan, combine Madeira, vinegar, sugar, currants, and red pepper. Bring to a boil over high heat; boil rapidly, uncovered, until reduced to 1¼ cups. Set aside.

Peel onions as previously directed, then arrange in a single layer in a wide frying pan. Pour oil over onions. Cook over medium heat until lightly browned (5 to 7 minutes), shaking pan

to turn onions. Transfer browned onions to Madeira sauce. Repeat with any remaining onions.

Bring onions in sauce to a boil over high heat; reduce heat, cover, and simmer until onions are tender-crisp when pierced (about 10 minutes). Remove from heat and let cool, then season to taste with salt. If made ahead, cover and refrigerate for up to 2 weeks. Serve at room temperature. Makes 6 to 8 servings.

SLOW-COOKED ONIONS

Per serving: 111 calories, 2 g protein, 10 g carbohydrates, 8 g total fat, 24 mg cholesterol, 105 mg sodium

Melt ¼ cup **butter** or margarine in a wide frying pan over medium-low heat. Add 3 large **onions,** sliced; cook, stirring often, until onions are soft and golden (about 40 minutes). If made ahead, cover and keep warm over low heat until ready to serve. Spoon over roasted or barbecued meats such as beef, pork, or lamb. Makes 6 to 8 servings.

■ *See also* **Corn & Onion Sauté** *(page 77).*

Parsnips

Parsnips are a fair-skinned cousin of carrots. Native to the eastern Mediterranean region, they were probably first known to the early Greeks and Romans in their wild form. *(Photo on page 56.)*

Parsnips require a long, cool growing season and are generally harvested in late autumn, after the first frost. The root isn't harmed by frozen ground—in fact, its flavor is improved. At low temperatures, the root's starch converts to sugar, giving the vegetable a delicately sweet, nutty taste.

Nutrition. Parsnips are a good source of vitamins A and C and potassium, though cooked parsnips have only about ¼ as much vitamin C as raw ones. One cup of diced parsnips has 102 calories.

■ **Season.** November through March.

■ **Selection.** Choose small to medium-size parsnips that are smooth, firm, and well shaped. Avoid large roots, since these are likely to have a woody core.

■ **Amount.** Allow about ¼ pound per person.

■ **Storage.** Refrigerate, unwashed, in a plastic bag for up to 10 days.

■ **Preparation.** Trim and discard tops and root ends. Peel with a vegetable peeler, then rinse. Leave whole; or dice, slice, shred, or cut into julienne strips.

■ **Cooking methods.** For more information on the cooking methods listed here, see "A Glossary of Techniques," page 122.

Baking. Cut 1 pound parsnips into ½-inch-thick sticks 3 to 4 inches long. Arrange in a shallow layer in a baking dish; generously dot with butter or margarine. Cover and bake in a 325° oven until tender when pierced (45 to 60 minutes).

Boiling. In a wide frying pan, boil 1 pound whole parsnips, covered, in 1 inch water until tender when pierced (10 to 20 minutes). Drain.

Boil 1 pound ¼-inch slices in ½ inch water for 5 to 10 minutes. Drain.

Butter-steaming. Cut parsnips into ¼-inch slices. Butter-steam up to 5 cups, using 2 to 4 tablespoons butter or margarine. Cook, stirring, for 1 minute. Add 6 to 8 tablespoons liquid, cover, and cook just until tender to bite (4 to 6 more minutes).

Microwaving. Cut 1 pound parsnips into ½-inch cubes. Place in a 1½-quart nonmetallic baking dish and sprinkle with ¼ cup water; cover. Microwave on **HIGH (100%)** for 8 to 9 minutes, stirring after 4 minutes. Let stand, covered, for 5 minutes. Parsnips should be tender when pierced.

Steaming. Arrange whole parsnips or ¼-inch slices on a rack. Steam until tender when pierced (15 to 25 minutes for whole parsnips, 7 to 15 minutes for slices).

Stir-frying. Cut parsnips into ¼-inch slices. Stir-fry up to 5 cups, using 1 to 2 tablespoons salad oil, for 1 minute. Add 6 to 8 tablespoons liquid, cover, and continue to cook just until tender to bite (4 to 6 more minutes).

■ **Serving ideas.** Add diced or sliced raw parsnips to stews and hearty soups during the last 15 to 20 minutes of cooking. Or offer small raw parsnips, cut into strips, with a dip for an appetizer. Bake parsnips as previously directed,

adding apple wedges, a sprinkling of brown sugar, and a splash of orange juice.

MALTESE SOUP

Per serving: 296 calories, 14 g protein, 23 g carbohydrates, 18 g total fat, 299 mg cholesterol, 793 mg sodium

4	cups *each* chopped parsnips, cauliflower, romaine lettuce leaves, and spinach leaves
2	cups chopped kohlrabi
½	cup chopped celery
½	cup (¼ lb.) butter or margarine
1	medium-size onion, finely chopped
6	cups regular-strength chicken broth
8	eggs

In a food processor, coarsely purée parsnips. Then coarsely purée—one vegetable at a time—cauliflower, romaine, spinach, kohlrabi, and celery. Set all puréed vegetables aside, keeping types separate.

Melt butter in a 5- to 6-quart pan over medium-high heat. Add parsnips, cauliflower, kohlrabi, celery, and onion. Cook, uncovered, stirring often, until vegetables begin to brown (about 25 minutes). Add broth, stirring constantly, and bring to a boil. Add romaine and spinach; return to a boil.

Pour soup into a 4- to 5-quart ovenproof tureen or bowl. Break eggs onto surface of soup, keeping them apart from each other. Bake, uncovered, in a 350° oven until whites are firm but yolks are still soft when touched (about 12 minutes). Makes 8 servings.

PARSNIP TWISTS

Per ½ cup: 66 calories, .57 g protein, 9 g carbohydrates, 4 g total fat, 0 mg cholesterol, 5 mg sodium

8	medium-size parsnips (about 2 lbs. *total*)
	Salad oil
	Salt

Prepare parsnips as previously directed. Shred coarsely, using a food processor or a sharp hand grater; you should have about 8 cups. In a wok or deep 3- to 4-quart pan, heat about 1 inch of oil to 375°F on a deep-frying thermometer. Drop about ½ cup of the shredded parsnips into oil. Cook, stirring, until light gold and crisp (about 30 seconds). With a large wire skimmer or slotted spoon, quickly lift out parsnips; drain on paper towels. Repeat with remaining parsnips. Lightly sprinkle with salt. Serve warm or cool; store airtight up to 3 days. Makes about 2 quarts.

SHREDDED PARSNIP SALAD

Per serving: 322 calories, 2 g protein, 14 g carbohydrates, 30 g total fat, 26 mg cholesterol, 277 mg sodium

Prepare 2 medium-size **parsnips** (about ½ lb. *total*) as previously directed. With a food processor or a sharp hand grater, shred parsnips to make about 2 cups. In a bowl, combine shredded parsnips with 1 cup thinly sliced **celery,** ½ cup **mayonnaise,** and 2 tablespoons **lemon juice.** Gently mix until well blended. Serve on large **butter lettuce leaves;** sprinkle with **coarsely ground pepper.** Makes 3 or 4 servings.

Peas

Peas have been around for a long, long time. In fact, peas found at an archeological site on the border between Burma and Thailand have been carbon-dated to 9750 B.C. In ancient times, these legumes were generally dried and used in soup, porridge, and similar fare. It wasn't until the 17th century that eating fresh peas came into vogue among members of the French court.

Over the years, many new strains of peas have been developed—especially in England, where they flourish in the cool, moist climate. In fact, the ordinary green or garden peas that you shell before eating are often referred to as English peas. These peas are picked still immature, when their sugar content is highest. As they mature, some of the sugar is converted to starch and the protein content increases (mature peas are picked for drying).

In addition to green (shell) peas, there are two types of edible-pod peas. The first is the snow pea, also called Chinese pea pod, sugar pea, and—in Pennsylvania—Mennonite pea. Snow peas contain tiny peas inside flat, tender pods 3 to 4 inches long.

The second type of edible-pod pea, a fairly recent arrival in the marketplace, is the sugar snap pea. Sugar snaps combine the best characteristics of both ordinary green peas and snow peas: they have crisp, tender, shiny pods enclosing plump, sweet, nicely rounded peas.

Continued on next page

Green or shell peas (in basket, rear) must be shelled before eating. But to enjoy edible-pod peas—sugar snaps (lower left) and snow peas (right)—simply remove ends and strings.

Nutrition. Peas are an excellent source of fiber and also provide vitamins A and C. A ¼-pound serving of raw shelled peas has 95 calories; the same amount of edible-pod peas has 60 calories.

■ **Season.** April through August for green or shell peas, February through June for edible-pod peas.

■ **Selection.** *For green peas:* Select small, plump, bright green pods that are firm, crisp, and well filled with medium-size peas. *For edible-pod peas:* Look for firm, crisp, bright green pods.

■ **Amount.** Allow about ½ pound unshelled green peas per serving (½ pound unshelled peas yields about ½ cup shelled). Allow about ¼ pound edible-pod peas per serving.

■ **Storage.** Refrigerate all peas, unwashed, in a plastic bag for up to 3 days.

■ **Preparation.** *For green peas:* Remove peas from pods and rinse. *For edible-pod peas:* Break off both ends and remove strings (see photo above). Rinse.

■ **Cooking methods.** For more information on the cooking methods listed here, see "A Glossary of Techniques," page 122.

Boiling. Shell 2 pounds green peas. In a 3-quart pan, boil peas, covered, in ½ inch water until tender to bite (5 to 10 minutes). Drain.

In a 5-quart pan, boil 1 pound edible-pod peas, uncovered, in 12 cups water until tender-crisp to bite (30 seconds). Drain.

Butter-steaming. Butter-steam up to 5 cups shelled green peas, using 1 to 2 tablespoons butter or margarine. Cook, stirring, for 1 minute. Add 3 to 4 tablespoons liquid, cover, and cook just until tender to bite (2 to 3 more minutes).

Butter-steam up to 5 cups edible-pod peas, using 1 to 2 tablespoons butter or margarine. Cook, stirring, for 3 minutes. Add 1 tablespoon liquid, cover, and cook just until tender-crisp to bite (30 more seconds).

Microwaving. Shell 2 to 2½ pounds green peas. Place peas in a 1½-quart nonmetallic baking dish; sprinkle with ¼ cup water. Cover. Microwave on **HIGH (100%)** for 8 to 12 minutes, stirring after 5 minutes. Let stand, covered, for 5 minutes. Peas should be tender to bite.

Place 1 pound edible-pod peas in a 2-quart nonmetallic baking dish. Cover. Microwave on **HIGH (100%)** for 4 to 5 minutes, stirring after 2 minutes. Let stand, covered, for 4 minutes. Peas should be tender-crisp to bite.

Steaming. Arrange shelled green peas or whole edible-pod peas on a rack. Steam until green peas are tender to bite (8 to 12 minutes) or until edible-pod peas are tender-crisp to bite (3 to 5 minutes).

Stir-frying. For all peas, prepare and cook as for butter-steaming (above), but substitute 1 tablespoon salad oil for the butter or margarine.

■ **Serving ideas.** Top hot cooked green peas with butter and season with nutmeg, fresh mint, tarragon, chives, thyme, or crumbled cooked bacon. Or combine with tiny boiled onions, small thin-skinned potatoes, or sautéed mushrooms. Stir lightly cooked, cooled peas (any kind) into rice, pasta, or green salads; use edible-pod peas in stir-fries. Offer raw edible-pod peas with a dip as an appetizer. Season hot cooked edible-pod peas with butter or soy sauce.

PEA PODS WITH MINT SAUCE

Per serving of pea pods: 37 calories, 2 g protein, 6 g carbohydrates, .96 g total fat, 0 mg cholesterol, 10 mg sodium

Per tablespoon mint sauce: 65 calories, .30 g protein, .46 g carbohydrates, 7 g total fat, 8 mg cholesterol, 45 mg sodium

In a food processor or blender, whirl ¼ cup *each* **sour cream** and **mayonnaise** and 2 tablespoons **fresh mint leaves** until mint is finely chopped. Transfer sauce to a small bowl. If made ahead, cover and refrigerate until next day.

Arrange 1 pound **edible-pod peas,** prepared as previously directed, on a platter around bowl of sauce. Garnish sauce with **mint sprigs.** Makes 5 or 6 servings.

FRENCH PEA & LETTUCE SOUP

Per serving: 110 calories, 7 g protein, 12 g carbohydrates, 4 g total fat, 26 mg cholesterol, 776 mg sodium

- 2 **tablespoons butter or margarine**
- 1 **teaspoon ground nutmeg**
- 1 **cup chopped green onions (including tops)**
- 2 **cups shelled green peas (about 2 lbs. unshelled)**
- ¼ **cup chopped parsley**
- 6 **cups regular-strength chicken broth**
- 4 **to 5 cups lightly packed shredded iceberg lettuce**

Melt butter in a 4- to 5-quart pan over medium-high heat; add nutmeg, onions, peas, and parsley. Cook, stirring frequently, until onions are soft but still bright green (about 3 minutes).

Add broth and bring to a boil over high heat. Add lettuce; reduce heat to low and simmer, uncovered, just until lettuce is wilted (about 3 more minutes). Serve at once. Makes 6 servings.

PEA-JICAMA SALAD

Per serving: 62 calories, 2 g protein, 10 g carbohydrates, .15 g total fat, 0 mg cholesterol, 2 mg sodium

- 2 **cups shelled green peas (about 2 lbs. unshelled)**
  Ice water
- 1½ **cups peeled, diced jicama**
- ¾ **cup seasoned rice vinegar; or ¾ cup white wine vinegar plus 2 tablespoons sugar**
- ¼ **cup finely chopped fresh mint**
- 8 **to 16 large butter lettuce leaves**
  Mint sprigs

In a 2- to 3-quart pan, boil peas over high heat in 1 inch water, stirring occasionally, just until bright green and hot through (2 to 3 minutes). Drain. Pour peas into ice water to cool; when cool, drain again.

Mix jicama and vinegar and let stand for at least 15 minutes or up to 5 hours. Mix peas, jicama mixture, and chopped mint. Line each of 8 salad plates with 1 or 2 lettuce leaves; spoon pea mixture onto lettuce with a slotted spoon. Garnish with mint sprigs. Spoon any remaining dressing over salad, if desired. Makes 8 servings.

■ *See also* **Cauliflower & Pea Stir-Fry** *(page 73)*.

Peppers

When Columbus discovered the New World, he was searching for precious black pepper. But what he carried back to Europe were *green* peppers—long, spicy vegetables. These New World peppers quickly caught on in Europe, then spread to Africa and Asia and were incorporated into the cuisines of countries all over the world.

Today, hundreds of pepper varieties are grown worldwide. Some are sweet; the rest have pungent, spicy flavors—varying in degree from mild to wild—and are generally referred to as hot or chile peppers.

The sweet peppers you're most likely to find in produce markets include green, red, yellow, and purple bell peppers; tapered red pimentos; and long, pointy Hungarian sweet yellow wax peppers. In some areas, you may also see slender, thin-walled Italian frying peppers. If left on the vine after reaching maturity, most peppers will ripen further, turning red and becoming sweeter; red bells are simply green bells that have been allowed to ripen fully.

Chile peppers differ in flavor and hotness depending on the type. Among the most familiar chiles, the mildest is the Anaheim (also called California green chile or long green chile). Blackish green, heart-shaped pasilla (also called ancho or poblano) is also relatively mild, with a touch of bitterness. These two varieties are extensively used to add mild heat to all kinds of Mexican dishes; they're also the favored choice for *chiles rellenos* (stuffed chiles).

Somewhat hotter are yellow wax peppers (short, conical, and waxy surfaced) and long, tapering Hungarian hot yellow wax peppers. These are frequently pickled to eat as a relish, or chopped and added to sauces.

Of the really hot chiles, the three most commonly available are short, tapering Fresno; thick-fleshed, cylindrical jalapeño; and short, slim, cylindrical serrano—the hottest of them all. Not for the timid, these chiles add a fiery note to all kinds of dishes.

A recent newcomer on the chile market is the Mexi-bell, which has the appearance and texture of a bell pepper but the taste of a mild chile.

There's no sure way to predict how hot a chile will be, but in general, the smaller varieties pack the most chile power. Heat is concentrated in the interior veins or ribs near the seed heart—not in the seeds themselves, as is commonly believed. The seeds taste extra hot because they're in close contact with the veins.

Nutrition. All peppers are rich in vitamin C; red peppers are a good source of vitamin A, as well. Peppers are low in calories—about 35 for a large raw green or yellow bell pepper, 50 for a large red bell, 21 for a long green chile or 4 jalapeños.

■ **Season.** All year for some varieties; peak July through October for most types.

■ **Selection.** Choose bright, glossy peppers that are firm and well shaped; avoid those with soft spots and gashes.

■ **Amount.** For peppers served as a vegetable, allow 1 medium-size sweet pepper per person. Use hot peppers according to individual taste.

■ **Storage.** Refrigerate, unwashed, in a plastic bag for up to 5 days.

■ **Preparation.** For sweet peppers, rinse, then remove stem, seeds, and pith. Leave whole, cut in half lengthwise, cut crosswise into rings, slice, dice, or cut into strips.

When handling hot peppers (chiles), wear rubber gloves to protect your hands from the volatile oil concentrated in the interior veins; it can cause severe burns. Otherwise, preparation is the same as for sweet peppers.

To peel, see the following instructions for "Roasting."

■ **Cooking methods.** When cooking bell peppers you can use any color, but since purple bells fade to khaki when heated, cooking them hardly

justifies the premium you pay for the color.

For more information on the cooking methods listed here, see "A Glossary of Techniques," page 122.

Grilling. Rinse whole bell peppers or chiles; pat dry. Grill until tender and streaked with brown (8 to 10 minutes).

Roasting. Place whole bell peppers, fresh pimentos, or Anaheim or pasilla chiles slightly apart in a rimmed shallow baking pan. Roast, uncovered, in a 400° oven until skin is browned and looks blistered (25 to 30 minutes). Remove from oven and place in a plastic or heavy paper bag. Close tightly and let sweat for 30 minutes. Pull off skins. Cut peppers into halves; discard seeds and stems. Use peppers, refrigerate airtight for up to 3 days, or freeze in 1-cup portions for longer storage.

Sautéing. Cut about 1 pound medium-size pimentos, bell peppers, or other sweet peppers into ¼-inch strips. Melt 2 tablespoons butter or

Sweet pepper choices include (from top to bottom) familiar green and red bells, red pimento, and golden and purple bells. Purple bells are green inside.

Green Anaheim

Hungarian yellow wax

Pasilla
(ancho, poblano)

Red Fresno

Yellow wax

Jalapeño

Red Anaheim

Serrano

Green Fresno

Brightly-colored fresh chiles, mild to hot in flavor, make their market appearance in the heat of summer. To preserve their spicy flavor for all-year use, can them in a piquant pickling mixture.

Chopped hot peppers can add zest to sauces, stews, soups, and dips such as guacamole. For an appetizer, serve quartered Anaheim chiles with string cheese pulled into fine threads.

HUNGARIAN PEPPER STEW

Per serving: 94 calories, 3 g protein, 12 g carbohydrates, 5 g total fat, 0 mg cholesterol, 23 mg sodium

> 2 pounds Hungarian sweet yellow wax peppers or bell peppers (use yellow, green, or red, or a combination)
> 2 to 3 tablespoons bacon drippings or salad oil
> 1 large onion, sliced
> 1 tablespoon sweet Hungarian paprika
> 2 large tomatoes, peeled and chopped
> Salt

Cut Hungarian peppers in halves lengthwise or bell peppers into eighths lengthwise; then cut each section crosswise into thin slices.

Heat drippings in a wide frying pan over medium heat; add onion and cook, stirring often, until soft. Add any green or yellow peppers and cook, stirring, for about 1 minute. Add red peppers and cook for about 2 more minutes. Remove from heat and add paprika.

Return pan to medium-high heat and cook, stirring, until peppers begin to soften. Add tomatoes, cover, and cook until juices are released from vegetables (about 2 minutes). Then uncover and cook, stirring occasionally, until almost all liquid has evaporated and peppers are tender-crisp to bite (5 to 15 more minutes, depending on type of peppers). Season to taste with salt. Makes 6 to 8 servings.

PETER PIPER'S PEPPER PICKLES

Per serving: 48 calories, .46 g protein, 12 g carbohydrates, .08 g total fat, 0 mg cholesterol, 58 mg sodium

For each quart, you'll need about 5 cups **chiles** (any variety). Wash all chiles. Cut 2 small slits in each of the small chiles (Fresno, jalapeño, serrano, yellow wax). Cut large chiles (Anaheim, Hungarian hot wax, pasilla) into 2-inch lengths; remove seeds, if desired. Cook chiles in **boiling water** to cover until barely tender when pierced (5 to 7 minutes). Drain thoroughly. Pack in a wide-mouth quart jar with 1 clove **garlic.** Combine 1 cup *each*

margarine (or heat 2 tablespoons olive oil) in a wide frying pan over medium heat. Add peppers and cook, stirring often, until tender when pierced (10 to 15 minutes).

Stir-frying. Cut bell peppers into 1-inch squares. Stir-fry up to 5 cups, using 1 to 2 tablespoons salad oil, for 1 minute. Add 2 to 3 tablespoons liquid, cover, and cook just until peppers are tender to bite (3 to 5 more minutes).

■ **Serving ideas.** Stuff whole or halved sweet peppers with a meat, rice, or vegetable mixture, then bake. Use raw sweet peppers as a crisp crudité or a crunchy addition to seafood, poultry, meat, or green salads. Spread red bell strips with Brie and serve as an appetizer. Add sautéed sweet peppers to sauces, omelets, scrambled eggs, and pizzas; or use to garnish grilled meats. Drizzle roasted sweet peppers with olive oil to serve on an antipasto tray.

distilled **white vinegar** and **sugar** and ½ teaspoon **salt;** stir until sugar is dissolved. Pour over chiles to cover. Screw on lid and shake jar well; refrigerate for at least 1 day or up to 2 weeks before using. Makes 1 quart (20 to 24 servings).

PEPPERED PEPPERS

Per serving: 92 calories, 1 g protein, 7 g carbohydrates, 7 g total fat, 0 mg cholesterol, 14 mg sodium

  2 **tablespoons olive oil or salad oil**
  1 **medium-size onion, finely chopped**
  2 **teaspoons** *each* **coarsely ground black pepper and ground cumin**
  2 **cloves garlic, minced or pressed**
  2 *each* **medium-size red and green bell peppers,** seeded and cut into 1-inch squares
  ¼ **cup dry white wine**
     Salt

Pour oil into a wide frying pan over medium-high heat; add onion, ground pepper, cumin, and garlic. Cook, stirring often, until onion is soft (about 10 minutes). Stir in bell peppers, then pour in wine. Reduce heat, cover, and simmer until peppers are tender-crisp to bite (4 to 5 minutes). Season to taste with salt. Makes 4 to 6 servings.

STUFFED CHILES

Per serving: 175 calories, 7 g protein, 10 g carbohydrates, 13 g total fat, 32 mg cholesterol, 268 mg sodium

     Chorizo Stuffing (recipe follows)
 16 **green or red Anaheim or pasilla chiles, small pimentos, or small green, red, or yellow bell peppers**

Prepare Chorizo Stuffing; set aside.

Slit peppers lengthwise, leaving stems intact. Remove seeds and pith. Fill equally with stuffing; place side by side, stuffed side up, in a 10- by 15-inch rimmed baking pan.

Bake, uncovered, in upper third of a 400° oven until chiles are soft and light brown (about 25 minutes). Makes 16 servings.

Chorizo Stuffing. Remove casings from ¾ pound **chorizo sausage.** Crumble meat into a wide frying pan over medium-high heat; add 1 large clove **garlic** (minced or pressed), ¾ teaspoon **ground cumin,** and ½ teaspoon **oregano leaves.** Cook, stirring often, until meat is browned (about 10 minutes).

Meanwhile, discard stems and any

tough or wilted leaves from 2 pounds **spinach.** Plunge remaining leaves into cold water to clean; lift out and drain, then coarsely chop. Add to meat mixture with ½ pound **mushrooms,** finely chopped. Cook over high heat until liquid has evaporated (about 10 minutes). Remove from heat and stir in 2 cups **soft bread crumbs,** ¾ cup shredded **jack cheese,** and 1 **egg.** Mix well, then season to taste with **salt.**

■ *See also* ***Brussels Sprouts & Red Bell Peppers** (page 67)*.

Potatoes

Potatoes have been labeled as "fattening" for years. "Unfair!" say nutritionists, pointing out that a medium-size potato is no higher in calories than a large apple.

Native to the Andes, the potato was carried from the New World to Europe by Spanish explorers. Over time, this lowly tuber has become one of the world's most important vegetables, though European cooks were slow to accept it as an edible root (the vine was initially grown only for its showy flowers).

Potatoes fall into two basic groups. *Thin-skinned* types—round whites, long whites such as the White Rose, and round reds—are firm and waxy textured, ideal for boiling and steaming. They're often called "new potatoes," since they come to market directly from the field.

Thick-skinned *russets* have a dry, mealy texture that makes them the best choice for baking and frying. The most common russet, the Burbank variety, is sometimes called "Idaho," since so many are grown in that state; it's also grown on a large scale in Washington and Oregon.

While most potatoes are white fleshed, some yellow-fleshed types are now marketed in this country. Look for Finnish yellows and Yukon golds.

Nutrition. Potatoes are naturally low in fat and sodium and rich in potassium and (if unpeeled) vitamin C. Both the carbohydrates and iron in potatoes are almost totally usable when digested. One large baked potato has about 145 calories.

■ **Season.** Thin-skinned potatoes do not store well—but frequent diggings make them available almost all year. Autumn-harvested thick-skinned russets can be kept in storage and are found in markets all year round.

■ **Selection.** Choose firm, smooth potatoes with no wrinkles, sprouts, cracks, bruises, decay, or bitter green areas (caused by overexposure to light). Avoid potatoes with an overall greenish color; they make some people ill. If you plan to cook several at a time, choose potatoes of uniform size.

■ **Amount.** Allow 1 large or 2 small thin-skinned potatoes (about 6 oz. *total)* or 1 medium-size russet (about 6 oz.) per serving.

■ **Storage.** It's best to buy only as many potatoes as you can use in 1 to 2 weeks. Store in a cool (50°F), dark, well-ventilated area—*not* in an airtight plastic bag.

■ **Preparation.** Scrub gently in cold water with a vegetable brush; remove sprouts and cut out any decayed or green areas. To preserve nutrients, leave skins on during cooking. To preserve whiteness, cover peeled potatoes with cold water for a short time before cooking.

■ **Cooking methods.** For more information on the cooking methods listed here, see "A Glossary of Techniques," page 122.

Baking. Russets are best for baking—they'll have crisp, slightly shriveled skin and a fluffy interior. Pierce potatoes in several places with a fork. Place on a baking sheet or on oven rack; bake, uncovered, in a 400° oven until potatoes feel soft when squeezed (45 to 60 minutes for a 6- to 8-oz. potato). Or bake with roasts in a 325° oven for about 1½ hours.

To bake potatoes in pan drippings, use whole small thin-skinned potatoes or halved russets. Arrange around meat or poultry in roasting pan 1½ hours before serving; turn in drippings to coat. Bake, turning and basting occasionally, until tender when pierced.

Boiling. Use russets or thin-skinned potatoes; firm thin-skinned potatoes work best, especially for salads. In a 3-quart pan, boil 1 to 2 pounds potatoes (about 3 inches in diameter), covered, in 1 to 2 inches water until tender when pierced (20 to 30 minutes). Drain.

Continued on next page

French-frying. Russets make the best fries—crisp outside, soft inside. For each serving, peel 1 large russet potato and cut into ¼-inch strips; place in ice water while cutting additional potatoes. In a deep-fat fryer or heavy pan, heat 2 inches of salad oil to 380°F on a deep-frying thermometer. Drain potatoes and pat dry with paper towels. Fill a wire basket 2 inches deep with potato strips; immerse in oil and cook until well browned (5 to 7 minutes). Drain on paper towels, sprinkle with salt, and keep warm in a 300° oven for up to 30 minutes.

To make ahead (or for extra crispness), fry potatoes only 4 minutes; drain. Just before serving, refry in hot oil for 3 to 4 minutes; drain, salt, and serve.

Microwaving. Use any variety of potato, but to ensure even cooking, choose potatoes of uniform size. A microwaved russet has softer skin and a wetter interior than an oven-baked one.

Pierce potatoes in several places with a fork. Place on a double layer of paper towels in bottom of microwave; if cooking more than 2 at a time, arrange like spokes. Microwave on **HIGH (100%):** 3 to 4 minutes for a 4- to 5-ounce potato, 4 to 5 minutes for a 6- to 8-ounce potato. Add 2 to 3 minutes for each additional potato. Turn halfway through cooking time. Let stand, covered, for 5 to 10 minutes. Potatoes should be tender when pierced.

Steaming. Thin-skinned potatoes, especially round reds, are most attractive for steaming. Arrange whole thin-skinned potatoes (3 inches in diameter) or ½-inch-thick slices on a rack. Steam until tender throughout when pierced (30 to 35 minutes for whole potatoes, 8 to 10 minutes for slices).

■ **Serving ideas.** Favorite potato toppings include butter, sour cream, bacon bits, chives, parsley, dill weed, and cheese such as Cheddar, Swiss, or Parmesan. Add raw potato chunks to stews and hearty soups for the last 20 minutes of cooking. Use cooked potatoes in quiches, meat pies, omelets, and salads. Combine leftover mashed potatoes with chopped green onion and bell pepper, then shape into patties and pan-fry in butter or margarine.

CRISP POTATO PANCAKES

Per serving: 181 calories, 3 g protein, 13 g carbohydrates, 13 g total fat, 100 mg cholesterol, 161 mg sodium

> 2 tablespoons lemon juice
> 4 cups water
> 1 large russet potato (at least 8 oz.)
> ¼ cup minced onion
> 2 tablespoons all-purpose flour
> 1 egg
> 1 tablespoon milk
> Salt and pepper
> 4 to 6 tablespoons butter or margarine

In a large bowl, combine lemon juice and water. Peel and finely shred potato; you should have 2 cups. Immediately submerge in lemon water; stir well, then lift out potato and drain on paper towels. Place potato in a bowl; mix in onion, flour, egg, and milk. Season to taste with salt and pepper.

Melt 2 to 3 tablespoons of the butter in a wide frying pan over medium heat. When bubbly, add about 2 tablespoons of the potato mixture for each pancake and spread into a 4-inch circle; don't worry if small holes appear. Cook 3 or 4 pancakes at a time, turning once, until golden brown on both sides (4 to 5 minutes per side); add more butter to pan as needed.

As pancakes are cooked, lift out with a wide spatula and place slightly apart on a rimmed baking sheet. Let cool completely; cover and let stand for up to 6 hours.

To serve, bake, uncovered, in a 400° oven until browned and crisp (8 to 10 minutes). Makes 4 servings.

POTATOES GRATIN

Per serving: 367 calories, 15 g protein, 25 g carbohydrates, 23 g total fat, 120 mg cholesterol, 360 mg sodium

> 1 clove garlic, halved
> 2½ tablespoons butter or margarine
> 3 tablespoons lemon juice
> 6 cups water
> About 2 pounds thin-skinned potatoes
> Salt, pepper, and ground nutmeg
> ¾ cup thinly sliced green onions (including tops)
> 2 cups (8 oz.) shredded Swiss cheese
> 1 egg yolk
> 1½ cups half-and-half, light cream, or milk

Rub a shallow 2-quart baking dish liberally with cut sides of garlic; then generously coat with ½ tablespoon of the butter. Discard garlic.

In a large bowl, combine lemon juice and water. Peel potatoes, if desired; then cut into paper-thin slices, dropping into lemon water as sliced.

Drain potatoes well. Arrange about ¼ of the slices in an even layer in baking dish. Sprinkle lightly with salt, pepper, and nutmeg; top with ¼ of the onions and ½ cup of the cheese. Repeat layers 3 more times, ending with cheese.

Place egg yolk in a small bowl; beat lightly. Heat half-and-half to scalding; pour slowly into egg yolk, beating constantly until blended. Pour egg mixture over potatoes. Dot with remaining 2 tablespoons butter.

Bake, uncovered, in a 350° oven until potatoes are tender when pierced (about 1½ hours). Makes 6 to 8 servings.

MASHED POTATOES

Per serving: 276 calories, 5 g protein, 30 g carbohydrates, 16 g total fat, 49 mg cholesterol, 202 mg sodium

> 2 pounds russet potatoes
> ⅓ cup butter or margarine, softened
> ⅓ cup warm milk
> Salt and pepper

Boil potatoes as previously directed; drain and peel. Mash with a potato masher or electric mixer until smooth. Beat in butter, then slowly beat in milk. Season to taste with salt and pepper. Makes about 4 servings.

PICNIC POTATO SALAD

Per serving: 337 calories, 6 g protein, 16 g carbohydrates, 28 g total fat, 110 mg cholesterol, 475 mg sodium

> 2½ pounds medium-size thin-skinned potatoes
> 12 green onions (including tops), thinly sliced
> 4 hard-cooked eggs, chopped
> 1 cup thinly sliced celery
> 12 slices bacon, crisply cooked, drained, and crumbled
> 1 jar (4 oz.) sliced pimentos, drained
> 1 cup chopped dill pickles
> 1½ cups mayonnaise
> 1 tablespoon prepared horseradish
> 2 teaspoons prepared mustard
> 1 tablespoon dill pickle liquid
> Salt and pepper

Boil potatoes as previously directed; drain. Peel, if desired, then cut into cubes and place in a large bowl. Add onions (reserving some green tops for garnish), eggs, celery, bacon, pimentos, and pickles.

Continued on page 102

Sweet potato

Russet

Round white

Market "yam"

Long white

Round red

Thin-skinned and russet potatoes nestle beside moister, sweeter-fleshed sweet potatoes. For details on the best way to prepare each type, check individual listings.

...Potatoes continued

Combine mayonnaise, horseradish, mustard, and pickle liquid. Stir into potato mixture, season to taste with salt and pepper, and garnish with reserved onion tops. Cover and refrigerate for at least 4 hours or until next day. Makes 12 to 14 servings.

■ *See also* ***Jicama with Fried Potatoes*** *(page 85),* ***Add-On Vichyssoise*** *(page 89),* ***Golden Mashed Potatoes*** *(page 103),* ***Autumn Squash Soup*** *(page 114).*

Pumpkin   see Squash, page 111

Radicchio   see Salad Greens, page 104

Radishes

Radishes are an ancient vegetable, probably first eaten in China, then in Greece and Egypt. These root vegetables come in various sizes, shapes, and colors—long, mild-flavored white ones called "icicles," the familiar red "button" radishes, and round white and black ones, too. A variety called Easter Egg even produces several different colors. The giant of the family is daikon, also called Japanese or Oriental radish—a long, tapered white radish that tastes a bit hotter than ordinary radishes.

In the United States, radishes are usually eaten raw, but in other cuisines they're often added to soups, steamed like carrots, or pickled and used as a relish. The green, leafy tops are also edible—try adding them to a mixed vegetable soup or sautéing them to serve as a green vegetable. Daikon, pickled or raw, accompanies many Oriental dishes as a condiment.

Nutrition. Radishes are very low in calories—less than 1 calorie for a medium-size radish, about 85 calories for a 1-pound daikon. Radishes and daikon are good sources of vitamin C.

■ **Season.** All year.

■ **Selection.** Look for smooth, crisp, firm radishes that are well formed. Bright green tops indicate freshness. Choose firm, white, small to medium-size daikon, 1 to 1½ inches in diameter.

■ **Amount.** For radishes served as a relish, allow 2 or 3 per person. Amount of daikon per person depends on the use.

■ **Storage.** Topped radishes keep best, though tops are desirable for certain presentations. Refrigerate, unwashed, in a plastic bag for up to 1 week (10 days to 2 weeks for daikon).

■ **Preparation.** Rinse well. Cut off and discard roots; leave tops intact for a relish tray, or cut off and discard.

Leave radishes whole, or slice, shred, or quarter. Peel daikon, then slice or shred.

■ **Cooking methods.** Though radishes are generally served raw, daikon and even regular radishes may be stir-fried in combination with other vegetables. See page 126 for more information on stir-frying.

Stir-frying. Add thinly sliced daikon or radishes when stir-frying a combination of vegetables. Cook until just tender-crisp to bite (4 to 6 minutes).

■ **Serving ideas.** Arrange whole radishes (with tops) on a serving plate with a crock of soft unsalted butter and some coarse salt. Dip radishes into butter, then salt lightly and eat out of hand. Slice radishes or daikon and add to a green salad, or shred them into cabbage or carrot slaw. Use whole or sliced radishes or shredded daikon to garnish meat, poultry, or fish platters. For an easy sandwich, spread a slice of French bread with butter and top with a layer of sliced radishes.

SALTED RADISHES

Per serving: 5 calories, .17 g protein, 1 g carbohydrates, .15 g total fat, 0 mg cholesterol, 282 mg sodium

Trim root ends from 2 bunches of **radishes,** then cut off all but about 2 inches of the tender stems and leaves. Arrange radishes in a single layer in a 10-inch pie pan. Sprinkle with 2 tablespoons **salt.** Rest a plate on radishes

From large white daikon to familiar red or multicolored Easter Egg, radishes add zip to salads and other dishes.

and weight it down by setting heavy objects on plate. Refrigerate until radishes are soft (about 2 days).

Rinse radishes well in cold water; drain, then cut off stem sections. Set aside. Thinly slice radishes, then arrange in a serving bowl with stem sections. Serve as an accompaniment to Japanese or other Asian dishes. Makes 2 cups.

CUCUMBER & RADISH SALAD

Per serving: 86 calories, 3 g protein, 16 g carbohydrates, 3 g total fat, 0 mg cholesterol, 247 mg sodium

- 1 English cucumber (about 1¼ lbs. *total*)
- 1 pound radishes with tops (about 10 oz. if topped) Szechwan-style Dressing (recipe follows)

Run tines of a fork lengthwise down all sides of cucumber, piercing skin. Cut cucumber crosswise into ¼-inch slices.

Trim tops and root ends from radishes. With a sharp knife, cut narrow V-shaped lengthwise gashes at intervals around sides of each radish, then thinly slice crosswise.

Stir dressing together in a serving bowl, then add radishes and cucumber; mix well. Cover and refrigerate until cold (2 to 3 hours) or until next day. Makes 4 to 6 servings.

Szechwan-style Dressing. Stir together 2 tablespoons **rice vinegar** or white wine vinegar, 2 tablespoons **sugar,** 2 teaspoons *each* **soy sauce** and **sesame oil,** and ½ teaspoon **liquid hot pepper seasoning.**

DAIKON SOUP

Per serving: 44 calories, 6 g protein, 5 g carbohydrates, .08 g total fat, 24 mg cholesterol, 1010 mg sodium

In a 3-quart pan, combine 4 cups **regular-strength beef broth;** 1 clove **garlic,** minced or pressed; 2 teaspoons **soy sauce;** and 1 teaspoon **sesame oil** (optional). Bring to a boil over high heat; add 2 cups thinly sliced **daikon.** Reduce heat, cover, and simmer until daikon is tender when pierced (10 to 15 minutes). Garnish with thinly sliced **green onion** (including top). Makes 4 servings.

■ *See also* **Green Pasta with Spinach Pesto** *(page 109).*

Rhubarb   see Fruit, page 54

Rocket   see Salad Greens, page 104

Rutabagas

Similar to and sometimes mistaken for its cousin the turnip, the rutabaga is a relative newcomer among vegetables; the first reference to it appeared in the 17th century. Rutabagas thrive in cold climates and soon spread from their probable area of origin in Eastern Europe to gain popularity in northern Europe. In fact, the English word "rutabaga" derives from Swedish *rotabagge.* Most rutabagas sold in the United States today are grown in Canada. *(Photo on page 56.)*

Rutabagas are larger, rounder, denser, and sweeter than turnips, with a lower water content and a more pronounced flavor. Though white and purple varieties exist, commercial rutabagas almost always have yellow to orange skin and flesh.

Nutrition. Rutabagas contain more vitamin A and C than turnips and are a good source of potassium. One cup of cooked cubed or sliced rutabagas provides about 60 calories.

■ **Season.** Almost all year; peak October through March.

■ **Selection.** Choose small to medium-size rutabagas (3 to 4 inches in diameter) that are smooth, firm, and heavy for their size. Lightweight rutabagas may be woody.

■ **Amount.** Allow about ⅓ pound per person.

■ **Storage.** Store, unwrapped, in a cool (50°F), dry, dark place with good ventilation for up to 2 months. Store, unwrapped, at room temperature or in the refrigerator for up to 1 week.

■ **Preparation.** Rinse and peel with a vegetable peeler. Leave whole; or quarter, slice, dice, or cut into julienne strips.

■ **Cooking methods.** For more information on the cooking methods listed here, see "A Glossary of Techniques," page 122.

Baking. Peel medium-size rutabagas; cut into ¼-inch-thick slices. Arrange in a shallow baking dish. Generously dot with butter or margarine; sprinkle lightly with water. Cover and bake in a 400° oven until tender when pierced (30 to 45 minutes).

Boiling. In a 4- to 5-quart pan, boil 1 to 2 pounds peeled whole rutabagas (3 to 4 inches in diameter), covered, in 2 inches water until tender when pierced (25 to 35 minutes). Drain.

Cut 1 to 2 pounds peeled rutabagas into ½-inch-thick slices; boil in a wide frying pan, covered, in ½ to 1 inch water for 7 to 10 minutes. Drain.

Butter-steaming. Cut peeled rutabagas into ¼-inch-thick slices. Butter-steam up to 5 cups, using 1 to 2 tablespoons butter or margarine. Cook, stirring, for 1 minute. Add 4 to 5 tablespoons liquid, cover, and cook just until tender-crisp to bite (5 to 6 more minutes).

Steaming. Arrange whole peeled rutabagas (3 to 4 inches in diameter) or ½-inch-thick slices on a rack. Steam until tender when pierced (30 to 45 minutes for whole rutabagas, 9 to 12 minutes for slices).

Stir-frying. Cut peeled rutabagas into ¼-inch-thick slices. Stir-fry up to 5 cups, using 1 tablespoon salad oil, for 1 minute. Add 4 to 5 tablespoons liquid, cover, and cook just until tender-crisp to bite (5 to 6 more minutes).

■ **Serving ideas.** Serve thinly sliced raw rutabagas as a crudité with dips; add shredded rutabagas to mixed green salads. Stir rutabaga chunks into hearty soups, stews, and New England-style boiled dinners during the last 20 minutes of cooking. Mash cooked rutabagas and season as you would sweet potatoes, with butter, brown sugar, and cinnamon.

GOLDEN MASHED POTATOES

Per serving: 225 calories, 4 g protein, 36 g carbohydrates, 8 g total fat, 24 mg cholesterol, 106 mg sodium

- 3 pounds rutabagas
- 4 pounds Finnish yellow, Yukon gold, or russet potatoes
- ¼ to ½ cup hot milk
- ½ cup (¼ lb.) butter or margarine, melted
- ¼ teaspoon ground nutmeg Salt and white pepper

Peel rutabagas and potatoes, then cut into 2-inch chunks. In a 6- to 8-quart pan, bring 2 inches water to a boil; add rutabagas, reduce heat, cover, and simmer for 15 minutes. Add potatoes; cover and simmer until vegetables are

...Rutabagas continued

very tender when pierced (about 20 more minutes). Drain well.

Place half the vegetables at a time in large bowl of an electric mixer and beat until smooth, adding hot milk to moisten mixture to the desired consistency. Mix in butter and nutmeg; season to taste with salt and white pepper. Makes 12 servings.

RUTABAGAS WITH SOY BUTTER SAUCE

Per serving: 171 calories, 2 g protein, 16 g carbohydrates, 12 g total fat, 36 mg cholesterol, 823 mg sodium

Peel 4 medium-size **rutabagas** and cut lengthwise into thin slices. Boil as previously directed just until tender when pierced (about 5 minutes). Drain.

While rutabagas are cooking, melt ¼ cup **butter** or margarine in a small pan over medium heat. Add 2 teaspoons firmly packed **brown sugar;** stir until well blended. Stir in 2 tablespoons **soy sauce,** 1 tablespoon **lemon juice,** and 1 teaspoon **Worcestershire.** Simmer, uncovered, for 2 to 3 minutes. Pour over cooked, drained rutabagas and mix well. Makes 4 servings.

■ *See also **Autumn Squash Soup** (page 114).*

Salad Greens

From familiar iceberg lettuce to colorful radicchio, salad greens are generally milder and more tender than those we call "greens with a bite" (see page 83). Their flavors range from bland to pleasantly bitter, their textures from crispy to delicate and soft.

Lettuces are doubtless the best-known salad greens. The four main market types— the lettuces most people think of when they hear "salad"— are butterhead, iceberg, looseleaf, and romaine. Other greens often included in salads are the chicories (including Belgian endive and escarole), watercress, tangy arugula, and radicchio.

Nutrition. All salad greens are low in calories and high in fiber; most are good sources of vitamin A. One cup of raw chicory, escarole, radicchio, or most types of lettuce has about 10 calories; watercress has only 7. A whole head of iceberg lettuce has 70 calories, a head of Belgian endive about 8.

■ **Ten greens.** The most common salad greens are discussed below. Turn to pages 107 and 109 for information on sorrel and spinach, both frequently used as salad greens.

Arugula (rocket, roquette). The bright green, serrated leaves of arugula have a spicy, mustardy tang—sharper than watercress, but not as hot as horseradish. The flowers, too, are edible.

Belgian endive (French endive, Witloof chicory). Because they're protected from light as they grow, Belgian endive's small, smooth, slender heads are almost white in color. The flavor is strong and pleasantly bitter. Most Belgian endive really does come from Belgium.

Butterhead lettuce (Bibb, Boston, buttercrunch, limestone). These lettuces are named for their delicate, almost buttery flavor. The loose-leafed heads are small, the leaves soft and pliable.

Chicory (curly endive). Chicory's tousled-looking heads are dark green outside, paler within. The outer leaves have a bitter flavor reminiscent of dandelion greens; the narrow, ragged inner leaves taste sweeter, though they're still slightly bitter.

Escarole. This sturdy, broad-leafed variety of endive has a strong, slightly bitter flavor, less pronounced in the creamy white center leaves.

Iceberg lettuce (crisphead). The best-selling lettuce, available all year, iceberg is known for its crisp texture and firm, light green head. It's very mild in flavor.

Looseleaf lettuce. These lettuces take their name from the way they grow: the leaves branch from the stems rather than forming heads. All looseleaf lettuces are tender and delicately flavored, but they come in assorted colors (red, bronze, dark green, chartreuse) and textures (smooth, puckered, ruffly, frilled).

Radicchio (red chicory, Italian red lettuce). Radicchio comes in a variety of sizes, shapes, and colors—many shades of red, as well as green and variegated red and green. The variety most often seen in U.S. markets is a reddish purple. Radicchio's flavor is similar to that of escarole and Belgian endive.

Romaine lettuce (Cos). Hailing from the Greek island of Cos, romaine has upright clusters of big, crunchy leaves that are exceptionally crisp.

Watercress. Its spicy, tingling flavor makes watercress a popular addition to salads and sandwiches; it's frequently used as a garnish, too. The dark green, round-leafed sprigs grow alongside or even partially submerged in water.

■ **Season.** Generally speaking, salad greens are available all year, though there are peak times for some of them: September through May for Belgian endive, August through December for chicory and escarole.

■ **Selection.** *Leafy greens and watercress* should be crisp and fresh looking, with deeply colored leaves free of brown spots, yellowed leaves, and decay. The white core at the base of *radicchio* should be firm, unblemished, and free of holes. *Belgian endive* should be crisp looking, with creamy white leaves tinged with light yellow at the tips; choose heads that are 4 to 6 inches long. Select *iceberg lettuce* with fresh outer leaves; heads should give a little under pressure.

■ **Amount.** Depends on the use. In general, allow about 1 head Belgian endive per person. To serve 4, allow 1 large head leaf lettuce, chicory, or escarole; 1 small head iceberg or romaine; 2 medium-size heads radicchio; or 1 large or 2 small bunches of watercress.

■ **Storage.** Rinse with cold water, shake off excess, and dry well. Wrap in paper towels and refrigerate in a plastic bag—iceberg and romaine for up to 5 days, other salad greens for up to 2 days.

■ **Preparation.** Tear salad greens into bite-size pieces. If desired, cut out core and shred iceberg. Remove tough stems from watercress; use leaves and tender part of stems.

■ **Cooking methods.** While salad greens are most often served raw, some types may also be cooked. For more information on the cooking methods listed here, see "A Glossary of Techniques," page 122.

Butter-steaming. Coarsely shred iceberg lettuce. Butter-steam up to 5

Iceberg

Escarole

Chicory

Butter lettuce

Green leaf lettuce

Red leaf lettuce

Romaine

Radicchio

Arugula

Watercress

Belgian Endive

Limestone lettuce

cups, using 1 to 2 tablespoons butter or margarine. Cook, stirring, for 30 seconds; then cover and cook just until tender-crisp to bite (2 to 3 more minutes).

Grilling. Cut radicchio heads in halves. Brush with salad oil or melted butter or margarine. Grill, turning frequently, until streaked with brown and tender when pierced (6 to 10 minutes).

■ **Serving ideas.** Toss one or more greens with your favorite dressing for a simple salad; try mixing sharp and mild flavors. Use small leaves as dippers and larger leaves as wrappers or edible serving containers for poultry, meat, or seafood mixtures. Add shredded lettuce to tacos and soups just before serving. Spread bread with sweet butter and top with watercress for a simple but elegant sandwich; add cheese for something heartier.

ENDIVE SALAD WITH WATERCRESS SAUCE

Per serving: 255 calories, 12 g protein, 3 g carbohydrates, 19 g total fat, 161 mg cholesterol, 403 mg sodium

 Watercress Sauce
 (recipe follows)
3 heads Belgian endive
 (about ¼ lb. *each*)
2 ounces Swiss cheese
6 paper-thin slices pastrami
 (about ¼ lb. *total*)
3 hard-cooked eggs, halved
 lengthwise
 Watercress sprigs

Prepare Watercress Sauce; set aside. Trim off and discard any discolored portion of endive bases, then cut heads in half lengthwise. Pull each half apart into 3 sections. On each of 6 salad plates, arrange 3 endive sections side by side.

Cut cheese into thin strips and lay equally on endive. Drape a slice of pastrami over each serving.

To serve, spoon equal portions of sauce beside endive leaves; garnish each plate with an egg half and watercress. Makes 6 servings.

Watercress Sauce. Blend ¾ cup **sour cream;** ¼ cup **milk;** 2 tablespoons *each* **cider vinegar** and chopped **watercress leaves;** ½ teaspoon *each* **Dijon mustard, sugar,** and **dry tarragon;** and 1 clove **garlic,** minced or pressed.

RADICCHIO WITH BUTTER LETTUCE

Per serving: 66 calories, 3 g protein, 8 g carbohydrates, 3 g total fat, 5 mg cholesterol, 74 mg sodium

3 slices bacon
 Salad oil (if needed)
1 tablespoon *each* red wine
 vinegar and minced
 shallot
½ teaspoon Dijon mustard
1 medium-size orange
2 cups lightly packed butter
 lettuce leaves
3 cups lightly packed
 radicchio leaves
 Salt and pepper
 Whole chives

In a wide frying pan, cook bacon over medium heat until crisp. Lift out, drain, and break into 1-inch pieces; set aside. Measure drippings and add oil, if needed, to make 3 tablespoons. Return to pan with bacon, vinegar, shallot, and mustard.

Using a sharp knife, cut peel and all white membrane from orange; cut between sections and lift them out. In a large bowl, mix lettuce and radicchio with orange sections. Heat bacon mixture to simmering and pour over salad. Mix quickly, season to taste with salt and pepper, and arrange at one end of a large platter. Garnish other end with a spray of chives radiating out from salad. Makes 4 servings.

ROMAINE & TANGERINE SALAD

Per serving of salad: 76 calories, 2 g protein, 8 g carbohydrates, 5 g total fat, 0 mg cholesterol, 10 mg sodium

Per tablespoon dressing: 76 calories, .08 g protein, 6 g carbohydrates, 6 g total fat, 0 mg cholesterol, 9 mg sodium

 Honey & Poppy Seed
 Dressing (recipe follows)
 Small inner leaves from 2
 large heads romaine
 lettuce (about 30 leaves)
1 cup peeled tangerine or
 mandarin orange
 segments
6 tablespoons pecan halves
 or sliced almonds

Prepare dressing; set aside.

Divide romaine leaves equally among 6 individual plates. Top equally with tangerines; sprinkle with pecans. Pass dressing to spoon over salads. Makes 6 servings.

Honey & Poppy Seed Dressing. In a blender (or a bowl), combine ⅓ cup **salad oil,** ¼ cup **honey,** 3 tablespoons **white wine vinegar,** 1 tablespoon minced **shallot,** and 1½ teaspoons *each* **poppy seeds** and **Dijon mustard.** Whirl (or beat with a whisk) until

blended. If made ahead, cover and refrigerate until next day. Makes about ¾ cup.

CREAM OF LETTUCE SOUP

Per serving: 142 calories, 4 g protein, 4 g carbohydrates, 12 g total fat, 50 mg cholesterol, 597 mg sodium

4 cups regular-strength
 chicken broth
4 cups firmly packed
 chopped butter lettuce or
 green leaf lettuce
¼ cup butter or margarine
1 cup half-and-half or light
 cream
 Salt and white pepper
 Chopped parsley
 Lemon wedges

Pour broth into a 3-quart pan; bring to a boil over high heat. Stir in lettuce; reduce heat, cover, and simmer until lettuce is completely limp (8 to 10 minutes).

Pour lettuce mixture, a portion at a time, into a blender or food processor; add butter and whirl until mixture is smooth.

Return to pan, stir in half-and-half, and heat until steaming. Season to taste with salt and white pepper, then pour into bowls and garnish with parsley. Pass lemon wedges to squeeze into soup. Makes about 6 servings.

■ *See also* **Cherry Salad with Sesame Dressing** *(page 20),* **Maltese Soup** *(page 95),* **French Pea & Lettuce Soup** *(page 96),* **Salsify Salad** *(page 107).*

Salsify

Also known as "oyster plant" for its delicate, oysterlike flavor, salsify was first commonly used in Europe in the late 16th century. Though still a favorite in European countries today, it has yet to achieve the same popularity in the New World.

Salsify looks something like parsnips. The roots are light brown and smoothly tapered, growing up to 10 inches long; the flesh is off-white. *Scozonera*, or black salsify, is a dark-skinned relative.

Nutrition. Salsify is a fairly good source of potassium; it has no measurable sodium. One cup of cooked salsify supplies anywhere from 16 to 94 calories, depending on whether the root is freshly pulled (calories increase with storage).

A note of caution: Salsify can cause gastric distress and should be consumed in moderation.

■ **Season.** Late autumn through early spring.

■ **Selection.** Look for stiff, evenly shaped, medium-size roots with no obvious flabbiness.

■ **Amount.** Allow about ⅓ pound per person.

■ **Storage.** Refrigerate, unwashed, in a plastic bag for up to 1 week.

■ **Preparation.** Rinse well, then peel. Immediately plunge into acidulated water (3 tablespoons vinegar or lemon juice per quart water) to prevent discoloration. Cut into sticks, slice, or dice.

■ **Cooking methods.** For more information on the cooking methods listed here, see "A Glossary of Techniques," page 122.

Boiling. Peel 1 to 1½ pounds salsify and cut into ¼-inch-thick slices. In a 3- to 4-quart pan, boil salsify, covered, in 2 inches acidulated water until tender when pierced (3 to 6 minutes). Drain.

Butter-steaming. Cut salsify into ¼-inch-thick slices. Butter-steam up to 5 cups, using 1 to 2 tablespoons butter or margarine. Cook, stirring, for 30 seconds. Add 4 to 5 tablespoons acidulated water, cover, and cook just until tender to bite (3 to 6 more minutes).

■ **Serving ideas.** Roll cooked salsify in melted butter in a frying pan, lightly sprinkle with sugar, and cook until glazed. Sprinkle cooked salsify with freshly grated Parmesan cheese or serve it with béchamel sauce.

Sharp-tasting sorrel leaves can be slivered for cooking or using raw in salads.

SALSIFY SALAD

Per serving: 379 calories, 12 g protein, 29 g carbohydrates, 35 g total fat, 57 mg cholesterol, 505 mg sodium

- ½ cup *each* mayonnaise and sour cream
- 2 tablespoons minced cornichons or dill pickles
- 2 tablespoons minced parsley
- 1 teaspoon lemon juice
- 1½ teaspoons Dijon mustard
- 1½ pounds salsify
- 1 large head Belgian endive
- 1 large head radicchio or red leaf lettuce
  Italian parsley or watercress sprigs
- ¼ pound thinly sliced prosciutto or smoked ham

Stir together mayonnaise, sour cream, cornichons, minced parsley, lemon juice, and mustard; set aside.

Peel salsify, then cut into sticks about 4 inches long and ½ inch thick. In a wide frying pan, bring 1 inch water to a boil over high heat. Add salsify; then reduce heat, cover, and simmer until barely tender when pierced (about 1 minute). Drain. While salsify is still hot, gently stir in mayonnaise mixture; let cool.

Meanwhile, trim and discard base of endive; rinse leaves and pat dry. Also separate radicchio leaves, rinse, and pat dry.

Spoon salsify equally onto 4 dinner plates. Garnish with endive, radicchio, parsley sprigs, and prosciutto. Makes 4 servings.

Scallions *see Onions, page 93*

Shallots *see Onions, page 93*

Sorrel

Long a staple in French cooking, tart-flavored sorrel has attracted quite a few fans in the United States as well. The smooth, bright green, arrow-shaped leaves taste like spinach—but sharper, with a lemony tang. And like spinach, sorrel is good both raw and cooked. Sorrel wilts after picking, but it retains its characteristic tartness even when wilted.

Nutrition. Sorrel is an excellent source of vitamins A and C and also provides fiber and iron. One cup of raw sorrel has only about 12 calories.

■ **Season.** July through October.

■ **Selection.** Select young, fresh-looking leaves that are free of blemishes.

■ **Amount.** Allow ¼ to ⅓ pound per person.

■ **Storage.** Wrap, unwashed, in paper towels. Refrigerate in a plastic bag for up to 2 days.

■ **Preparation.** Remove and discard tough stems and midribs. To wash, plunge into a large quantity of cold water; lift out and drain. Chop or tear into bite-size pieces; or stack leaves and cut into shreds.

■ **Cooking methods.** Heat causes sorrel's color to fade quickly. For more information on butter-steaming, see "A Glossary of Techniques," page 122.

Butter-steaming. Coarsely shred sorrel leaves. Butter-steam up to 5 cups lightly packed leaves, using 1 to 2 tablespoons butter or margarine. Cook, stirring, for 30 seconds. Then cover and cook just until leaves are wilted (2 to 3 more minutes).

■ **Serving ideas.** Use tender sorrel leaves in place of lettuce in hamburgers or hot or cold meat and cheese sandwiches. Offer finely shredded or chopped sorrel in tacos and tostadas, tuck it into a luncheon omelet with chopped green onions and sautéed mushrooms, or stir it into your favorite gazpacho before chilling. Toss in a salad as you would spinach, using a sweet-sour dressing.

Continued on page 109

ADDING FLAVOR WITH HERBS

Add a sprig of greenery, and familiar foods take on new character. Fresh herbs contribute pleasing aromas and flavors, from subtle to pungent, and using them creatively is one of the keys to good cooking.

Most of the herbs shown in the photograph below can be found in well-stocked produce markets; you might also try growing your own. The peak season for most herbs is July through September, though you'll find parsley and cilantro all year. Look for herbs with all-over green color; yellowing indicates old plants, while black, watery areas are a sign of bruising.

Rinse herbs under cold running water, then shake off excess moisture, wrap in a dry cloth or paper towel, and refrigerate in a plastic bag for up to 4 days (1 week for parsley). To use, pull or cut off leaves; chop or mince. Use whole leaves, sprigs, or blossoms for garnish.

You can freeze or dry herbs for longer storage. To freeze, wash herbs, pat dry, and freeze in airtight bags or foil; frozen herbs will darken and become limp when thawed, so do not thaw them before adding to the food you are cooking.

WHITE WINE HERB VINEGAR

Rinse and pat dry enough **fresh herb sprigs** (tarragon, thyme, or equal parts lemon thyme and marjoram or oregano) to loosely fill a glass jar. If desired, add 1 large clove **garlic** (peeled). Fill jar with **white wine vinegar,** cover with wax paper or plastic wrap, and secure lid. Let stand at room temperature for 3 weeks, then strain through several layers of cheesecloth into another jar. Use within several months.

FRESH HERB MAYONNAISE

To 1 cup **mayonnaise,** add 2 teaspoons **lemon juice** and about ½ cup chopped **fresh herbs** (basil, dill, marjoram, oregano, or savory; or use about ¼ cup tarragon). Mix well, then cover and refrigerate at least until next day or for up to 1 month.

WHIPPED HERB BUTTER

In a blender or food processor, combine 1 cup (½ lb.) **butter** or margarine (softened), 2 teaspoons **lemon juice,** and about ⅓ cup finely chopped **fresh herbs** (basil, chives, marjoram, oregano, or savory). Whirl until thoroughly blended; cover and refrigerate at least until next day or for up to 2 weeks.

CREAM OF SORREL SOUP

Per cup: 174 calories, 4 g protein, 12 g carbohydrates, 13 g total fat, 48 mg cholesterol, 386 mg sodium

> 3 tablespoons butter or margarine
> 1 medium-size onion, chopped
> 1 medium-size potato, peeled and diced
> 2 cans (14½ oz. *each*) regular-strength chicken broth
> 4 cups finely shredded sorrel
> ⅓ cup whipping cream
> Salt and pepper
> Ground nutmeg or sour cream

Melt butter in a 4-quart pan over medium heat. Add onion and cook, stirring often, until soft. Stir in potato and broth. Reduce heat, cover, and simmer until potato mashes easily (about 20 minutes). Stir in sorrel and cook for 3 more minutes.

In a blender, whirl vegetable mixture, a portion at a time, until smooth. Return to pan, stir in whipping cream, and season to taste with salt and pepper. Heat through. Ladle into small bowls; dust with nutmeg. Or cover and refrigerate until cold; serve cold, topping each serving with a dollop of sour cream. Makes about 5 cups.

BEEF & SORREL SCRAMBLE

Per serving: 289 calories, 33 g protein, 6 g carbohydrates, 14 g total fat, 327 mg cholesterol, 439 mg sodium

> ½ teaspoon salt
> 1 pound lean ground beef
> 1 medium-size onion, chopped
> 1 clove garlic, minced or pressed
> ¼ pound mushrooms, sliced
> ⅛ teaspoon *each* pepper, ground nutmeg, and oregano leaves
> 2 cups chopped sorrel
> 4 eggs, lightly beaten
> Grated Parmesan cheese

Sprinkle salt into a wide frying pan over medium heat; add beef and cook, stirring, until browned and crumbly. Stir in onion, garlic, and mushrooms; cook, stirring often, until onion is soft. Stir in pepper, nutmeg, oregano, and sorrel. Pour in eggs and cook, stirring gently to allow uncooked eggs to flow underneath, just until set to your liking. Pass cheese to sprinkle over individual servings. Makes 4 servings.

Spinach

One of the world's best-known vegetables, spinach was cultivated in ancient Persia more than 2,000 years ago. A versatile performer in the kitchen, it's equally tasty cooked or raw.

Though there are a number of spinach varieties, they fall into two broad groups: smooth-textured types and those having ruffly or crinkled leaves. There's no difference in flavor or nutrient content. *(Photo on page 72.)*

New Zealand spinach is a coarser-leafed relative of regular spinach. It can be used interchangeably with regular spinach in recipes.

Nutrition. Spinach is an excellent source of vitamin A and potassium and a good source of vitamin C, riboflavin, and (when cooked) iron. About ¾ pound of raw spinach (an average-size bunch) has only 90 calories.

■ **Season.** All year.

■ **Selection.** Choose bunches having crisp, tender, deep green leaves; avoid yellowing bunches and those with blemished leaves.

■ **Amount.** Allow ⅓ to ½ pound per person for cooked spinach, about ¼ pound per person for spinach served raw in salads.

■ **Storage.** Discard yellow, damaged, and wilted leaves. Remove and discard tough stems and midribs. To wash, plunge into a large quantity of cold water; lift out and drain. Pat dry, wrap in a dry cloth or paper towels, and refrigerate in a plastic bag for up to 3 days. (Spinach washed immediately before cooking need not be dried; cook it in the water that clings to the leaves.)

■ **Preparation.** Leave whole or tear into bite-size pieces; or stack leaves and cut into shreds.

■ **Cooking methods.** For more information on the cooking methods listed here, see "A Glossary of Techniques," page 122.

Boiling. In a 4- to 5-quart pan, boil about 1½ pounds spinach, covered, in water that clings to leaves until wilted and bright green in color (2 to 4 minutes). Drain.

Butter-steaming. Use leaves whole or coarsely chop. Butter-steam up to 5 cups lightly packed leaves, using 1 to 2 tablespoons butter or margarine. Cook, stirring, for 30 seconds. Then cover and cook just until leaves are wilted (2 to 3 more minutes).

Microwaving. Arrange 1 pound spinach in a 3-quart nonmetallic baking dish. Cover and microwave on **HIGH (100%)** for 5 to 7 minutes, stirring after 3 minutes. Let stand, covered, for 2 minutes. Spinach should be bright green and look wilted.

Steaming. Arrange spinach on a rack. Steam until wilted and bright green in color (3 to 5 minutes).

Stir-frying. Use leaves whole or coarsely chop. Stir-fry up to 5 cups lightly packed leaves, using 1 tablespoon salad oil, for 30 seconds. Then cover and cook just until leaves are wilted (2 to 3 more minutes).

■ **Serving ideas.** Enjoy raw spinach dressed with a vinaigrette or in mixed green and vegetable salads. Season hot cooked spinach with melted butter, nutmeg, or grated lemon peel; add crisply cooked and crumbled bacon or chopped hard-cooked egg to either cooked spinach or spinach salad. Include chopped cooked spinach in stuffings for poultry or fish, or serve it as a low-calorie alternative to rice as a bed for curried, creamed, and sauced entrées.

GREEN PASTA WITH SPINACH PESTO

Per serving: 629 calories, 27 g protein, 60 g carbohydrates, 32 g total fat, 107 mg cholesterol, 487 mg sodium

> 10 ounces spinach
> Spinach Pesto (recipe follows)
> 10 ounces dry spinach noodles
> ½ cup minced red onion
> 1 cup radishes, thinly sliced
> Salt and pepper
> Grated Parmesan cheese

Clean spinach as previously directed, then cut leaves into thin shreds. Lightly pack enough spinach to measure 1 cup; reserve for pesto. Set remaining shredded leaves aside.

Prepare Spinach Pesto and set aside. Cook noodles in boiling water according to package directions until just tender to bite; drain and transfer to a large shallow bowl. Pour pesto on noodles; sprinkle with shredded spinach, onion, and radishes. Mix with 2 forks to blend. Season to taste with salt and pepper. Pass cheese to sprinkle over individual servings. Makes 4 servings.

Spinach Pesto. In a blender or food processor, combine 1 cup **reserved shredded spinach**, 1 clove **garlic**, ¼ cup **pine nuts**, 1 cup (about 5 oz.) grated **Romano cheese**, 1 cup **plain yogurt**, and ¼ cup **olive oil** or salad oil. Whirl until puréed.

SPINACH CRÊPES

Per serving: 260 calories, 11 g protein, 26 g carbohydrates, 13 g total fat, 173 mg cholesterol, 171 mg sodium

   ½ **pound spinach**
   3 **eggs**
   1 **tablespoon salad oil**
   1 **cup all-purpose flour**
  1½ **cups milk**
     About 2 tablespoons
     butter or margarine
     Sour cream

Clean spinach as previously directed, then coarsely chop. In a blender or food processor, whirl spinach, eggs, and oil until smooth; add flour and whirl to blend. Add milk and whirl until smooth; stop to scrape container sides as needed.

Set a 6- to 7-inch crêpe pan or flat-bottomed frying pan over medium heat. When hot, add ¼ teaspoon butter; spread butter over pan bottom as it melts. Add about 3 tablespoons of the spinach batter and tilt pan so batter coats pan bottom. Cook until top looks dry (about 1 minute). With a wide spatula, turn over and cook for 20 to 30 more seconds. Turn out onto a flat surface. Cover and keep hot. Repeat with remaining batter, adding about ¼ teaspoon butter to pan each time and stacking crêpes as cooked.

Fold or roll crêpes; top with sour cream. Makes 5 or 6 servings.

■ *See also* **Carambola Spinach Salad** *(page 18),* **Cauliflower-Spinach Toss** *(page 72),* **Maltese Soup** *(page 95),* **Spinach-stuffed Tomatoes** *(page 120).*

Sprouts

Alfalfa and mung bean sprouts are the best known sprouts, but any number of seeds and beans—including clover, sunflower seeds, radish seeds, wheat berries, and lentils—can be sprouted for a crunchy addition to salads, sandwiches, and other dishes.

Some sprouts, like tiny alfalfa and larger, crispy mung bean, are mild in flavor. Others, such as mustard, radish, cress, and chia, are more peppery. While most sprouts are eaten raw or used as a garnish, mung bean sprouts are also a common ingredient in cooked Asian dishes.

Nutrition. Sprouts have a very high ratio of protein to calories; they contain some vitamin C. One cup of raw mung bean sprouts has 37 calories; 3½ ounces of alfalfa sprouts provide about 29 calories.

■ **Season.** All year.

■ **Selection.** Select small, tender examples of all varieties. Bean sprouts should be crisp and white with beans attached.

■ **Amount.** Allow about ¼ pound mung bean sprouts per person when cooked as a vegetable.

■ **Storage.** Refrigerate, unwashed, in a plastic bag for up to 3 days.

■ **Preparation.** Rinse and drain sprouts; discard discolored mung bean sprouts.

■ **Cooking methods.** Use the following methods for mung bean sprouts. For more information on the cooking methods listed here, see "A Glossary of Techniques," page 122.

Butter-steaming. Butter-steam up to 5 cups bean sprouts, using 1 to 2 tablespoons butter or margarine. Cook, stirring, for 1 minute. Add 1 tablespoon liquid, cover, and cook until tender-crisp to bite (½ to 1½ more minutes).

Microwaving. Rinse 1 pound mung bean sprouts in cold water just before using. Arrange in a 2-quart nonmetallic baking dish; cover and microwave on **HIGH (100%)** for 4 to 5 minutes, stirring after 2 minutes. Let stand, covered, for 2 minutes. Bean sprouts should be tender-crisp to bite.

Add interest to salads or sandwiches with a handful of sprouts (clockwise from top): mung bean, clover, lentil, sunflower, or alfalfa.

Stir-frying. Stir-fry up to 5 cups bean sprouts, using 1 tablespoon salad oil, for 1 minute. Add 1 tablespoon liquid. Cover and cook until tender-crisp to bite (½ to 1½ more minutes).

■ **Serving ideas.** Use raw alfalfa sprouts or other tiny sprouts in salads, tuck them into meat or cheese sandwiches, sprinkle over thick soups or cottage cheese, or mix into scrambled eggs just before removing from heat. Add raw mung bean or other larger sprouts to salads. Season lightly cooked sprouts with butter, ginger, or soy sauce. Also include larger sprouts in stir-fry combinations.

SPROUT & VEGETABLE MEDLEY

Per serving: 117 calories, 3 g protein, 10 g carbohydrates, 8 g total fat, 24 mg cholesterol, 116 mg sodium

   4 **tablespoons butter or**
     margarine
   1 **large onion, thinly sliced**
   2 **cups** *each* **thinly sliced**
     zucchini and carrots
   ¼ **cup water**
   3 **cups mung bean sprouts**
     Salt and pepper

Melt 2 tablespoons of the butter in a wide frying pan over medium heat. Add onion and cook, stirring often, until soft and golden (about 15 minutes). Remove from pan; set aside.

Melt remaining 2 tablespoons butter in pan. Add zucchini, carrots, and water. Cover and cook, stirring occasionally, until vegetables are just tender to bite (about 5 minutes). Add bean sprouts, return onion to pan, and heat through. Season to taste with salt and pepper. Makes 6 servings.

Squash

Both summer and winter squash were important foods in the native American diet—and both were exported to Europe soon after Columbus's arrival in the New World. Though "summer" and "winter" do refer to the main months of availability, peak season isn't the chief difference between the two types.

Summer squash are picked when still immature and tender skinned. Hard-shelled winter squash, on the other hand, are allowed to reach maturity before being harvested. In a category of its own is spaghetti squash; it falls somewhere between summer and winter squash in skin hardness. (Also in the squash family is the chayote; see page 75.)

Nutrition. Summer squash are high in vitamin C and extremely low in calories—a cup of cooked squash provides only about 25 calories. Winter squash are low in sodium and an excellent source of vitamin A; their calorie count ranges from about 90 to 130 per cup (cooked). Spaghetti squash, high in folic acid and low in sodium, has about 45 calories per cup when cooked. All squash are high in fiber.

SUMMER SQUASH

Distinguished by their edible skins and seeds, summer squash vary widely in shape and skin color—but all types have a mild, delicate flavor that makes them largely interchangeable in use. Despite the name, summer

New summer squash varieties have come along by the basketful in recent years; baby-size squash and squash blossoms are a favorite with restaurant chefs.

squash are generally available almost all year round.

Most popular among the group is the zucchini (also called Italian squash or courgette)—typically straight, slim, and dark green. Some newer zucchini varieties are solid yellow in color. English squash looks like a fatter, paler zucchini, while global squash is rounded. Other favorite kinds of summer squash include yellow straightneck; yellow, curving crookneck; and pale green, dark green, white, or yellow (Sunburst) pattypan, scallop, or scallopini squash, shaped something like a top with a scalloped edge.

■ **Season.** All year; peak July through September.

■ **Selection.** Select small to medium-size, firm squash with smooth, glossy, tender skin. Squash should feel heavy for their size.

■ **Amount.** Allow ¼ to ⅓ pound per person.

■ **Storage.** Refrigerate, unwashed, in a plastic bag for up to 5 days.

Continued on next page

...Squash continued

■ **Preparation.** Trim off and discard ends. Rinse squash, but do not peel. Leave whole, dice, or cut into slices or julienne strips.

■ **Cooking methods.** For more information on the cooking methods listed here, see "A Glossary of Techniques," page 122. You can also substitute shredded zucchini for carrots in the recipe for Carrot Cake on page 70.

Boiling. In a 3-quart pan, boil 1 to 1½ pounds whole squash, covered, in 1 inch water until tender when pierced (8 to 12 minutes). Drain.

Boil 1 to 1½ pounds of ¼-inch slices in ½ inch water for 3 to 6 minutes. Drain.

Butter-steaming. Cut squash into ¼-inch slices. Butter-steam up to 5 cups, using 1 to 2 tablespoons butter or margarine. Cook, stirring, for 1 minute. Add 2 to 4 tablespoons liquid, cover, and cook just until tender-crisp to bite (3 to 4 more minutes).

Microwaving. Cut 1 to 1½ pounds squash into ¼-inch slices. Arrange in a 1½-quart nonmetallic baking dish. Add 2 tablespoons butter or margarine, cut into 6 pieces; cover. Microwave on **HIGH (100%)** for 6 to 7 minutes, stirring after 3 minutes. Let stand, covered, for 3 minutes. Squash should be tender when pierced.

Steaming. Arrange whole squash or ¼-inch slices on a rack. Steam until tender when pierced (10 to 12 minutes for whole squash, 4 to 7 minutes for slices).

Stir-frying. Cut squash into ¼-inch slices. Stir-fry up to 5 cups, using 1 tablespoon salad oil, for 1 minute. Add 2 to 4 tablespoons liquid, cover, and cook just until tender-crisp to bite (3 to 4 more minutes).

■ **Serving ideas.** Offer raw summer squash as a snack, add to a relish tray with other raw vegetables, or serve as an appetizer with your favorite dip. Shredded raw squash mixed with a complementary dressing makes a colorful slaw. Dress hot cooked squash with butter seasoned with basil, oregano, or dill weed. Or top with shredded Cheddar, Swiss, jack, or Parmesan cheese and slip under the broiler until bubbly.

ZUCCHINI OMELETS

Per serving: 174 calories, 11 g protein, 3 g carbohydrates, 13 g total fat, 278 mg cholesterol, 265 mg sodium

½	**pound small zucchini**
4	**eggs**
1½	**tablespoons minced parsley**
⅛	**to ¼ teaspoon ground nutmeg**
	Salt and pepper
4	**teaspoons butter or margarine**
½	**cup shredded Swiss cheese**

Prepare zucchini as previously directed, then finely shred. With your hands, squeeze as much liquid from zucchini as possible. Measure zucchini; you should have 1 cup. With a fork, beat together zucchini, eggs, and parsley until blended; beat in nutmeg, then season to taste with salt and pepper.

Melt 1 teaspoon of the butter in an 8- to 9-inch omelet pan or flat-bottomed frying pan over medium heat. Add ¼ of the zucchini mixture and spread over pan bottom. Cook until bottom is lightly browned and top is still moist.

Remove from heat. Fold ⅓ of omelet over center; slide unfolded edge onto a plate, then flip folded portion over on top. Keep warm. Repeat with remaining 3 teaspoons butter and remaining zucchini mixture to make 3 more omelets. Sprinkle evenly with cheese and serve hot. Makes 4 servings.

COOL GOLDEN CHOWDER

Per serving: 148 calories, 5 g protein, 19 g carbohydrates, 7 g total fat, 24 mg cholesterol, 269 mg sodium

2	**tablespoons butter or margarine**
1	**medium-size onion, chopped**
1	**cup chopped carrots**
2½	**cups chopped crookneck squash, straightneck squash, or golden zucchini**
1	**can (14½ oz.) regular-strength chicken broth**
1	**cup fresh corn kernels cut from cob**
¼	**teaspoon thyme leaves Salt and pepper**
½	**cup milk Chopped parsley Sunflower seeds**

Melt butter in a 3-quart pan over medium heat; add onion and cook, stirring often, until soft. Stir in carrots, squash, and broth. Bring to a boil; then reduce heat, cover, and simmer for 10 minutes. Add corn; cover and simmer until carrots are tender to bite (about 5 more minutes).

In a blender or food processor, whirl soup, a portion at a time, until smooth. Add thyme and season to taste with salt and pepper. Cover and refrigerate for at least 4 hours or until next day. Stir milk into cold soup; garnish with parsley. Pass sunflower seeds to sprinkle on individual servings. Makes 4 or 5 servings.

■ *See also* **Vegetable Purée** *(page 71),* **Sprout & Vegetable Medley** *(page 110).*

WINTER SQUASH

Richly hued squash with yellow or orange flesh were a winter staple for early American settlers. Harvested in autumn, they could be kept for months thanks to their thick, hard shells.

Besides their later harvest date, winter squash also differ from their summer cousins in that only the flesh is eaten (though the seeds can be eaten if toasted and husked).

Depending on the type, winter squash range in flavor from very mild to distinctly nutty, with varying degrees of sweetness. Textures differ, too—from smooth to pebbly outside, fibrous to creamy within. All these squash can be used in much the same way.

The photograph on page 113 shows five longtime favorites and five relative newcomers. The smallest common winter squash is the acorn (usually 1 to 3 lbs.), with sweet, slightly fibrous flesh. Next comes the butternut (2 to 5 lbs.), with sweet, nutty, creamy-textured flesh. The giants of the family are banana squash (10 to 70 lbs.), Hubbard (9 to 12 lbs.), and pumpkin—on record as reaching weights of several hundred pounds. Banana squash is slightly sweet, Hubbard somewhat sweeter; both have creamy flesh. Pumpkin has a mild, watery flavor and fibrous texture.

Newer to the marketplace are extra-sweet Delicata and Japanese (Kabocha) varieties, sweet Chinese and Sweet Dumpling, and mild Golden Acorn.

■ **Season.** All year for some types; peak September through March for most kinds.

Hubbard

Banana

Butternut

Pumpkin

Chinese

Japanese

Acorn

Sweet Dumpling

Golden Acorn

Delicata

As Halloween approaches, pumpkins and the other members of the colorful winter squash clan appear in markets.

■ **Selection.** Choose hard, thick-shelled squash that feel heavy for their size. Banana and Hubbard squash are usually sold cut; select pieces with thick, bright yellow-orange flesh. The smaller pumpkins are the best for eating; choose larger ones for decorative uses or serving containers.

■ **Amount.** Allow ⅓ to ½ pound per person. Or serve baked halves of the smaller squashes (or whole Sweet Dumplings) as hearty individual servings.

■ **Storage.** Store whole squash, unwrapped, in a cool (50°F), dry, dark place with good ventilation for up to

2 months. Wrap cut pieces in plastic wrap and refrigerate for up to 5 days.

■ **Preparation.** Rinse. Cut acorn, butternut, Chinese, Delicata, Golden Acorn, Japanese (Kabocha) squash, or pumpkin in half lengthwise; or cut a "lid" off Japanese squash or pumpkin. Cut Sweet Dumpling in half crosswise; use top half as lid. Cut banana or Hubbard squash into serving-size pieces.

Remove and discard seeds and fibers. Bake unpeeled. For other cooking methods, peel with a sharp knife and cut into cubes, spears, or slices.

■ Cooking methods.
For more information on the cooking methods listed here, see "A Glossary of Techniques," page 122.

Baking. Prepare all squash as previously directed. Place, cut side down, in a greased rimmed baking pan. Bake all except pumpkin, covered, in a 400° to 450° oven until flesh is tender when pierced (30 to 45 minutes). Bake small pumpkin, uncovered, in a 350° oven until flesh is tender when pierced (1 to 1¼ hours).

Boiling. Prepare all squash as previously directed, then peel and cut into ½-inch-thick slices. In a wide frying pan, boil 1½ to 2 pounds squash, covered, in ½ inch water until tender when pierced (7 to 9 minutes). Drain.

Butter-steaming. Prepare squash (especially banana, Hubbard, or pumpkin) as previously directed. Peel and cut into 1-inch cubes. Butter-steam up to 5 cups, using 2 tablespoons butter or margarine. Cook, stirring, for 1 minute. Add 3 to 5 tablespoons liquid, cover, and cook just until squash is tender to bite (6 to 8 more minutes).

Microwaving. As previously directed, prepare 2 medium-size squash such as acorn or butternut (about 1½ lbs. *each*) or a 1-pound piece of squash such as banana. (Pumpkin is not recommended for microwaving.) Place squash, cut side up, in a 9- by 13-inch nonmetallic baking dish. Spread cut surfaces with 1 to 2 tablespoons butter or margarine; cover. Microwave on **HIGH (100%)** for 10 to 13 minutes, rotating dish ½ turn after 5 minutes. Let stand, covered, for 5 minutes. Flesh should be tender when pierced.

Steaming. Prepare all squash as previously directed, then peel and cut into ½-inch-thick slices. Arrange on a rack. Steam until tender when pierced (9 to 12 minutes).

■ Serving ideas.
Top hot cooked winter squash with melted butter seasoned with allspice, cardamom, cinnamon, or nutmeg. Or sprinkle with brown sugar and toasted nuts. Small chunks of peeled squash are a tasty addition to soups and stews. Make a squash slaw using peeled, shredded raw squash, raisins, chopped nuts, and a seasoned mayonnaise.

Use baked whole or half squash as serving containers for meat stew or baked beans. Or hollow out a pumpkin to serve as a soup tureen.

AUTUMN SQUASH SOUP

Per serving: 292 calories, 12 g protein, 54 g carbohydrates, 6 g total fat, 20 mg cholesterol, 1023 mg sodium

- ¼ cup salad oil
- 4 medium-size onions, chopped
- 2 teaspoons thyme leaves
- ½ teaspoon ground nutmeg
- 1 pound rutabagas, peeled and diced
- 2 pounds thin-skinned potatoes, peeled and cubed
- 16 cups peeled, cubed banana, Hubbard, acorn, or Golden Acorn squash, or pumpkin (about 7 lbs.)
- 3½ quarts regular-strength chicken broth
- 1 large pumpkin shell (about 6-qt. capacity), top cut off, seeds and fibers scraped out
- Boiling water

Heat oil in an 8- to 10-quart pan over medium-high heat. Add onions, thyme, and nutmeg and cook, stirring frequently, until onions are soft (about 15 minutes). Add rutabagas, potatoes, and squash; cook, stirring occasionally, until vegetables begin to soften (about 30 minutes). Pour in broth and bring to a boil over high heat; then reduce heat, cover, and simmer until squash mashes easily (about 1½ hours).

Whirl vegetables and broth, a portion at a time, in a blender or food processor until smooth. If made ahead, let cool, then cover and refrigerate until next day.

Return soup to pan and bring to a boil, stirring often; keep warm. While you are reheating soup, heat pumpkin shell: fill it with boiling water and let stand until shell feels warm (about 20 minutes). Drain water and pour in soup. Serve hot. Makes 10 to 12 servings.

CUSTARD SQUASH PIE

Per serving: 549 calories, 9 g protein, 50 g carbohydrates, 36 g total fat, 248 mg cholesterol, 252 mg sodium

- 1½ to 2 pounds squash, such as banana, Hubbard, acorn, Golden Acorn, or Japanese (Kabocha)
- 4 eggs
- 1½ cups whipping cream
- 2 teaspoons ground cinnamon
- ½ teaspoon ground nutmeg
- ⅔ to 1 cup firmly packed brown sugar
  Unbaked 9- or 10-inch pie shell
  Sweetened whipped cream

Prepare and bake squash as previously directed. Scrape cooked squash from shell and whirl in a blender or food processor until smooth. Measure 2 cups squash and spoon into a strainer; let stand for about 10 minutes to drain off any excess liquid.

In a large bowl, beat together eggs, the 1½ cups whipping cream, cinnamon, and nutmeg. Stir in squash and sugar to taste. Pour squash mixture into pie shell and bake in a 350° oven until custard appears set in center when pan is gently shaken (1 hour to 1 hour and 10 minutes).

Serve warm or at room temperature, topped with sweetened whipped cream. Makes 6 to 8 servings.

SPAGHETTI SQUASH

The pale yellow flesh of spaghetti squash separates into strands when cooked—hence the name. And like spaghetti, this squash is an ideal foil for all kinds of sauces, thanks to its mild, almost nutlike flavor.

Spaghetti squash is oblong, with pale to bright yellow skin. An average-size squash weighs 3 to 4 pounds.

While spaghetti squash is believed to have originated in the New World, the variety that's most popular today was developed in Japan during this century.

■ Season.
August through February.

■ Selection.
Spaghetti squash should have a hard, thick shell and feel heavy for its size.

■ Amount.
Allow about ½ pound per person.

■ Storage.
Store whole squash, unwrapped, at room temperature for up to 2 months.

To serve baked spaghetti squash, cut cooked squash in half and remove seeds. Use a fork to remove spaghetti-like strands.

■ **Preparation.** Rinse; do not peel. Then proceed as directed for baking or microwaving.

■ **Cooking methods.** For more information on the cooking methods listed here, see "A Glossary of Techniques," page 122.

Baking. Pierce shell of medium-size squash in several places to allow steam to escape. Place whole squash in a rimmed baking pan. Bake, uncovered, in a 350° oven for 45 minutes; turn squash over and continue to bake until shell gives to pressure (15 to 45 more minutes).

Microwaving. Cut 1 small spaghetti squash (1¼ lbs.) in half lengthwise; remove seeds. Place squash, cut sides up, in a 9- by 13-inch nonmetallic baking dish. Spread cut surfaces with 1 to 2 tablespoons butter or margarine; cover. Microwave on **HIGH (100%)** for 10 to 12 minutes, rotating each piece ½ turn after 5 minutes. Let stand, covered, for 5 minutes. Shell should give to pressure.

■ **Serving ideas.** Cooked spaghetti squash is a crisp-textured, low-calorie base for almost any topping. Try butter seasoned with basil or oregano and minced parsley; or toss the strands with butter and grated Parmesan cheese. You can also use spaghetti squash in place of pasta, with your favorite sauce.

SPAGHETTI SQUASH HASH BROWNS

Per serving: 184 calories, 5 g protein, 22 g carbohydrates, 10 g total fat, 30 mg cholesterol, 144 mg sodium

- 1 **spaghetti squash (4 to 5 lbs.)**
- ⅓ **cup all-purpose flour**
- ½ **cup grated Parmesan cheese**
  About 4 tablespoons butter or margarine
  Salt and pepper
  Sour cream
  Parsley sprigs

Prepare and bake spaghetti squash as previously directed. Cut in half lengthwise, discard seeds, and scoop flesh into a bowl; you should have about 6 cups. Add flour and cheese. Using 2 forks, lift squash strands to mix well.

Melt 1 tablespoon of the butter in a wide frying pan over medium-high heat. Spoon ¼ cup squash mixture into pan. With a fork, quickly pat and press to form an evenly thick cake about 3 inches in diameter. Repeat to make more cakes, leaving about ½ inch between cakes. Cook cakes until bottoms are lightly browned (2 to 3 minutes), then turn over and cook until lightly browned on other side (2 to 3 more minutes). Transfer to a platter; keep warm.

Continue until all squash mixture has been used, adding more butter to pan as needed. Season to taste with salt and pepper; serve with sour cream and garnish with parsley. Makes 6 to 8 servings.

Sunchokes

Also known as Jerusalem artichokes, sunchokes are the knotty, brown-skinned roots of a sunflower relative. Their common name notwithstanding, they're *not* artichokes; nor do they have any connection with Jerusalem (they're American natives). Though once considered a specialty item, sunchokes are now readily available in many supermarkets.

Beneath their thin skin, sunchokes have crisp, white flesh with a mellow, nutlike flavor; you can enjoy them raw or cooked, hot or chilled.

Nutrition. Sunchokes are a good source of vitamin B and iron. A 3½-ounce serving (raw) contains 7 calories just after harvesting, about 75 after storage.

A note of caution: Since sunchokes contain a starch that many people cannot digest efficiently, they should be eaten in moderation until a tolerance is established.

■ **Season.** October through April.

■ **Selection.** Choose firm sunchokes that are free of mold.

■ **Amount.** Allow ¼ to ⅓ pound per person.

■ **Storage.** Refrigerate, unwashed, in a plastic bag for up to 1 week.

■ **Preparation.** Scrub well or peel with a vegetable peeler. Leave whole; or slice, dice, or shred. Submerge peeled and cut sunchokes immediately in a bowl of acidulated water (3 tablespoons vinegar or lemon juice per quart water) to prevent discoloration.

Continued on next page

Prepare sunchokes by scrubbing well, slicing, and submerging in lemon water to prevent browning.

…Sunchokes continued

■ **Cooking methods.** In addition to the following, slices and finger-size sunchoke pieces can be deep-fried like potatoes. For more information on the cooking methods listed here, see "A Glossary of Techniques," page 122.

Boiling. In a 3-quart pan, boil 1 to 1½ pounds whole medium-size sunchokes, covered, in 1 inch water until tender when pierced (10 to 20 minutes). Drain.

In a wide frying pan, boil ¼- to ½-inch slices, covered, in ½ inch water for 5 to 10 minutes. Drain.

Butter-steaming. Cut sunchokes into ¼-inch slices. Butter-steam up to 5 cups, using 2 tablespoons butter or margarine. Cook, stirring, for 1 minute. Add 2 to 3 tablespoons liquid, cover, and cook just until tender-crisp to bite (3 to 5 more minutes).

Steaming. Arrange whole sunchokes or ¼-inch slices on a rack. Steam until tender when pierced (15 to 20 minutes for whole sunchokes, 5 to 10 minutes for slices).

■ **Serving ideas.** With their crisp texture and nutlike flavor, sunchokes make a good substitute for water chestnuts in salads and stir-fry combinations. Season hot cooked sunchokes with butter, tarragon, or lemon juice; or top them with hollandaise sauce (page 66). Mix shredded raw sunchokes with a mayonnaise dressing for a sunchoke slaw.

To make speedy sunchoke pickles, save the pickling liquid when you finish a jar of dill pickles. Cut sunchokes crosswise into ¼-inch slices, drop into pickling liquid to cover, screw on lid, and refrigerate for at least 24 hours or up to 2 weeks.

SUNCHOKE SALAD

Per serving: 350 calories, 7 g protein, 6 g carbohydrates, 30 g total fat, 154 mg cholesterol, 399 mg sodium

- 1 pound sunchokes
- 1 cup sliced celery
- ½ cup thinly sliced green onions (including tops)
- 2 hard-cooked eggs, diced
- 5 slices bacon, crisply cooked, drained, and crumbled
- ½ cup mayonnaise
- 2 tablespoons sweet pickle relish
- 1 teaspoon Dijon mustard
  Salt and pepper
  Chopped parsley

Prepare sunchokes as previously directed; cut into ¼-inch slices and steam as previously directed. Let cool.

In a large bowl, combine sunchokes, celery, onions, eggs, and bacon. Stir together mayonnaise, relish, and mustard; pour over sunchoke mixture and mix well. Season to taste with salt and pepper. Cover and refrigerate for about 4 hours. Garnish with parsley. Makes 4 to 6 servings.

■ *See also Fava Bean Sauté (page 62).*

Sweet Potatoes & Yams

Though sweet potatoes and yams are often considered interchangeable, they're actually two different plants. The first is native to and grown in the Americas, while the second is cultivated primarily in tropical areas. The "yams" marketed in the United States are actually a type of sweet potato. *(Photo on page 101.)*

Sweet potatoes fall into two categories: moist-fleshed (our common market "yams") and dry-fleshed. The skin color of moist-fleshed types ranges from light copper to dark red and purple; the bright orange flesh is sweet and moist when cooked. Dry-fleshed sweet potatoes have cream-colored to yellow flesh that's dry and mealy after cooking; their skin may be yellowish gray, tan, or brown. Both types of sweet potatoes vary in shape from round to slim and tapering.

Pale-fleshed true yams are sweeter and moister than sweet potatoes. Though rarely sold in American supermarkets, they're sometimes available in Hispanic and Asian markets.

Nutrition. Sweet potatoes are an excellent source of vitamin A, a good source of vitamin C and potassium. One sweet potato, baked or boiled in its skin, has about 165 calories.

■ **Season.** All year; peak October through March.

■ **Selection.** Choose firm, well-shaped sweet potatoes with bright, uniformly colored skin.

■ **Amount.** Allow 1 medium to large sweet potato per person.

■ **Storage.** Store, unwrapped, in a cool (50°F), dry, dark place with good ventilation for up to 2 months or at room temperature for up to 1 week.

■ **Preparation.** Scrub well. Leave whole; or peel, then slice, dice, or shred.

■ **Cooking methods.** You may use either "yams" or dry-fleshed sweet potatoes in our recipes. For more information on the cooking methods listed here, see "A Glossary of Techniques," page 122.

Baking. Pierce skin in several places; rub with butter or margarine. Arrange in a single layer in a rimmed baking pan. Bake, uncovered, in a 400° oven until soft when squeezed (45 to 50 minutes).

Boiling. In a 3-quart pan, boil 4 whole medium-size (3-inch-diameter) sweet potatoes, covered, in 2 inches water until tender throughout when pierced (20 to 30 minutes). Drain.

Microwaving. Pierce skin of medium-size sweet potatoes with a fork. Place on a double layer of paper towels on floor of microwave; if cooking more than 2 at a time, arrange like spokes. Microwave on **HIGH (100%)**, turning halfway through cooking. Allow 4 to 5 minutes for 1 potato; add 2 to 3 minutes to the total cooking time for each additional potato. Let stand for 5 to 10 minutes, wrapped in foil or a clean towel. Potatoes should feel soft when squeezed.

Steaming. Arrange whole medium-size (3-inch-diameter) sweet potatoes on a rack. Steam until tender throughout when pierced (30 to 40 minutes).

■ **Serving ideas.** Serve hot cooked sweet potatoes with butter seasoned with lemon peel and juice, orange peel and juice, brown sugar, or chopped pecans. Substitute cooked sweet potatoes for thin-skinned potatoes in your favorite potato salad recipe. Or mash cooked sweet potatoes as you would russet potatoes; add butter and a sweet spice such as cinnamon or nutmeg.

SWEET POTATOES WITH TEQUILA & LIME

Per serving: 259 calories, 2 g protein, 23 g carbohydrates, 17 g total fat, 47 mg cholesterol, 187 mg sodium

¾ cup (¼ lb. plus ¼ cup) **butter or margarine**
2 pounds **sweet potatoes**
2 tablespoons **sugar**
2 tablespoons **tequila**
1 tablespoon **lime juice**
Salt and pepper
Lime wedges

Place a 12- to 14-inch frying pan over medium heat; add butter and stir until melted. Set aside.

Peel sweet potatoes, then shred, using a food processor or coarse holes of a grater. Immediately mix with butter in pan, then sprinkle with sugar. Cook over medium heat until potatoes begin to caramelize and look slightly translucent (about 15 minutes); turn occasionally with a wide spatula.

Stir in tequila and lime juice. Cook, stirring, for 3 more minutes. Season to taste with salt and pepper. Pour into a bowl; garnish with lime wedges. Makes 6 to 8 servings.

SWEET POTATO & GINGER SALAD

Per serving: 378 calories, 2 g protein, 61 g carbohydrates, 8 g total fat, 0 mg cholesterol, 8 mg sodium

½ pound **sweet potatoes**
2 tablespoons **lemon juice**
1 small **pineapple (about 3 lbs.)**
1 cup peeled, finely **shredded jicama**
2 tablespoons **salad oil**
2 teaspoons **honey**
1 teaspoon *each* minced **fresh ginger and grated lemon peel**
Finely chopped parsley
Red leaf lettuce leaves

In a 5-quart pan, bring about 12 cups water to a boil over high heat. Peel and shred sweet potatoes; immediately add to boiling water. Cook for 30 seconds; then drain well and mix with lemon juice.

Cut off pineapple peel. Cut about half the pineapple into 4 crosswise slices and set aside. Core and finely chop remaining pineapple; drain briefly.

Squeeze excess liquid from jicama. Mix jicama, chopped pineapple, oil, honey, ginger, and lemon peel with sweet potatoes. (At this point, you

may cover and let stand at room temperature for 3 to 4 hours.)

Place an equal portion of potato mixture atop each pineapple slice. Sprinkle with parsley and present on a lettuce-lined platter. Makes 4 servings.

Swiss Chard

Swiss chard is actually a type of beet—but it develops lush leaves rather than a fleshy root. No one seems to know why it's called "Swiss." It is believed to have originated in the Mediterranean and Near East, but today it's particularly popular in parts of France.

Swiss chard almost gives you two vegetables in one. The enlarged white or scarlet stem has a delicate taste reminiscent of celery; the wide leaves resemble spinach and are treated much the same way, though raw chard has a noticeable beetlike flavor.

Nutrition. Swiss chard is an excellent source of vitamin A, potassium, and iron and also provides some calcium. One cup of cooked leaves and stems has only 26 calories.

Red or green Swiss chard leaves should be cut or torn from center stems before cooking.

■ **Season.** Much of the year; peak July through October.

■ **Selection.** Look for bunches with fresh, glossy leaves and heavy white or red stems.

■ **Amount.** Allow ⅓ to ½ pound per person.

■ **Storage.** Refrigerate, unwashed, in a plastic bag for up to 3 days.

■ **Preparation.** To clean, plunge into a large quantity of cold water; lift out and drain. Cut off discolored stem bases and discard. Cut leaves from stems (leaves cook faster). Slice stems crosswise; leave leaves whole or shred.

■ **Cooking methods.** You can substitute small, tender chard leaves in most recipes using cooked spinach or "greens with a bite" (see pages 109 and 83). For more information on the cooking methods listed here, see "A Glossary of Techniques," page 122.

Boiling. Prepare 1½ to 2 pounds Swiss chard, cutting stems crosswise into ¼-inch slices and shredding leaves. In a wide frying pan, boil stems, covered, in ¼ inch water for 2 minutes. Add leaves and cook just until stems and leaves are tender-crisp to bite (1 to 2 more minutes).

Butter-steaming. Use up to 5 cups *total* chard stems and leaves—stems cut into ¼-inch slices, leaves cut into shreds. Butter-steam stems, using 2 tablespoons butter or margarine. Cook, stirring, for 1 minute. Add 1 tablespoon liquid; cover and cook for 2 more minutes. Add leaves, cover, and cook just until stems and leaves are tender-crisp to bite (1½ to 2½ more minutes).

Microwaving. Prepare 1¼ to 1½ pounds Swiss chard, cutting stems crosswise into ¼-inch slices and shredding leaves. Place stems in a 2-quart nonmetallic baking dish with 2 tablespoons water; cover. Microwave on **HIGH (100%)** for 3 minutes. Add leaves and microwave for 4 to 5 more minutes. Let stand, covered, for 2 minutes. Stems and leaves should be tender-crisp to bite.

Steaming. Arrange sliced chard stems on a rack. Steam for 3 minutes. Add shredded leaves and steam until just tender-crisp to bite (2 to 4 more minutes).

Continued on next page

Stir-frying. Use up to 5 cups *total* chard stems and leaves—stems cut into ¼-inch slices, leaves cut into shreds. Stir-fry stems, using 1 tablespoon salad oil, for 1 minute. Add 1 tablespoon liquid; cover and cook for 2 more minutes. Add leaves, cover, and cook just until stems and leaves are tender-crisp to bite (1 to 2 more minutes).

■ **Serving ideas.** Dress hot cooked chard with butter seasoned with basil, nutmeg, oregano, or crumbled bacon. Add sliced stems to chowders and hearty soups during the last 10 minutes of cooking, shredded leaves during the last 4 to 5 minutes. Cook stems and leaves in stir-fry combinations.

FLORENTINE-STYLE SWISS CHARD

Per serving: 73 calories, 3 g protein, 5 g carbohydrates, 5 g total fat, 0 mg cholesterol, 167 mg sodium

    2   pounds green Swiss chard
    1   tablespoon lemon juice
    3   tablespoons olive oil
        Salt and freshly ground
        black pepper
        Lemon wedges

Clean chard as previously directed; cut stems from leaves. Leave stems and leaves whole.

In a 5- to 6-quart pan, bring 12 cups water to a boil over high heat. Push stems down into water. Cook, uncovered, until soft (about 4 minutes). Lift out and let cool.

At once, push leaves gently down into boiling water and cook until limp (1 to 2 minutes). Lift out and drain, then immediately immerse in ice water. When cool, drain.

Select 8 of the largest, most perfect leaves and set aside. Chop remaining leaves and stems together. Mix with lemon juice and 2 tablespoons of the oil; season to taste with salt and pepper. Lay out reserved leaves; mound an equal amount of chopped chard on each. Fold each leaf to enclose filling; set, seam side down, on a serving dish. If made ahead, cover and refrigerate until next day.

Serve at room temperature, drizzled with remaining 1 tablespoon oil. Offer lemon wedges to squeeze over top. Makes 8 servings.

■ *See also **Minestrone** (page 62).*

Tomatillos

Tomatillos look like green cherry tomatoes enclosed in papery husks. Beneath the husk, you'll find a sticky-skinned fruit with an acidic flavor similar to that of green tomatoes. An essential ingredient in Mexican *salsa verde*, tomatillos can be eaten both raw and cooked. *(Photo on page 119.)*

Nutrition. Tomatillos are a good source of vitamin C; they also provide vitamin A, thiamin, and niacin. Four tomatillos have about 35 calories.

■ **Season.** All year.

■ **Selection.** Look for smooth, firm tomatillos without bruises or noticeable shriveling.

■ **Amount.** For salads, allow about ¼ pound per person.

■ **Storage.** Refrigerate, unwashed, in an open container for up to 1 week.

■ **Preparation.** Remove husks. Wash well and cut out core.

■ **Cooking methods.** Tomatillos aren't usually served on their own as a cooked vegetable; instead, they're cooked with other ingredients to make sauces. They may also be roasted separately, then added to a green chile salsa or other sauce.

Roasting. Spread prepared tomatillos in a single layer in an ungreased 10- by 15-inch rimmed baking pan. Bake in a 500° oven until lightly singed (about 15 minutes). Let cool.

■ **Serving ideas.** Add chopped raw tomatillos to gazpacho, guacamole, or salsa. To make a refreshing appetizer, stack thin slices of jicama, apple, and tomatillo, then drizzle with lime juice and sprinkle with coarse salt.

TOMATILLO & CHEESE SALAD

Per serving: 270 calories, 7 g protein, 1 g carbohydrates, 19 g total fat, 19 mg cholesterol, 147 mg sodium

Prepare 1 pound **tomatillos** as previously directed; thinly slice and arrange on a platter. Combine ¼ cup **olive oil** and 2 tablespoons **lime juice;** sprinkle over tomatillos, then sprinkle with 1 cup (about 5 oz.) grated **Parmesan cheese.** Season to taste with **pepper.** Makes about 4 servings.

TOMATILLO LIME SAUCE

Per ¼ cup: 76 calories, .41 g protein, 1 g carbohydrates, .07 g total fat, 0 mg cholesterol, 5 mg sodium

In a blender or food processor, whirl 1 pound **tomatillos** (husked and cored), 2 tablespoons **lime juice,** and 1½ cups lightly packed **fresh cilantro (coriander) sprigs** until puréed; season to taste with **salt.** Serve, or cover and refrigerate for up to 2 days. Use as an accompaniment to beef, pork, chicken, turkey, or rich fish such as salmon. Makes about 2 cups.

Tomatoes

Debates have long raged over whether the tomato is a fruit or a vegetable, but legally it's a vegetable—the U.S. Supreme Court so ruled in 1893. The question became a matter for the courts because of different trade regulations governing fruits and vegetables.

Tomatoes range in size from pop-in-the-mouth cherry types to 1- to 2-pound giants. The tomatoes most familiar to many of us are round and red, but you can also find (or grow) yellow, orange, and even pink ones. Pear-shaped, Roma-type tomatoes are usually very meaty and good for canning and sauces; the rounder and cherry types are most often used raw or in baked dishes.

Though tomatoes are native to South America, it wasn't until a century ago that they became a popular U.S. crop. Today, California and Florida are the leading domestic producers; many tomatoes are also imported from Mexico.

Nutrition. Tomatoes are a good source of potassium and vitamin A; they also provide vitamin C, phosphorus, and other minerals. One large raw tomato, unpeeled, has about 40 calories.

■ **Season.** All year; peak July through September.

■ **Selection.** Choose smooth, well-formed tomatoes that are firm (but not hard) and heavy for their size. Color varies according to variety and ripe-

Tomatillo

Round red (slicing)

Yellow cherry

Red Pear

Yellow Roma

Saladrette

Red cherry

Red and yellow tomato varieties of various sizes and small green, husk-covered tomatillos range from extra-sweet to puckery tart in flavor.

ness. Tomatoes picked ripe are richly colored; those picked before ripening are paler. Tomatoes picked early and commercially ripened may have a rich red color, but they're less flavorful than vine-ripened tomatoes. (You're most likely to find vine-ripened tomatoes in late summer.)

■ **Amount.** Allow 1 medium-size tomato per person. One large tomato yields about 1 cup when coarsely chopped.

■ **Storage.** Store, unwashed, at room temperature, stem end up, until slightly soft. Refrigerate very ripe tomatoes, unwrapped, for up to 4 days.

■ **Preparation.** *To peel,* submerge tomatoes in boiling water for 15 to 30 seconds, then lift out and plunge immediately into cold water; when cool, lift out and slip off skins. Or hold tomato on a fork over a flame until skin splits, then peel.

For either peeled or unpeeled tomatoes, cut out core; leave whole or slice, chop, or cut into wedges.

To seed, cut in half crosswise and squeeze out seeds.

■ **Cooking methods.** For more information on baking, see "A Glossary of Techniques," page 122.

Baking. Core medium-size tomatoes and cut in half crosswise; squeeze out juice and seeds. Place, cut side up,

...Tomatoes continued

in a baking dish. Drizzle with olive oil or salad oil. Bake, uncovered, in a 400° oven until just soft throughout (20 to 25 minutes).

■ **Serving ideas.** Cherry tomatoes make a delicious, nutritious snack; you can also serve them with a dip as an appetizer or use them as a garnish. Season chopped tomatoes with onion, green chiles, and fresh cilantro (coriander) for a salsa to serve with Mexican dishes. Dress sliced tomatoes, cucumbers, sweet onion, and green bell pepper with a vinaigrette for a simple salad. Tuck sliced tomatoes into sandwiches or stuff whole, seeded ones with an egg, poultry, or seafood salad. Use chopped tomatoes in soups, stews, and sauces.

TOMATO-BASIL SOUP

Per cup: 95 calories, 2 g protein, 9 g carbohydrates, 6 g total fat, 20 mg cholesterol, 190 mg sodium

- 3 tablespoons butter or margarine
- 1 large onion, sliced
- 1 large carrot, shredded
- 4 large ripe tomatoes, peeled, seeded, and coarsely chopped (about 4 cups)
- ½ cup lightly packed fresh basil leaves or 2 teaspoons dry basil
- ¾ teaspoon sugar
- ⅛ teaspoon white pepper
- 1 can (14½ oz.) regular-strength chicken broth
  Salt
  Fresh basil leaves or minced parsley

Melt butter in a 3-quart pan over medium heat. Add onion and carrot; cook, stirring often, until onion is slightly soft. Stir in tomatoes, the ½ cup basil leaves, sugar, and white pepper. Bring to a boil, stirring to prevent sticking; then reduce heat, cover, and simmer until onion is very soft (10 to 15 minutes).

In a blender or food processor, whirl tomato mixture, a portion at a time, until smooth. (At this point, you may let cool, then cover and refrigerate until next day.)

Return tomato mixture to pan over medium heat; add broth and season to taste with salt. Heat until steaming. Garnish each serving with basil leaves. Makes about 5 to 6 cups.

To peel tomatoes, first dip in boiling water for 15 to 30 seconds, then plunge into cold water; pull skin off cooled tomatoes in strips.

TOMATO & EGG SUPPER

Per serving: 282 calories, 14 g protein, 7 g carbohydrates, 22 g total fat, 506 mg cholesterol, 127 mg sodium

- 3 tablespoons olive oil; or 1½ tablespoons butter or margarine and 1½ tablespoons salad oil
- 4 large cloves garlic, chopped
- 6 Roma tomatoes (about 1 lb. *total*), cut in half lengthwise
- 8 eggs
- 3 tablespoons chopped parsley
  Salt and pepper

Heat oil in a wide frying pan over medium heat. Add garlic and tomatoes, cut side down. Cook, uncovered, turning once, until tomatoes are browned (about 10 minutes). Reduce heat to low and slide eggs into pan between tomatoes. Cover and cook just until whites of eggs are firm. Sprinkle with parsley and season to taste with salt and pepper. Makes 4 servings.

BROILED PARMESAN TOMATOES

Per serving: 33 calories, 3 g protein, 3 g carbohydrates, 1 g total fat, 5 mg cholesterol, 39 mg sodium

Cut 2 to 4 medium-size **tomatoes** in half crosswise and place, cut side up, in a 9-inch square baking pan. Sprinkle with ¼ to ½ cup grated **Parmesan cheese.** Broil 4 to 6 inches below heat

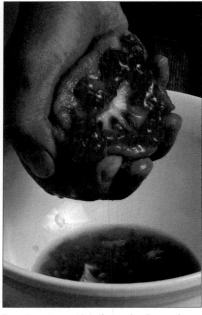

To seed tomatoes, cut in half crosswise, then gently squeeze each half to remove seeds and juice; chop or slice tomatoes to use.

just until cheese is lightly toasted and tomatoes are warm (about 10 minutes). Makes 4 to 8 servings.

SPINACH-STUFFED TOMATOES

Per serving: 127 calories, 8 g protein, 11 g carbohydrates, 7 g total fat, 16 mg cholesterol, 156 mg sodium

- ¾ pound spinach
- 8 medium-size tomatoes
- 1 tablespoon butter or margarine
- 1 tablespoon salad oil
- 1 medium-size onion, chopped
- 1¼ cups (about 6¼ oz.) grated Parmesan cheese
- 2 tablespoons fine dry bread crumbs
- ⅛ teaspoon ground nutmeg

Discard spinach stems and any yellow or wilted leaves. Plunge spinach into a large quantity of cold water to clean; lift out, drain, pat dry, and coarsely chop. Set aside.

Cut off top fourth of each tomato; reserve for other uses. With a small spoon, scoop out pulp to make hollow shells. Chop pulp; let drain in a colander.

Melt butter in oil in a wide frying pan over medium-high heat. Add onion; cook, stirring, until soft. Stir in drained tomato pulp and spinach; cook, stirring, until spinach is wilted (3 to 4 minutes). Stir in 1 cup of the cheese, bread crumbs, and nutmeg.

Fill each tomato with spinach mixture and arrange in an ungreased baking pan; sprinkle evenly with remaining ¼ cup cheese. Broil 4 inches below heat until cheese is lightly browned (3 to 4 minutes). Makes 8 servings.

■ See also **Vegetable Purée** (page 71), **Freezer Tomato Sauce** (page 126).

Turnips

Turnips have been used for centuries for both food and medicines, and they're good to eat from top to bottom—both the mature root and the leaves of the young plant are edible (see "Greens with a Bite," page 83). Though once grown to be quite large—up to 36 pounds, according to eyewitnesses—they're considerably smaller today. The globe-shaped roots have reddish purple skin, crisp white flesh, and a sweet-to-hot flavor. (Photo on page 56.)

Nutrition. Turnips are an excellent source of vitamin C and a good source of potassium and iron. One cup of cooked turnips has 36 calories.

■ **Season.** October through March.

■ **Selection.** Choose firm, smooth, small to medium-size (2- to 3-inch diameter) turnips that feel heavy for their size. If they have tops, leaves should be bright green and tender.

■ **Amount.** Allow about 1 medium-size turnip per person.

■ **Storage.** Remove tops; if desired, cook tops separately (see "Greens with a Bite," page 83). Refrigerate, unwashed, in a plastic bag for up to 1 week.

■ **Preparation.** Rinse and peel. Leave whole; or cube, slice, cut into quarters or julienne strips, or shred.

■ **Cooking methods.** For more information on the cooking methods listed here, see "A Glossary of Techniques," page 122.

Baking. Peel medium-size turnips; cut into ¼-inch-thick slices. Arrange in a shallow baking dish. Generously dot with butter or margarine; sprinkle lightly with water. Cover and bake in a 400° oven until tender when pierced (30 to 45 minutes).

Boiling. In a 4- to 5-quart pan, boil 1½ to 2 pounds peeled, whole 2- to 3-inch-diameter turnips, covered, in 2 inches water until tender when pierced (20 to 30 minutes). Drain.

Cut 1 to 2 pounds peeled turnips into ½-inch-thick slices; boil in a wide frying pan, covered, in ½ inch water for 6 to 8 minutes. Drain.

Butter-steaming. Cut peeled turnips into ¼-inch-thick slices. Butter-steam up to 5 cups, using 2 tablespoons butter or margarine. Cook, stirring, for 1 minute. Add 4 to 5 tablespoons liquid, cover, and cook just until tender-crisp to bite (4 to 5 more minutes).

Microwaving. Cut 1 pound peeled turnips into ½-inch cubes. Arrange in a 1½-quart nonmetallic baking dish. Add 3 tablespoons water; cover. Microwave on **HIGH (100%)** for 7 to 9 minutes, stirring after 3 minutes. Let stand, covered, for 3 minutes. Turnips should be tender when pierced.

Steaming. Arrange peeled, whole 2- to 3-inch-diameter turnips or ½-inch-thick slices on a rack. Steam until turnips are tender when pierced (25 to 35 minutes for whole turnips, 7 to 9 minutes for slices).

Stir-frying. Cut peeled turnips into ¼-inch-thick slices. Stir-fry up to 5 cups, using 1 tablespoon salad oil, for 1 minute. Add 4 to 5 tablespoons liquid, cover, and cook just until tender-crisp to bite (4 to 5 more minutes).

■ **Serving ideas.** Serve thinly sliced raw turnips as a crudité with dips. Or mix shredded raw turnips with salad oil and lemon juice accented with mint for a refreshing salad. Dress hot cooked turnips with butter, basil, dill, caraway seeds, or crumbled bacon. Or glaze cooked turnips in a mixture of melted butter and brown sugar.

TURNIPS WITH MUSTARD GREENS

Per serving: 152 calories, 4 g protein, 11 g carbohydrates, 12 g total fat, 0 mg cholesterol, 64 mg sodium

> 2 turnips, each about 2½ inches in diameter, peeled and cut into ⅛-inch julienne strips
> 3 tablespoons each distilled white vinegar, water, and sugar
> 2 teaspoons toasted sesame seeds
> 3 tablespoons salad oil
> 4 cups lightly packed mustard greens
> 1 small red bell pepper, seeded and diced

In a wide frying pan, combine turnips, vinegar, water, and sugar. Cover and bring to a boil over high heat; boil just until turnips are tender-crisp to bite (about 3 minutes). Uncover and quickly mix in sesame seeds, oil, and mustard greens. Stir just until greens are slightly wilted. Pour into a shallow serving dish and sprinkle with bell pepper. Makes 4 servings.

BEEF & TURNIP STEW

Per serving: 406 calories, 50 g protein, 10 g carbohydrates, 17 g total fat, 147 mg cholesterol, 1364 mg sodium

> ⅓ cup soy sauce
> 2 tablespoons each sugar and dry sherry
> 2½ cups water
> 3 pounds boneless beef chuck, cut into 1½-inch cubes
> 2 star anise; or 1 teaspoon crushed anise seeds and 1 cinnamon stick (about 3 inches long)
> 3 thin slices fresh ginger, each about 1 by 3 inches
> 2 green onions (including tops), cut into 2-inch lengths
> About 1 pound small turnips, peeled and cut into 1½-inch cubes

In a 4- to 5-quart pan, combine soy, sugar, sherry, water, beef, anise, ginger, and onions. Cover and bring to a simmer over medium heat. Simmer, covered, until meat is almost tender (about 1½ hours).

Add turnips and continue to simmer until turnips and meat are very tender when pierced (45 to 50 more minutes). Skim and discard fat. Makes about 6 servings.

A Glossary of Techniques

BAKING

Certain vegetables cook to perfection in the dry, continuous heat of the oven. Baking intensifies the naturally mellow-sweet flavor and preserves the nutritional value of such vegetables as corn, potatoes, and winter squash; at the same time, it tames the pungency of garlic and onions. Some fruits, too, are well suited to this method of cooking.

"Roasting" also refers to cooking in dry heat. This term is most often used for meats and poultry cooked uncovered in the oven, but through popular usage it's also frequently applied to certain vegetables—corn on the cob, garlic, and peppers, for example.

When you tuck vegetables into the same oven with meats or chicken, you save energy—your own included. The vegetables require minimal preparation and cook with little or no attention. Some—onions and potatoes, for example—can be roasted alongside meat in the pan drippings. In this case, use the oven temperature specified for roasting the meat and add 20 to 30 minutes to the cooking time suggested for the vegetable. You can use the same procedure for certain fruits, such as dates and figs, adding them to the roasting pan for the last 15 minutes of cooking. (Also see recipe above right).

Potatoes and some squash are baked whole and unwrapped, with their skins providing adequate protection against moisture loss. Other vegetables, such as beets and husked corn on the cob, should be wrapped in foil to hold in moisture during cooking. In the individual listings, you'll find specific instructions on preparation for each vegetable, plus oven temperature and cooking time.

One basic rule applies to all baking: never overcrowd the oven. For even cooking, the heat must have room to circulate. As long as you observe this rule, you can bake ten potatoes as quickly as one.

To test doneness, check the individual listings. Most baked vegetables should be tender when pierced. Potatoes should yield to pressure when squeezed; spaghetti squash is done when its shell gives to pressure.

Season baked or roasted vegetables to taste with salt and pepper, or with one or more of the seasonings suggested for each vegetable (see "Serving ideas").

■ **Baked fruit.** Fruits play a starring role in pies, cobblers, and many other baked desserts—including such all-time favorite treats as baked apples and pears (see pages 8 and 45). But glazed, baked fruits prepared according to the following recipe also make a succulent accompaniment to roast pork, ham, and poultry.

The individual listings tell you which fruits are appropriate for baking and give basic preparation instructions and cooking time.

Roasting peppers mellows their flavor, also makes peeling them an easy task. Roast in a 400° oven until skin browns and looks blistered (25 to 30 minutes), then seal in a plastic bag for 30 minutes; pull off skin.

SPICY BAKED FRUIT

- ¼ cup butter or margarine
- 1 teaspoon *each* ground ginger and coriander
- ¼ teaspoon curry powder
- 2 tablespoons *each* honey and lime juice
- 1½ to 2 pounds fruit, prepared as directed in individual listings

In a small pan, combine butter, ginger, coriander, and curry powder; cook over low heat until bubbly. Stir in honey and lime juice.

Arrange fruit in a baking pan, cut side up, or place in roasting pan alongside meat or poultry. Brush butter mixture over fruit.

Bake in a 325° oven, basting occasionally, until hot and tender (see individual listings for specific cooking times). Pour any remaining butter mixture over baked fruit, then serve with meat or poultry. Makes 8 servings.

BOILING

Boiling is one of the most widely used cooking methods for vegetables. In the individual listings, you'll find specific recommendations for basic preparation, pan size, amount of water, and cooking time. Keep in mind that vegetables cook more evenly if they're uniform in size and shape.

For most vegetables, we recommend a fairly small amount of water—½ to 2 inches—to minimize nutrient loss. To boil, bring the designated amount of water to a rolling boil over high heat; add vegetables. When water returns to a boil, cover pan (unless instructed otherwise), reduce heat to medium (water should boil throughout cooking time), and begin timing.

Total cooking time depends on the freshness and maturity of the vegetables and on personal taste. Test for doneness after the minimum suggested time; if necessary, continue to cook, testing frequently, until vegetables are done to your liking.

Drain vegetables immediately; reserve liquid to use in soups, stock, or sauces, if you wish. Serve hot, seasoning as desired (see "Serving ideas" for each vegetable). Or, to serve cold, immediately plunge drained cooked vegetables into cold water; when cool, drain again.

BUTTER-STEAMING

Butter-steaming is almost identical to stir-frying (see page 126), yielding the same tender-crisp, brightly colored vegetables. The difference is that butter or margarine replaces the salad oil in which the vegetables are quick-cooked over high heat.

Though many vegetables are equally good stir-fried or butter-steamed, some taste better when cooked in butter; for these, we suggest butter-steaming rather than stir-frying. See the individual listings for guidelines on preparation, amount of butter and additional liquid, and cooking time.

To butter-steam, place a wok or wide frying pan over high heat. When the pan is hot, add butter or margarine and cut-up vegetables. Cook, uncovered, stirring constantly, for time given under individual listings. Add specified amount of liquid (water or regular-strength chicken or beef broth), cover, and continue to cook, stirring occasionally, for time indicated. Add a few more drops of liquid if vegetables appear dry.

(*Note:* In some cases, you won't need to add liquid or cover the pan during cooking. Follow the individual directions closely—don't pour in liquid or cover the cooking pan unless instructed to do so.)

When butter-steaming, don't crowd the wok or frying pan. Cook no more than 5 cups of cut-up vegetables in a 12- to 14-inch wok or 10-inch frying pan. If you want to prepare more than you can cook at one time, have ready the total amount of vegetables you'll need; then cook in 2 batches.

Total cooking time varies, depending on the freshness and maturity of the vegetable and on personal preference. Test after the minimum suggested cooking time; if you prefer softer vegetables, continue cooking, testing frequently, until vegetables are done to your liking. Season as desired (see "Serving ideas" for each vegetable) and serve at once.

GRILLING

Grilling fresh fruits and vegetables alongside meat, fish, or poultry is an easy way to add color, flavor, and nutrition to barbecue meals. And the distinctive flavor imparted by grilling gives a new dimension to familiar produce.

To grill fruits and vegetables, follow the basic recipes below; refer to the individual listings for guidelines on preparation and cooking time.

GRILLED VEGETABLES

> About 2 pounds vegetables, prepared as directed in individual listings
> ⅓ to ½ cup olive oil*, salad oil*, melted butter or margarine*, or basting sauce used on an accompanying entrée
> *If desired, add 2 tablespoons chopped fresh thyme, rosemary, oregano, or tarragon (or 2 teaspoons dry herbs) to oil or melted butter

If using small vegetables, thread on thin metal or bamboo skewers, making sure vegetables lie flat. (If using bamboo skewers, soak in hot water for 30 minutes before threading vegetables.)

Coat prepared vegetables with oil, butter, or basting sauce. Place on a lightly greased grill 4 to 6 inches above a partly dispersed bed of medium coals. Cook, turning frequently, until vegetables are streaked with brown and tender when pierced (see individual listings for specific cooking times).

Serve hot or at room temperature. Makes 6 to 8 servings.

GRILLED FRUIT

> 1½ to 2 pounds fruit, prepared as directed in individual listings
> ½ cup (¼ lb.) melted butter or margarine,* or basting sauce used on an accompanying entrée
> *If desired, add 3 tablespoons firmly packed brown sugar to melted butter, then season with 1 teaspoon ground cinnamon or ginger

Thread small pieces of fruit on thin metal or bamboo skewers, making sure fruit lies flat. (If using bamboo skewers, soak in hot water for 30 minutes before threading fruit.)

Firm fruits like cantaloupe are good choices for grilling. Thread on skewers, then brush with butter or a basting sauce used on barbecued entrée for same meal.

Coat prepared fruits with butter or basting sauce. Place on a lightly greased grill 4 to 6 inches above a partly dispersed bed of medium coals. Cook, turning frequently, until fruits are hot and streaked with brown (see individual listings for specific cooking times).

Serve hot or at room temperature. Makes 6 to 8 servings.

MICROWAVING

The microwave might have been created expressly for the purpose of cooking fresh vegetables—they are done in minutes, often without the addition of any nutrient-depleting liquid. And maximum retention of vitamins and minerals isn't the only advantage of microwaving—you get extra-bright color, garden-fresh flavor, and delightfully crisp texture, too.

The individual listings give details on preparation, container size, and cooking and standing time for each vegetable. To ensure even cooking, be sure the vegetables you use—whether whole or cut up—are of uniform size and shape. **Cook all vegetables on HIGH (100%).**

To hold in steam, cover the non-metallic cooking dish with either its lid or heavy-duty plastic wrap. (Check the package to make sure the plastic wrap you use is recommended for use in the microwave; lightweight wraps may split and melt into the food.) *Caution:* **When uncovering a dish after cooking, be sure to start at the edge farthest from you; escaping steam can cause burns.**

Cooking time depends on the freshness, moisture content, and maturity of the vegetable. Quantity makes a difference, too; if you double the amount, increase the initial cooking time by about 60 percent. Remove the vegetables from the microwave after the shortest suggested cooking time, then let stand for the recommended time before testing for doneness. Most microwaved vegetables should be tender-crisp when pierced; if overcooked, they'll dry out and

Microwaving preserves vegetable color, crispness, and nutrients. Heavy-duty plastic wrap—or a natural covering like corn husks (minus corn silk)—holds in steam.

become tough. If the vegetables are still too crisp for your liking, microwave them further in 1-minute increments.

To serve, season to taste (see "Serving ideas" for each vegetable).

Pan-frying *see Sautéing*

POACHING

Gentle simmering in a sweetened liquid enhances the delicate flavors of many fruits—and makes for a cool, elegant dessert. Our poaching syrup is based on a fruity white wine. You can choose from an entire palette of fruits, from apricots to litchis to pineapple; see individual listings for specific instructions on quantities, preparation, and cooking times.

FRUIT WITH WHITE WINE

 1½ **cups water**
  1 **cup sugar**
  1 **tablespoon lemon juice**
   Yellow part of peel pared in a strip from ½ large lemon
 1¼ **cups fruity white wine such as Gewürztraminer, Johannisberg Riesling, or Chenin Blanc**
   Fruit, prepared as directed in individual listings

In a 2- to 3-quart pan, combine water, sugar, lemon juice, and lemon peel. Bring to a boil over high heat; boil rapidly, uncovered, until reduced to 1 cup (about 10 minutes). Remove pan from heat and stir in wine; you should have 2¼ cups liquid.

Bring wine syrup to a boil in 2- to 4-quart pan. Add fruit; then reduce heat, cover, and simmer, turning fruit in syrup occasionally, until fruit is tender (see individual listings for specific cooking times).

With a slotted spoon, carefully transfer fruit to a glass serving dish or other noncorrodible container. Let syrup cool to lukewarm; pour over fruit. Cover and refrigerate until cold (about 4 hours) or for up to 3 days.

To serve, spoon poached fruit into individual bowls. Ladle some of the syrup into each bowl. Makes about 4 servings.

Roasting *see Baking*

White wine poaching syrup complements the natural flavor of many fruits; see individual listings for suggested fruits and poaching time for each.

SAUTÉING

Sautéing (sometimes called pan-frying) is a method of cooking foods in a frying pan over medium-high to high heat, using a small amount of fat—butter or margarine, olive oil, or salad oil. This quick-cooking technique is popular for many vegetables; sautéed garlic and onions are often used as seasoning in meat and vegetable dishes.

Fruits, too, are delicious when sautéed. Just remember that gentle handling is in order, since many fruits are quite delicate in texture. The following recipe makes an interesting spicy-sweet accompaniment for roasted poultry, pork, ham, or lamb; use any of the fruits suggested in the individual listings.

SAUTÉED FRUIT

> 3 tablespoons butter or
> margarine
> 1 small onion, coarsely
> chopped
> 1½ teaspoons finely chopped
> fresh ginger
> About 1½ cups fruit,
> prepared as directed in
> individual listings
> 1 to 2 tablespoons lime juice
> 2 to 4 tablespoons firmly packed
> brown sugar

Melt butter in a 10- to 12-inch frying pan over medium heat. Add onion and ginger; cook, stirring, until onion is barely soft (about 1 minute).

Add prepared fruit and turn gently to coat with butter. Cover and cook, turning occasionally, until fruit is heated through and very tender when pierced (2 to 5 minutes for most fruits).

Season fruit with lime juice and sugar; mix gently to blend well. Serve hot, as an accompaniment to roasted poultry, pork, ham, or lamb. Makes about 3 cups.

STEAMING

Steaming vegetables is a favorite way to preserve their nutritional content. Since the boiling water over which they're cooked doesn't actually touch the vegetables, depletion of nutrients in cooking liquid is kept to a minimum.

Cookware shops sell various utensils for steaming; the simplest and least expensive is a collapsible metal basket, available in two sizes to fit into ordinary pans. A metal colander also makes a suitable steaming basket—as long as you have a pan big enough to hold it. Whatever utensil you use, it should accommodate whole vegetables such as potatoes in a single layer, or cut-up or small vegetables (such as peas) in an even layer no deeper than 2 inches.

To steam, place rack or basket in pan; pour in water to a depth of 1 to 1½ inches (water should not touch bottom of rack). Bring water to a boil over high heat; then place vegetables on rack. Cover pan, reduce heat to medium or medium-high (water should boil throughout cooking time), and begin timing. If necessary, add boiling water to pan to maintain water level throughout cooking time.

Steaming takes slightly longer than boiling for most vegetables. Cooking time depends on freshness and maturity of vegetables—see individual vegetable listings for specific cooking times. Test after the minimum suggested cooking time; if necessary, continue to cook, testing frequently, until vegetables are as done as you like them.

Steaming is one of the easiest ways to cook vegetables. Steam whole vegetables such as potatoes in a single layer on rack; or steam slices or very small vegetables in a shallow layer. Water should not touch rack bottom.

Continued on next page

FREEZING FRUIT

Fruits are often available in abundance only during rather short seasons. To preserve them for year-round use, you may wish to try freezing them; check the individual listings to see which fruits are suitable for freezing.

Some fruits need no special preparation for freezing. In other cases, you'll get best results by freezing in a light syrup to help preserve color, shape, and flavor. The following syrup adds enough sweetening for many fruits, but you can always add more sugar when serving tarter fruits.

To freeze syrup-packed fruits, use rigid plastic or waxed cardboard containers with tight-fitting lids; glass canning jars also work well. You'll need to store the prepared fruits at 0°F or lower. Prepare no more fruit than your freezer can freeze solid within 24 hours (check manufacturer's instructions).

FREEZER FRUIT IN LIGHT SYRUP

Allow about 1 pound **fruit** for each pint. Peel or wash fruit as directed under individual listings. Pour ½ cup cold **Uncooked Syrup** (recipe follows) into each pint container. Cut fruit into syrup as directed, discarding any pits. Add enough additional syrup to each container to cover fruit, leaving at least ½ inch headspace for pint containers, 1 inch for quarts (if using narrow-mouth jars, leave ¾ inch headspace for pints, 1½ inches for quarts). Place crumpled wax paper or plastic wrap on top of fruit to keep it submerged in syrup. Cover with lids and freeze.

Uncooked Syrup. Combine 1½ cups **sugar** with 4 cups **water.** To control darkening, add ½ to ¾ teaspoon **ascorbic acid** (or a commercial antidarkening agent, following manufacturer's directions). Stir until sugar is dissolved. Refrigerate syrup until cold. Makes about 5 cups, enough for 8 pints (about 8 lbs.) fruit.

EXTENDING THE TOMATO SEASON

Whether you're taking advantage of a prolific garden or a bargain at a roadside stand, you can preserve the goodness of vine-ripened tomatoes by turning them into a well-seasoned sauce for the freezer. Such a sauce is a great starting point for easy, delicious winter meals. And because it's not canned, but just spooned into freezer containers, you can make it with a minimum of time and effort.

Choose containers of various sizes—ones you will be able to use up when thawed. One-cup containers hold enough sauce for a pizza topping. Pint and quart sizes are ideal for storing sauce for pasta dishes; a pint container makes two servings, while a quart will serve four.

FREEZER TOMATO SAUCE

Peel and core 5 pounds ripe **tomatoes** (about 12 medium-size); cut into eighths and set aside.

Heat 3 tablespoons **salad oil** in a 6-quart pan over medium heat; add 2 large **onions,** finely chopped, and 4 cloves **garlic,** minced or pressed. Cook until onions are soft (about 10 minutes). Add tomatoes, 1 teaspoon *each* **salt** and **paprika,** ¾ teaspoon *each* **pepper** and **dry rosemary,** ¼ teaspoon crushed **anise seeds,** 1 tablespoon *each* **dry basil, oregano leaves,** and **sugar,** and ¾ cup **dry red wine.**

Bring mixture to a boil, stirring with a wooden spoon to break up tomatoes. Reduce heat, cover, and simmer for 1 hour; stir several times. Then uncover and boil over medium-high heat, stirring often to prevent sticking, until reduced to 8 cups (about 50 more minutes).

Let cool, then ladle into rigid plastic or glass cup, pint, or quart containers; leave at least ½ inch headspace for cup and pint containers, 1 inch for quarts. Cover and freeze at 0°F or lower for up to 9 months. Makes 8 cups.

Bright colors, crisp texture are bonuses of stir-frying. Vegetables cook quickly over high heat, using little liquid.

…Steaming continued

Serve immediately, seasoning as desired (see "Serving ideas" for each vegetable). Or, to serve cold, immediately plunge cooked vegetables into cold water; when cool, drain well.

STIR-FRYING

Stir-frying utilizes high heat and quick cooking time to produce vegetables with tender-crisp texture, bright color, and rich, natural flavor. Whether you stir-fry in a wok or frying pan, the basic procedure is the same.

See individual vegetable listings for preparation techniques, amount of oil and liquid, and cooking time for each vegetable.

To stir-fry, place a wok or wide frying pan over high heat; when pan is hot, add oil and cut-up vegetables. Cook, uncovered, stirring constantly, for time given under individual listing. Add specified amount of liquid (water or regular-strength chicken or beef broth), cover, and continue to cook, stirring occasionally, for time indicated. Add a few more drops of liquid if vegetables appear dry. (*Note:* In some cases, you won't need to add liquid or cover the pan during cooking. Follow the individual directions closely—don't pour in liquid or cover the cooking pan unless instructed to do so.)

Two secrets to success. *Never crowd the wok or frying pan.* Cook no more than 5 cups cut-up vegetables in a 12- to 14-inch wok or 10-inch frying pan. To prepare more servings than you can cook at one time, have ready the total amount of cut-up vegetables you'll need, then cook in 2 batches. Stir-frying proceeds so quickly that you can keep the first portion warm, without flavor loss, while the second batch cooks.

Use the highest heat so the vegetables begin cooking at once. A slow start means slow cooking. As the vegetables cook, all or most of the liquid evaporates; because there's no cooking liquid to drain off, vitamins and minerals are retained.

Cooking time varies depending on the freshness and maturity of the vegetables and on your own preference. Test after the minimum suggested cooking time; if you prefer softer vegetables, continue cooking, testing frequently, until vegetables are done to your liking. Season as desired (see "Serving ideas" for each vegetable) and serve at once.

Index

Add-on vichyssoise, 89
Alfalfa sprouts. See Sprouts
Apples, 7–9
  crisp, 8
  gingered carrots &, 70
  honey crunch baked, 8
  molded Waldorf salad, 8
  pie, 17
Apricots, 9–10
  jam, 28
  -onion salad, 10
  pie, 17
  sorbet, 41
  upside-down gingercake, 10
Artichokes, 57–58
  with cream cheese, 58
  salad, bacon & rice, 58
Arugula. See Salad greens
Asian pear pie, 47
Asparagus, 58–59
  with lemon-ginger cream, 59
  with orange butter sauce, 59
  wrapped, with watercress
    mayonnaise, 59
Autumn kiwi fruit salad, 33
Autumn squash soup, 114
Avocados, 10–11
  cauliflower-spinach toss, 72
  guacamole, 10
  huevos rancheros, 11
  salad, citrus-, 24

Bacon & rice artichoke salad, 58
Baked cinnamon pears, 45
Baked lemon custard, 24
Baked marinated eggplant, 81
Baking fruits & vegetables, 122
Bananas, 11–13
  autumn kiwi fruit salad, 33
  flaming dessert, 12
  sorbet, 41
Beans, 59–62
  & bok choy with chive butter, 61
  & celery root soup, 75
  green, with bacon dressing, 61
  green, with garlic, 61
  minestrone, 62
  sauté, fava, 62
Bean sprouts. See Sprouts
Béarnaise sauce, 66
Béchamel sauce, 66
Beef
  & sorrel scramble, 109
  & turnip stew, 121
Beet greens. See Greens with a
  bite
Beets, 62–63
  & pears with dandelion
    greens, 84
  borscht, chilled, 63
  leaves, stuffed, 85
  pickle-packed, 63
  purée, 71
  vinaigrette, shredded, 63
Belgian endive. See Salad greens
Berries, 13–16, 18
  blueberry crunch coffee ring, 16
  with chantilly custard, 16
  compote, wine &, 16
  cranberry-orange relish, 18
  gooseberry or currant relish, 16
  jam, 28
  pie, 17
  rhubarb-strawberry pie, 54
  sorbet, 41
Bitter melon, 86
Bittersweet marmalade, 24
Blackberries. See Berries
Blueberries. See Berries
Blueberry crunch coffee ring, 16
Boiling vegetables, 122
Bok choy, 63–64
  with chive butter, beans &, 61
  with ginger vinaigrette, 64
Borscht, chilled beet, 63

Breadfruit, 86
Broccoli, 64–65
  & mushrooms, marinated, 65
  cream sauce, capellini with, 65
  oriental, 65
Broiled chicken with nectarines, 39
Broiled Parmesan tomatoes, 120
Brussels sprouts, 65, 67
  & red bell peppers, 67
  bean & celery root soup, 75
  marinated, 67
  southern sprouts, 67
Burdock, 86
Butters, 66
  whipped herb, 108
Butter-steamed kohlrabi &
  mushrooms, 87
Butter-steaming vegetables, 123
Buttery fig bar cookies, 29

Cabbage, 68–69
  minestrone, 62
  slaw, crisp, 68
  stir-fried napa, 68
  toasted, with noodles, 69
Cactus pads, 86
Cactus pears. See Prickly pears
Cantaloupe. See also Melons
  salad, minted pepino &, 47
Cape gooseberries. See Berries
Capellini with broccoli cream
  sauce, 65
Caper dressing, 74
Carambolas, 18
  spinach salad with passion fruit
    dressing, 18
Cardoon, 86
Caribbean stuffed chayotes, 76
Carrots, 69–70
  & apples, gingered, 70
  bisque, spiced, 70
  cake, 70
  purée, 71
  sprout & vegetable medley, 110
Cauliflower, 70, 72–73
  & pea stir-fry, 73
  fritters, golden, 72
  Maltese soup, 95
  -spinach toss, 72
Celeriac. See Celery root
Celery, 73–74
  hearts with caper dressing, 74
  stew, lamb &, 73
Celery root, 74–75
  salad, 74
  soup, bean &, 75
Chard. See Swiss chard
Chayote, 75–76
  Caribbean stuffed, 76
Cheesecake, frozen peach
  yogurt, 44
Cherimoyas, 18–19
  chiffon pie, 19
  sorbet, 41
Cherries, 19–20
  raisins, 20
  salad with sesame dressing, 20
  tart, dark, 20
Chicken
  broiled, with nectarines, 39
  minted, & pineapple, 49
  with port-flavored grape
    sauce, 30
  roast, with prune plums, 50
  stew with okra & fruit, 92
Chicory. See Salad greens
Chiles. See Peppers
Chilled beet borscht, 63
Chilled melon soup, 37
Chinese gooseberries. See Kiwi fruit
Chinese long beans. See Beans
Chinese pea pods. See Peas
Chives. See Onions
Chorizo stuffing, 99
Cilantro dressing, 42
Cilantro papaya salad, 42
Citrus, 20–24
  -avocado salad, 24
  baked lemon custard, 24
  bittersweet marmalade, 24
  cilantro papaya salad, 42
  cranberry-orange relish, 18

Citrus (cont'd.)
  feijoas in orange syrup, 26
  kumquat marmalade, 24
  quick lemon or lime curd, 24
  romaine & tangerine salad, 106
  spinach, date & orange salad, 26
Coconut, 21
Collards. See Greens with a bite
Cool golden chowder, 112
Cool vegetable buttermilk soup, 71
Corn, 76–77
  & onion sauté, 77
  fritters, old-fashioned, 77
  relish, refrigerator, 77
Cranberries. See also Berries
  -orange relish, 18
Cream of lettuce soup, 106
Cream of sorrel soup, 109
Crêpes, spinach, 110
Crisp cabbage slaw, 68
Crisp-fried onions, 94
Crisp persimmon pie, 48
Crisp potato pancakes, 100
Cucumbers, 77–78
  & radish salad, 103
  chips, quick refrigerator, 78
  cream soup, 78
Currants. See also Berries; Grapes
  relish, 16
Curried okra, 92
Curry dressing, 44
Curry sauce, 66
Custard squash pie, 114

Daikon. See also Radishes
  soup, 103
Dandelion greens. See Greens with
  a bite
Dark cherry tart, 20
Dates, 24–26
  & orange salad, spinach, 26
  cookie pillows, 26
Dijon vinaigrette, 45
Dragon's eyes. See Longans
Dressings
  caper, 74
  cilantro, 42
  curry, 44
  Dijon vinaigrette, 45
  fresh herb mayonnaise, 108
  herb, 38
  herb-mayonnaise, 58
  honey, 26
  honey & poppy seed, 106
  honey-yogurt, 33
  mint, 86
  orange, 8
  passion fruit, 18
  sesame-orange, 20
  shallot, 47
  Szechwan-style, 103
  vinaigrette, 66

Eggplant, 79–81
  baked marinated, 81
  with sesame sauce, 79
  soup, roasted, 79
Endive. See also Salad greens
  salad with watercress sauce, 106
Enoki with soy-mustard dip, 91
Escarole. See Salad greens

Fava bean sauté, 62
Feijoas, 26
  in orange syrup, 26
  sorbet, 41
Fennel, 81–82
  & onions, glazed, 82
  salad vinaigrette, 81
Fiddlehead ferns, 86
Figs, 29–30
  bar cookies, buttery, 29
  jam, 28
  proscuitto & yogurt salad, 29
  sorbet, 41
Finocchio. See Fennel
Flaming dessert bananas, 12
Florentine-style Swiss chard, 118
Freezer fruit in light syrup, 125
Freezer tomato sauce, 126
French pea & lettuce soup, 96
French quince candy, 53
Fresh herb mayonnaise, 108

Fresh horseradish, 75
Fresh melon pickles, 37
Fried plantain chips, 12
Frozen peach yogurt
  cheesecake, 44
Fruit with white wine, 124

Garlic, 82–83
  butter, 66
  croutons, 85
  pickles, 83
  soup, 82
Ginger, 75
Gingered carrots & apples, 70
Gingered papaya with
  ice cream, 42
Glazed fennel & onions, 82
Golden cauliflower fritters, 72
Golden mashed potatoes, 103
Gooseberries. See also Berries
  Chinese. See Kiwi fruit
  relish, 16
Graham cracker crust, 44
Grapefruit. See Citrus
Grapes, 30–32
  autumn kiwi fruit salad, 33
  sauce, port-flavored,
    chicken with, 30
  sherried cream with, 32
  in wine jelly, 30
Green beans with bacon
  dressing, 61
Green beans with garlic, 61
Green pasta with spinach
  pesto, 109
Greens. See Salad greens
Greens with a bite, 83–85
  beets & pears with dandelion
    greens, 84
  minestrone, 62
  stuffed beet leaves, 85
  turnips with mustard greens, 121
  wilted greens, 84
Grilling vegetables & fruits, 123
Guacamole, 10
Guavas, 32
  chiffon pie, 32
  pineapple. See Feijoas
  sorbet, 41

Heavenly mushrooms, 91
Herbs, 108
  -cheese butter, 66
  dressing, 38
  -mayonnaise dressing, 58
Hollandaise sauce, 66
Honey & poppy seed dressing, 106
Honey crunch baked apples, 8
Honey dressing, 26
Honey peach cobbler, 44
Honey-yogurt dressing, 33
Horseradish, fresh, 75
Hungarian pepper stew, 98

Jackfruit, 86
Jam, 28
Jerusalem artichokes. See
  Sunchokes
Jicama, 85–86
  with fried potatoes, 85
  salad, pea-, 96
  sweet potato & ginger salad, 117
  tabbouleh, 85

Kale. See Greens with a bite
Kiwano, 86
Kiwi fruit, 33
  jam, 28
  Pavlova, 33
  salad, autumn, 33
  sorbet, 41
Kohlrabi, 86–87
  & mushrooms, butter-
    steamed, 87
  Maltese soup, 95
  meat-stuffed, 87
Kumquats. See also Citrus
  marmalade, 24

Lamb
  & celery stew, 73
  kebabs, pomegranate, 52
  stew with okra & fruit, 92

Leeks, 87, 89
  add-on vichyssoise, 89
  au gratin, 89
Lemons. See also Citrus
  butter, 66
  cucumbers, 78
  custard, baked, 24
  dipping sauce, 72
  -ginger cream, asparagus
    with, 59
  guavas, 32
  or lime curd, quick, 24
Lettuce. See also Salad greens
  soup, French pea &, 96
Limequats. See Citrus
Limes. See also Citrus
  curd, quick lemon or, 24
Litchis, 34
Longans, 34
Loquats, 86
Lotus root, 86

Maltese soup, 95
Mandarins. See Citrus
Mangoes, 34–35
  flummery, 35
  jam, 28
  sorbet, 41
Marinated broccoli &
  mushrooms, 65
Marinated Brussels sprouts, 67
Marinated mushrooms, 91
Marmalade, bittersweet, 24
Mashed potatoes, 100
Meat-stuffed kohlrabi, 87
Melons, 35–38. See also Pepinos
  & smoked meat salad, 38
  minted pepino & cantaloupe
    salad, 38
  pickles, fresh, 37
  sorbet, 41
  soup, chilled, 37
Microwaving vegetables, 123
Minestrone, 62
Mint dressing, 86
Minted chicken & pineapple, 49
Minted pepino & cantaloupe
  salad, 47
Molded Waldorf salad, 8
Mornay sauce, 66
Mushrooms, 89–91
  enoki with soy-mustard dip, 91
  heavenly, 91
  kohlrabi &, butter-steamed, 87
  marinated, 91
  marinated broccoli &, 65
  shiitake & egg soup, 91
Mustard greens. See also Greens
  with a bite
  turnips with, 121

Nectarines, 38–39
  broiled chicken with, 39
  jam, 28
  pie, 17
  salad ring, 39
  sorbet, 41
  tart, 39
No-cook freezer jam, 28
Nopales, 86
Nutritional data, 5

Okra, 92
  & fruit, lamb stew with, 92
  curried, 92
Old-fashioned corn fritters, 77
Omelets, zucchini, 112
Onions, 93–94
  crisp-fried, 94
  knots with peanut sauce, 94
  pub, 94
  salad, apricot-, 10
  sauté, corn &, 77
  slow-cooked, 94
Oranges. See also Citrus
  cilantro papaya salad, 42
  dressing, 8
  relish, cranberry-, 18
  salad, spinach, date &, 26
  syrup, feijoas in, 26

Papayas, 39–40, 42
  & sausage sauté, 40

Papayas (cont'd.)
  gingered, with ice cream 42
  jam, 28
  salad, cilantro, 42
  sorbet, 41
Parsnips, 94–95
  Maltese soup, 95
  salad, shredded, 95
  twists, 95
Passion fruit, 42
  dressing, 18
  filling for pies & cakes, 42
  sorbet, 41
Pastry, flaky, 17
Pavlova, 33
Peaches, 43–44
  cobbler, honey, 44
  jam, 28
  pie, 17
  shrimp-stuffed, 44
  sorbet, 41
  soup, plum &, 51
  yogurt cheesecake, frozen, 44
Peanut sauce, 94
Pears, 44–47
  & cheese salad, 45
  baked cinnamon, 45
  beets &, with dandelion
    greens, 84
  jam, 28
  pie, 17
  pie, Asian, 47
  plate, prosciutto, 46
  sorbet, 41
Peas, 95–97
  -jicama salad, 96
  & lettuce soup, French, 96
  pea pods with mint sauce, 96
  stir-fry, cauliflower &, 73
Pepinos, 47
  & cantaloupe salad, minted, 47
  sorbet, 41
Peppered peppers, 99
Peppers, 97–99
  peppered, 99
  pickles, Peter Piper's, 98
  red bell, Brussels sprouts &, 67
  stew, Hungarian, 98
  stuffed chiles, 99
Persimmons, 47–48
  autumn kiwi fruit salad, 33
  drop cookies, 48
  pie, crisp, 48
  quick bread, 48
  sorbet, 41
Peter Piper's pepper pickles, 98
Pickle-packed beets, 63
Picnic potato salad, 100
Pie, fresh fruit, 17
Pineapple guavas. See Feijoas
Pineapples, 48–50
  autumn kiwi fruit salad, 33
  cherry salad with sesame
    dressing, 20
  minted chicken &, 49
  spears, spiced, 49
  sweet potato & ginger salad, 117
Plantains. See also Bananas
  chips, fried, 12
Plums, 50–51
  & peach soup, 51
  jam, 28
  pie, 17
  prune, roast chicken with, 50
Poaching fruits, 124
Pomegranates, 51–52
  lamb kebabs, 52
  syrup, 52
Potatoes, 99–102
  add-on vichyssoise, 89
  autumn squash soup, 114
  fried, jicama with, 85
  gratin, 100
  mashed, 100
  mashed, golden, 103
  pancakes, crisp, 100
  salad, picnic, 100
Prickly pears, 52–53
  dessert sauce, ruby, 53
  sorbet, 41
Prosciutto & yogurt salad, fig, 29
Prosciutto pear plate, 46
Pub onions, 94

Pummelos. See Citrus
Pumpkin. See Squash

Quick lemon or lime curd, 24
Quick refrigerator cucumber
  chips, 78
Quinces, 53
  candy, French, 53
  syrup, 53

Radicchio. See also Salad greens
  with butter lettuce, 106
Radishes, 102–103
  daikon soup, 103
  green pasta with spinach
    pesto, 109
  salad, cucumber &, 103
  salted, 102
Raspberries. See also Berries
  sauce, 33
Red currants. See Berries
Refrigerator corn relish, 77
Rhubarb, 54
  -raisin compote, 54
  -strawberry pie, 54
Roast chicken with prune
  plums, 50
Roasted eggplant soup, 79
Rocket. See Salad greens
Romaine. See also Salad greens
  & tangerine salad, 106
Ruby prickly pear dessert
  sauce, 53
Rutabagas, 103–104
  autumn squash soup, 114
  golden mashed potatoes, 103
  with soy butter sauce, 104

Salad greens, 104–106
  cherry salad with sesame
    dressing, 20
  cream of lettuce soup, 106
  endive salad with watercress
    sauce, 106
  French pea & lettuce soup, 96
  Maltese soup, 95
  radicchio with butter lettuce, 106
  romaine & tangerine salad, 106
  salsify salad, 107
Salad Savoy. See Cabbage
Salsify, 106–107
  salad, 107
Salted radishes, 102
Sapotes, 54–55
  breakfast smoothie, 55
  sorbet, 41
Sautéing vegetables & fruits, 124
Scallions. See Onions
Sesame orange dressing, 20
Shallots. See also Onions
  dressing, 47
Sherried cream with grapes, 32
Shiitake & egg soup, 91
Short-cook jam, 28
Shredded beets vinaigrette, 63
Shredded parsnip salad, 95
Shrimp-stuffed peaches, 44
Slow-cooked onions, 94
Snow peas. See Peas
Sorbet, fresh fruit, 41
Sorrel, 107, 109
  scramble, beef &, 109
  soup, cream of, 109
Southern sprouts, 67
Spaghetti squash. See also
  Squash
  hash browns, 115
Spiced butter, 66
Spiced carrot bisque, 70
Spiced pineapple spears, 49
Spicy baked fruit, 122
Spinach, 109–110
  crêpes, 110
  date & orange salad, 26
  Maltese soup, 95
  pesto, green pasta with, 109
  salad, carambola, 18
  -stuffed tomatoes, 120
  toss, cauliflower &, 72
Sprouts, 110–111
  & vegetable medley, 110

Squash, 111–115. See also Chayote
  cool golden chowder, 112
  custard squash pie, 114
  soup, autumn, 114
  spaghetti squash hash
    browns, 115
  sprout & vegetable medley, 110
  vegetable purée, 71
  zucchini omelets, 112
Starfruit. See Carambolas
Steaming vegetables, 125
Stir-fried napa cabbage, 68
Stir-frying vegetables, 126
Strawberries. See also Berries
  pie, rhubarb-, 54
Streusel topping, 17
Stuffed beet leaves, 85
Stuffed chiles, 99
Sunchokes, 115–116
  fava bean sauté, 62
  salad, 116
Sweet potatoes, 116–117
  & ginger salad, 117
  with tequila & lime, 117
Swiss chard, 117–118
  Florentine-style, 118
  Minestrone, 62
Szechwan-style dressing, 103

Tamarillos, 55
  sorbet, 41
  tipsy, 55
Tangelos. See Citrus
Tangerines. See also Citrus
  salad, romaine &, 106
Tangors. See Citrus
Taro, 86
Tipsy tamarillos, 55
Toasted cabbage with noodles, 69
Tomatillos, 118
  & cheese salad, 118
  lime sauce, 118
Tomatoes, 118–121
  & egg supper, 120
  -basil soup, 120
  broiled Parmesan, 120
  purée, 71
  sauce, freezer, 126
  spinach-stuffed, 120
Turnip greens. See Greens with
  a bite
Turnips, 121
  with mustard greens, 121
  stew, beef &, 121

Ugli fruit, 86

Vegetable buttermilk soup, cool, 71
Vegetable medley, sprout &, 110
Vegetable purée, 71
Vegetable purée dip, 71
Vegetable-sauced pasta, 71
Vichyssoise, add-on, 89
Vinaigrette dressing, 66
Vinegar, white wine herb, 108

Waldorf salad, molded, 8
Water chestnuts, 86
Watercress. See also Salad greens
  mayonnaise, 59
Watermelon. See Melons
Whipped herb butter, 108
White wine herb vinegar, 108
Wilted greens, 84
Wine & berry compote, 16
Wine jelly, grapes in, 30
Winter melon, 86
Wrapped asparagus with
  watercress mayonnaise, 59

Yams, 116

Zucchini. See also Squash
  omelets, 112
  purée, 71